Marxism and Educational Theory

D0218799

We live in a world where thousands make massive profits out of the labours of others, while those others exist as wage slaves, millions of whom die of starvation and poverty-related illlness every year. The fundamental aim of Marxism is the overthrow of the anarchic, exploitative and eco-destructive system of world capitalism and its replacement by world socialism and equality. To build a socialist world is a task of gargantuan proportions, but one that Marxists believe is eminently achievable.

This book addresses some of these challenges from within educational theory. The key theoretical issues addressed are:

* utopian socialism;
* poststructuralism and postmodernism;
* transmodernism;
* globalisation, neo-liberalism and environmental destruction;
* the New Imperialism;
* critical race theory.

Marxism and Educational Theory compellingly and informatively propels the debate forward in the pursuit of that socialist future. In that quest, suggestions are made to connect theoretical issues with the more practical concerns of the school and the classroom.

With a specially written foreword by Peter McLaren, this timely book will be of interest to academics and students interested in educational theory, the sociology of education, sociology, politics, philosophy and critical theory.

Mike Cole is Research Professor in Education and Equality and Head of Research at Bishop Grosseteste University College Lincoln, UK.

Marxism and Educational Theory

Origins and issues

Mike Cole

LONDON AND NEW YORK

First published 2008
by Routledge
2 Park Square, Milton Park, Abingdon, Oxon OX14 4RN

Simultaneously published in the USA and Canada
by Routledge
270 Madison Ave, New York, NY 10016

Routledge is an imprint of the Taylor & Francis Group, an informa business

Typeset in Times by Wearset Ltd, Boldon, Tyne and Wear
Printed and bound in Great Britain by Antony Rowe Ltd, Chippenham, Wiltshire

British Library Cataloguing in Publication Data
A catalogue record for this book is available from the British Library

Library of Congress Cataloging in Publication Data
Cole, Mike, 1946–
   Marxism and educational theory : origins and issues / Mike Cole.
      p. cm.
1. Socialism and education. 2. Socialism–Philosophy.
3. Education–Philosophy. 4. Social justice. I. Title.
   HX526.C483 2008
   370.1–dc22

2007019519

ISBN10: 0-415-33170-6 (hbk)
ISBN10: 0-415-33171-4 (pbk)

ISBN13: 978-0-415-33170-8 (hbk)
ISBN13: 978-0-415-33171-5 (pbk)

For my mum Gladys Rosina Cole, 1914–2005
And for my grandson Leo Cole Rochelle, 2004–

Contents

Foreword   vii
Acknowledgements   xxi

1   Introduction: personal and political reflections on a
    life in education   1

PART I
Origins   11

2   Socialism and Marxist theory   13

3   Marxist theory and education   28

4   Nietzsche, poststructuralism and postmodernism   37

PART II
Issues   51

5   Poststructuralism and postmodernism in educational theory:
    social change and social justice   53

6   Transmodernism in educational theory: a step closer
    to liberation?   68

7   Globalisation, neo-liberalism and environmental destruction   85

8   The New Imperialism: postmodern, transmodern and Marxist
    perspectives   98

9   Critical Race Theory and racialisation: a case study of
    contemporary racist Britain   112

10   Common objections to Marxism and a Marxist response   129

     Afterword   139
     Appendix: Robert Miles and the concept of racism   140
     Notes   142
     References   155
     Index   176

Foreword

It has been over five years since a cadre of what were identified as 'al Qaida oper-
atives' hijacked four jetliners undetected, completed the greatest act of non-state
terror in human history with no interference from the most sophisticated air force
on the planet, and the U.S. intelligence community managed to have their plot
solved the day it was carried out. The very next day Defense Secretary Donald
Rumsfeld called for an attack on Iraq (Secretary of State Colin Powell had per-
suaded President Bush that U.S. public opinion had to be prepared for an attack
on Iraq and that it would be easier to begin with an attack on Afghanistan). Just
48 hours after the World Trade Center towers came crashing down and thousands
of innocent victims were confirmed dead as a result of a deliberate act of mass
murder, President George W. Bush visited the National Cathedral and, flanked by
evangelist Billy Graham, a cardinal, a rabbi and an imam, intoned in a drawl
befitting a cowboy prophet a permanent and unyielding war on terror, noting
that America's "responsibility to history is already clear: to answer these attacks
and rid the world of evil". The neoconservatives who were members of the
Project for the New American Century (a think tank established in 1997 that
included many members of the former Reagan administration who were to
become members of the Bush Jr. administration, such as Donald Rumsfeld,
Richard Perle and Paul Wolfowitz) and who called for U.S. world economic,
moral, and military domination – a "pax Americana" – brayed that the events of
9/11 gave them a reason sufficient for urging preemptive strikes on "evil nations"
and demanding "total war". And once Bush's threat that nations are either with
the United States or against the United States won him approbation from the U.S.
public, Afghanistan was the first nation to be attacked, Iraq the second and
Lebanon the third (with Israel as our proxy) with perhaps attacks on Syria and
Iran to follow in a campaign against what President Bush now refers to as fighting "Islamic fascists".

The war in Iraq, supposititously proclaimed as a war in the larger battle for
freedom and democracy in the Middle East, for the liberation of the bedraggled
masses of strangers for whom the U.S. ruling elite has little sympathy but whom
are never the less deemed to be in need of colonial tutelage and avuncular care
(as in the "White Man's Burden") in order to create the kind of society that
serves as a reliable and malleable client regime of the United States, is a war for

oil and for fossil fuels and for remaking the Middle East politically and economically in the interests of the United States and the transnational capitalist class whom the government of the United States dutifully serves. Iraq's economy is being organized for opening up markets for both commodities and capital investment for the benefit of the transnational capitalist class. The moral crusades of Bush and Blair (and now Gordon Brown?) remain unperturbed by the hundreds of thousands of civilians slaughtered by advanced military operations of the U.S. and Great Britain in their war on terrorism (a phony war that allows them to destroy sovereign nations under the imperialist guise of self-protection) but are handwringingly hesitant about drawing the line between slaughter and too much slaughter.

Especially today, it is important to underscore that Marxists fervently aspire to a society unmarked by terrorism, whether this be a police state or "democratic" government terror against the working masses by means of physical violence (military or police acts of brutality, preemptive invasions and the destruction of civilian infrastructure) or economic violence (an institutionalized abandonment of the poor to suffering and death and the prosecution of such without challenge; the imposition of an implacable and merciless economic order on developing countries), or targeted assassinations of civilians in other countries, states, or territories (all of which can be considered terrorism from above), or individual acts of terrorism by radical groups (conservative or leftist) pursuing a strategy to destabilize the ruling regime (terrorism from below). When the United States ruling class supports regimes that traffic in torture, 'black sites', mercenary armies repression and military operations that amount to war crimes, they are nailing their colors to the mast, and it is no surprise that the predominant color is the color of money. It appears to be quite proper political conduct – even the order of the day – to protect the profits of American arms merchants (with their powerful Washington lobby), to the extent of supporting right-wing governments that contemptuously ignore international legal norms, that have taken military actions which have egregiously exceeded their legitimate right to self-defense, and that have resulted in the loss of hundreds of thousands of innocent civilian lives. These actions of astonishing callousness are congruent with the imperatives of the transnational capitalist class and any discussion of social conditions either domestic or foreign needs to be understood in relation to declining profit rates and a crisis-ridden world economic system, and this demands a Marxist approach.

Those tunneling their way through the hallways of the U.S. Congress are not only habituated to nativist and evangelical triumphalist propaganda, but are subjectively reconciled to the objective logics of the world market. Labor organizing, anti-sweatshop campaigns, green mobilizations, shack-dweller and landless peasant movements and debt repudiation coalitions are proliferating at breakneck pace, as the race is on to keep the social fabric in its entirety from imploding into the universe of capital and human beings from simply resigning themselves to a world of oppression. But the hydra-headed beast of capitalism only seems to grow more feral heads when one or more are cut off. Today Marx is still occasionally touted as a visionary, but the legacy of the ex-Soviet Union that in the West made it the poster-child of the "Marxist" gulag has not disappeared. If anything, this legacy has intensified and has led many young people to disregard Marx as a thinker worthy of serious study and socialist educators into despairing whether or not there is a viable future for socialism.

The Marxist tradition has never lacked in vociferous critics of the ex-Soviet Union and the Eastern Bloc police states who were willing go public with their criticisms. Some of the most strident and incisive criticisms of totalitarian communist regimes – their oligarchic state structures and command economies – have come from Marxists critics. Just as I do not wish to dwell on the crimes of Stalinism, or the excessive bureaucracy and authoritarian control of populations that for decades tragically deformed workers' states – tout court – in the eyes of many, or create some kind of historical "balance sheet" for the contributions of regimes that claimed to be inspired by the ideas of Marx and Engels, neither do I wish simply to conjure a retort that serves as little more than an expose of the spurious and contradictory character of much of Western democracy. What is necessary – and this is the main point of Cole's landmark book – is that readers (many of whom will be educators or prospective educators) need a serious engagement with the basic concepts and principles of Marxist theory. They would benefit enormously from the challenge of investigating the theory for themselves. Then they can better judge for themselves the history of socialism and communism, and the gains, the setbacks, and the crises that occurred within this history. This is important, especially today, when pro-capitalist and pro-imperialist writers are adventitiously distorting Marx's ideas – and even going so far as to argue that Marxism is responsible for the killing fields of rogue regimes or that its "ideology" can be traced to the roots of terrorism. A recent article in *The Australian* by Tanveer Ahmed is a case in point. Ahmed links political Islam to Marxism by arguing that many of the doctrinaire Islamists were once doctrinaire Marxists. According to Ahmed:

> the old Marxists are extending their influence in many of the Islamic political parties that are rapidly rising in popularity, in response to inept, autocratic Arab governments. Arab governments have closed off opportunity to such an extent that secular forces such as communism or liberalism have minimal outlets. ... The similarities of communism and Islam are considerable. Both demand a domination of the public space and share a dogmatic, ideological view of the world.
>
> (2006, p. 14)

Of course, comparing Marxism to Islam not only reveals a mind untutored in Marxism, but someone who is trying to strike deep chords of suspicion and doubt about socialism (or Islam for that matter) within a very gullible public who might otherwise conceivably be disposed to some or all of its major tenets. Tanveer fails to notice the obvious: that no system demands more of a domination of public space and a dogmatic, ideological view of the world than capitalism. He also disparages the fact that "like communism, Islam believes the collective must be preserved at the expense of the individuals. We are social beings first, individuals second." But even by the most brute capitalist standards, are we to truly believe that we are not social beings? Or that the lives of individuals are more important than our collective well-being as a society? Capitalism needs society, if nothing more than to exploit systematically its collective labor-power, which it accomplishes by means of the extraction of its surplus value. Is there any capitalist who would support Donald Trump – the American incarnation of the inborn drives of the capitalist id – purchasing the globe for himself and ordering all but the very few of his inner circle to drown themselves in the ocean? What Marxism does do is to emphasize the creation of a society where social interests are not pushed aside for individual gain, where human beings cease to be degraded, where human potential is activated in all spheres of social life, where the gap between mental and manual labor and between conception and execution is closed, and where human creativity flourishes. Ahmed also maintains that, "like communism, Islamism promises a better life for the poor, oppressed and alienated. It is cloaked in God, but its essence is strongly secularist." Is there any better description of free market capitalism in the United States, which is seen as a thoroughly Christian enterprise? Has Ahmed not been following the success of President Bush's faith-based initiative program?

Marxist analysis can help us explain how imperialism (both economic and military or a combination thereof) is becoming acceptable today (with the emergence of the U.S. as the world's sole superpower) after having been the object of scathing critiques in the preceding decades. What are the characteristics of current conceptions of progress and nation change that can lead people – even those who champion equality before the law, freedom of the press, and religious freedom and adhere to the principles of self-government and that all human beings are naturally equal and that certain fundamental moral principles are universally valid – to support unreservedly imperial rule? What is it about disenfranchised workers and farmers that can lead them to vote for a political party that clearly further disenfranchises them? How can constituencies such as these, who adamantly believe in law and order, support an administration that is proposing to cut a billion dollars in federal funding of local law enforcement agencies at a time of rising murder rates and other violent crimes throughout the United States? The answer, of course, is an exceedingly complex one, and a fuller and more comprehensive answer demands an historical materialist approach.

The collapse of Keynesian social policy and the ascendancy of neoliberal globalization – which has lowered costs in the interests of national capital as well as small entrepreneurs and has stimulated demand through the creation of public and personal debt – has made the rich much richer and driven the poor into a downward spiral that seems to know no end. After Thatcher and Reagan smashed the welfare state and set in train the neoliberal machinery (the supply side conditions of capital accumulation) that ratcheted up the devaluation of workers, that escalated the depletion of the global environment, that increased the scale of debt peonage and sparked the proliferation of financialization and structural adjustment programs, we find ourselves at a critical juncture in which finance capital, in all of its spectral and omnipresent power, has subordinated all social and environmental conditions to the imperatives of the global money markets. Labor is under vicious assault, as internationalized capital "which had earlier accommodated to the welfare state and trade unions in the interests of domestic peace" can now directly confront labor with disinvestment, virtually sapping its capacity to fight the interests of major capitalist investors (Tabb, 2006, p. 13). New statistical studies have demonstrated unequivocally that intergenerational class mobility in the United States is far below what the public perceives or can even guess – and that the United States "is a more class-bound society that is major Western European counterparts, with the exception of Britain" (Foster, 2006, p. 1).

In the United States, education is funded primarily through property taxes (whose distribution is drastically unequal) at approximately 40–50 percent, with state support at about 47 percent while the federal government spends less than 7 percent. Given that communities are segregated by "race" and class, schools that are largely dependent on local property taxes will be unequal amongst its 16,000 school districts nationwide. The desire to keep the tax rate flat, and the fact that only a fraction of the local population has children in the schools, creates a climate for austerity and anti-tax protests, and school budgets are often sacrificed. This has led the United States to be one of only two nations to spend less money educating poor children than wealthy children; the other was South Africa under Apartheid (Karp, 1997). The voucher system often touted as "free choice" for parents to opt out of the public school system and send their children to private schools pits "freedom" against "equality" since it suggests that free choice is antiseptically removed from social consequences and puts individual self-interest before the collective interest of public schools (who are increasingly serving communities of color) as monies for vouchers are siphoned away from the public school system. It denies the fact that school choice is really a move towards privatization and competition within self-regulated markets, and that the wealthy investor seeks to gain enormous profits from the privatization of education (not to mention that private schools can reject students who might require higher cost services such as special education, or who have low performance indices or a history of behavioral problems). The fight to equalize funding for school districts and to substantially increase funding of education overall is a worthy struggle, but educators such as Mike Cole have another agenda besides advancing reforms at the level of resource distribution. Cole's agenda is surely more ambitious: to create a society in which such dramatic disparities of economic and social resources do not exist in the first place and therefore do not have to be "remediated". It is not brute reality that intercedes against Cole's ambition, nor the inevitability of capitalism, it is the ideological machinery set in motion for the past hundred years by the capitalist class (who are now thoroughly transnationalized) who want to do everything in their power to discredit alternatives to capitalism and convince the general public to believe fervently that socialism is but an idealistic dream that sounds good on paper but that can never be accomplished in the "real" world. Of course current attempts by the transnational imperialist bourgeoisie to keep the dominant social order functioning so as to serve their economic and political interests have created world historical conditions that sound eerily similar to the famous description provided by Rosa Luxemburg in *The Junius Pamphlet*, written in 1916:

> Business thrives in the ruins. Cities become piles of ruins; villages become cemeteries; countries, deserts; populations are beggared; churches, horse stalls. International law, treaties and alliances, the most sacred words and the highest authority have been torn in shreds. Every sovereign "by the grace of God" is called a rogue and lying scoundrel by his cousin on the other side. Every diplomat is a cunning rascal to his colleagues in the other party. Every government sees every other as dooming its own people and worthy only of universal contempt. ... Violated, dishonored, wading in blood, dripping filth – there stands bourgeois society. This is it [in reality]. Not all spic and span and moral, with pretense to culture, philosophy, ethics, order, peace, and the rule of law – but the ravening beast, the witches' sabbath of anarchy, a plague to culture and humanity. Thus it reveals itself in its true, its naked form.

Capitalism has not changed in its love affair with imperialism. One of the most potent exponents of the anti-imperialism, Michael Parenti, writes:

> Capitalism is a system without a soul, without humanity. It tries to reduce every human activity to market profitability. It has no loyalty to democracy, family values, culture, Judeo-Christian ethics, ordinary folks, or any of the other shibboleths mouthed by its public relations representatives on special occasions. It has no loyalty to any nation; its only loyalty is to its own system of capital accumulation. It is not dedicated to "serving the community"; it serves only itself, extracting all it can from the many so that it might give all it can to the few.
>
> (1998, pp. 84–85)

It is true that Marx emphasized the positive as well as the exploitative and alienating features of capitalism. We have witnessed that capitalism has now reached the stage where it has overcome obstacles to its general development, as the vast majority of humanity has been drawn into a matrix of economically-based social contacts and dependencies, and as the productive powers of the economy have evolved such that socialism is possible not as the mere struggle for necessities but with the capacity for promoting the general interests of humanity once the victory of the working class is able to achieve the transformation of capitalism.

Manning Marable calls "the problem of global apartheid" the key issue facing the twentieth century. Marable describes this condition as "the racialized division and stratification of resources, wealth, and power that separates Europe, North

America, and Japan from the billions of mostly black, brown, indigenous, undocumented immigrant and poor people across the planet." The processes of global apartheid within the United States is represented by what Marable refers to as the New Racial Domain. This new domain of exploitation and suffering is different from the old racial domain of slavery, Jim Crow segregation, ghettoization, or strict residential segregation that were grounded in the political economy of U.S. capitalism, where anti-racism was grounded in the realities of domestic markets and the policies of the U.S. nation states. Whereas the struggles involving the old racial domain were debated "within the context of America's expanding, domestic economy, and influenced by Keynesian, welfare state public policies," the New Racial Domain, by contrast, "is driven and largely determined by the forces of transnational capitalism, and the public policies of state neoliberalism." Marable describes these forces as "an unholy trinity" or "deadly triad" which he names as unemployment, mass incarceration, and mass disenfranchisement. Marable, like Cole, avoids excessive subjectivism in his discussion of racism and traces the creation of the New Racial Domain to the point of capitalist production. He links it to the advent of neoliberal capitalism and to the emergence of the transnational capitalist class. He sees the social consequence of these policies inside the precincts of the United States as the creation of:

> an unequal, two-tiered, uncivil society, characterized by a governing hierarchy of middle-to upper-class "citizens" who own nearly all private property and financial assets, and a vast subaltern of quasi- or subcitizens encumbered beneath the cruel weight of permanent unemployment, discriminatory courts and sentencing procedure, dehumanized prisons, voting disenfranchisement, residential segregation, and the elimination of most public services for the poor.

If this perilous condition wasn't bad enough, Marable adds to it the race neutral, color-blind language that effectively functions as racism as well as the dismantling of unions, and a xenophobia and ethnic and religious intolerance against Muslims and Arab Americans that fires the new American hyperpatriotism in a way that could "potentially reinforce traditional white racism against all people of color." Cole shares Marable's concern, and his analysis of racism and his development of anti-racist initiatives in this book is an indispensable contribution to Marxist educational theory.

The key question today is what can be done to reverse the deepening ravages of capitalism both in war-torn countries and at home is a crucial question at this historical juncture. How can capitalism be defeated at a time when it is defining itself against the terrorism wrought by Islamic "evil-doers" and those who question the dictates of a wartime president, when it is advertising itself as the economic correlative to democracy? One of the central means of abolishing terrorism is effectively building various social movements strong enough to prevent assault against working-class and all aggrieved groups affected by capitalist terrrorism. Any socialist-driven opposition to imperialism, in order to be effective in combating those conditions that produce poverty, political terrorism (from above or from below), racism and all types of inhuman conditions, must possess a transnational sweep. In areas where these united fronts already exist already, including the anti-war movement, teachers, popular educators and educational activists should support, through mass work, the efforts of these coalitions so that they are able to work together with different forces in anti-imperialist efforts. In doing so, it is hoped that the ideas of critical educators can help to challenge liberal and bourgeois attitudes towards U.S. imperialism to solidify the relationship between the larger anti-imperialist struggle and the local struggles of workers, teachers, and other groups in the building of a world outside of the social law of value within capitalism. It has become clearer that economic power is the oxygen of educational power within capitalist societies. Nothing will change that short of a socialist revolution.

Marx's writings, especially today, tap a world-weary longing stretching back through the centuries, a longing that inspires men and women – comrades in struggle – to cross the divide between the oppressed and the oppressor that overlooks the bloody chasm produced by generations of class warfare and transcend that world-historical division by transforming the very nature of the power-ridden and socially corrosive capitalist state from below. There have been bold socialist experiments in the past, and they will continue well into the future. But they will not be carried out unopposed by the power of the capitalist state. Many educators know a little about Marxist theory but in the United States it is safe to say that they have not absorbed and digested Marx into their canon of liberal progressivism.

For over three decades Mike Cole has remained enthusiastic in his support for socialism and his commitment to bring discussions of socialism and Marxism into the debates over education has never dwindled. The struggle, while not easy, has always borne fruit. I recall visiting East Germany with Mike several decades ago and leaving our late night conversations outside of rust-splotched factory gates with a renewed interest in Marxist theory that has only grown stronger since those years. Mike's unyielding support of my work has been nothing short of inspirational and I am not the first to remark on the contagious nature of his scholarship. Mike's work has been of fundamental importance to many educators who are convinced that an alternative to the social universe of capital must be forged amid the debris of poverty and suffering left in the bloody wake of capital's ruthless global juggernaut. My students at the University of California, Los Angeles, are avid readers of Mike's work. They find his writings to be lucid, well-researched and convincing and always take pains in telling me how much they appreciate the coherence of his arguments. This is no small accomplishment, especially in graduate schools of education in post-9/11 United States.

And while objections to Marxism and socialism are less likely to be found among educators in the United Kingdom than in the United States (given that the U.K. has always had a long and distinguished history of socialist struggles),

Cole has confronted many of the same objections to socialism and Marxism as educators here in the U.S. are wont to wield. But growing inequality and lower real income for the working class than would be the case under socialism is an indisputable reality that is now, thanks to Mike Cole and other Marxist educators, gaining more recognition among the ranks of teachers in both United States and Britain. The contradictions of capitalism are becoming more difficult to ignore, even though the media propaganda that supports capital at all costs grows more sophisticated.

In *Marxism and Educational Theory: Origins and Issues*, Mike Cole canvasses a number of theoretical developments in the fields of social and sciences and philosophy that include poststructuralism, postmodernism, critical race theory, transmodernism, deconstruction, and the philosophy of Nietzsche. Cole is not content with dealing with these theories simply on their own terms, but pays attention to how they have been taken up and applied by prominent education thinkers. He both locates and evaluates these theories in terms of how they can help educators navigate the terrain of contemporary capitalism as it continues to be impacted by the globalization of capitalism and imperialism. Cole develops his work so that his text is accessible to novices in critical theory, yet there is much for veteran critics to relish in his work. If Cole's text isn't enough to make Marxist converts of postmodernism into "post-Marxist" affiliates, then it will surely provoke much thought and push to reader to consider further the value of Marxist analysis. Many of Cole's U.S. readers will identify his work with that of Bowles and Gintis, since at the time of the release of *Schooling in Capitalist America*, Cole was one of the most prominent exponents of their work. Those, like me, whose critical faculties were honed in the 1980s by course materials developed by the Open University or the Centre for Contemporary Cultural Studies at Birmingham University will also appreciate how Cole has dealt deftly with the classical and contemporary Marxist tradition in education, most of which has been taken from the British scene. And many will appreciate how he examines the saliency and efficacy of Marxist theory when engaging the concepts of "race", racism, Islamophobia, and state surveillance within contemporary educational debates.

As Marxist educators such as Cole know, the promised land of a fuller democracy and popular control is not a glimpse of a lush fragment of a dream or the verdant fields of the imagination but a real place-in-the-making. The moment that production ceases to be founded on the exploitation of human labor, and human labor ceases to be founded on the exploitation of nature, does not portend a mystical interlude when humanity finally expiates its past, but a moment that much be stretched from the present all the way into the future through the daily toil and struggle of socialist educators and cultural workers. It is a constant movement of the masses participating directly, step-by-step, while at the same time understanding why they must participate and what is at stake in their struggle, in the democratic workings of the social order.

The progressivism of the past, born of the tepid waters of liberal reformism, has now become outlived. Early on in his career, Cole knew this to be the case and, as always, was bent on taking teachers down the path of socialism by persuading them to become conscious not only of capital as a social relation but of the importance of adopting a new language of critique and possibility. As such, he is adamantly opposed to cut-and-dried abstractions passed off in some type of neoliberal "banking education" format. While he supports equalizing educational opportunity for those denied it by means of supporting local community initiatives and increasing government commitment for the redistribution of economic opportunity, Cole is aware that states and localities in capitalist societies have neither the fiscal capacity nor the political incentive to create the conditions that will abolish disadvantaged students. Cole wants his readers to make more than modest departures from mainstream thinking about Marxism and to reconsider Marxism and critical pedagogy as twin pillars in the struggle for the future. By revealing the major conflict in capitalist societies as the wrestling of freedom from necessity, Cole seeks to ground readers in cumulative insights of social transformation gleaned from his long history of socialist struggle (up to and including his recent teaching in Venezuela on behalf of the Bolivarian revolution). By analyzing social class not as inequality (a bourgeois term signifying differences of income, opportunity, and outcome) but as a structural relation that reflects the major antagonism of labor and capital, Cole deconditions his readers of everyday understandings of class and in their stead challenges them to reconsider Marxist analysis and class struggle as a means of repositioning their lives in the service of a socialist alternative to capitalism. He understands that only in a socialist society will there be real opportunities to bring about changes in the infrastructure necessary to make substantive gains for poor students – affordable housing, increased child care facilities, improved health care, antiracist and antisexist policy initiatives, etc.

Cole eschews both false optimism and cynical fatalism, but seeks through his scholarly and pedagogical work, a quickening of the revolutionary will so that the pulse of socialism can increase through educators' contact with the essential writings of Marxist theorists. Cole does not adhere to the belief that revolution is determined or inevitably results from its insurmountable contradictions, nor does he believe that society will undergo a massive upheaval by means of a special intercession on the part of educators that will bring socialist democracy to the gates of a new era if only the right path from below can be chosen. Cole is not suggesting that we force the practical tasks faced by educational progressives into the Procrustean bed of pre-dialectical orthodoxies or pseudo-orthodoxies; rather, he points to the living character of Marxist theory. Because he recognizes that consciousness does not arise mechanically from the underlying mode of production, he untiringly insists that we need an educational revolution, a consolidation of revolutionary consciousness and a project of human development that will help in the broader task of destroying class rule, of increasing the ability of the working class to participate in society more broadly by expressing their feelings and creativity and relating their study to the contextual specificity of their own social reality, and making socialism objectivity realizable. Of course, political-social conditions to ensure the necessary steps towards socialism are many and variegated and the weight of such conditions cannot be carried on Cole's shoulders alone, no matter how much he has accomplished single-handedly over the decades or with his comrades Dave Hill and Glenn Rikowski.

Cole is convinced that Marxist theory can contribute to transforming our current social order, one that is heterosexist, non-factual, racist and repugnantly moralistic and in the thrall of cultural and knowledge monopolies. He wants to end the educational transmission of capitalist ideologies that justify oppression and exploitation, to break the academy's loyalty to capitalism, to provide students and teachers with a full understanding of the productive process, to bring socialist principles together with socialist action (praxis), to replace a highly restrictive and imposed curriculum with one that is dedicated to fostering critical consciousness, to cultivate revolutionary convictions, and to combat the overwork of teachers and their lack of employment security. In short, he seeks to abolish the alienation brought about by mainstream capitalist education.

Mike is a man who lives dangerously and who refuses to countenance stereotypes. Once while visiting me in Hollywood, Mike was warned by some white locals to be careful travelling alone in South Central Los Angeles in the evenings, where his white face would surely invite trouble. Even the African-American taxi driver pleaded with him not to enter the pub that Mike had picked to visit. Mike ended up spending half the night in the pub discussing socialism with a score of patrons eager to hear his philosophy of socialist praxis. And on the ride back to Hollywood, an African-American taxi driver who had lost a leg in Vietnam discussed the politics of the Bush administration with him. Mike, of course, recommended some reading for the taxi driver, including some early works of Marx. There are dozens of these stories about Mike that fill the annals of popular discourse. Recently, on a visit to Romania, Mike and his partner, Susi, were told (indeed they were begged) not to go to the Republic of Moldovia because it was lawless and they would get shot, and, whatever they did, they must not enter Transdniestr. The Commonwealth Office advises contacting the British Consulate in Chisinau, Moldovia before attempting to enter Transdniestr. Ignoring this advice, Mike and his companions drove up to the border (having spent a gun-free and very pleasant few hours in Moldovia). As Mike tells the story:

> The first thing you see is a giant hammer and sickle and red emblem. We were told we could not enter because we had no "invite" but after some consultation with the major on duty, we were told we could enter if we each paid €10 (we were with a hired driver because Budget Rentacar doesn't allow travel to Moldovia nor Transdniestr, which is not recognised by any other country in the world, by the way). Transdniestr is still half state-owned, including the bar we drank in. There are no ATMs and no credit cards can be used. Went to a fantastic Ukrainian restaurant, and when the musicians moving from table to table came to our table, we asked them to play "The International". At that point, we heard this amazing voice from another table singing along in Russian (the official language). We joined his

table. He was an ex-Soviet army major. We spent the rest of the evening making toasts with Vodka:

Tony Blair - sheet!

George Bush - sheet!

Gorbachov - sheet!

Hugo Chavez - comrade!

The major then sang some songs in Russian. We didn't understand the words, but we did understand the chorus, which was "Lenin, Marx, Trotsky, Che Guevara, Luxemborg"

(Mike Cole, personal communication, 2007)

It is informal stories like these that help us to connect Mike the Marxist educational theorist to Mike the socialist humanist. That is how I have come to know Mike and to appreciate the full complement of his political theory.

The long-fallow subfield of critical education or critical pedagogy is ripe for new Marxist approaches to revolutionary transformation to be planted in its fertile soil which, when harvested, will sprout new grassroots movements for socialist transformation. The rich history of Marxist theory makes it a welcome domicile for students and cultural workers interested in pursuing social justice agendas both inside and outside their classrooms. Exploring the interstices between rage and hope for a voice that will be heard in our age of despair, Cole has produced a landmark text that will be visited and revisited by generations to come, as the struggle for a democratic socialist society proceeds apace both out of necessity and out of the diehard commitment, Argus-eyed observations, and fearless efforts of scholar-activists such as Mike Cole.

Peter McLaren
University of California
Los Angeles, USA

Acknowledgements

First of all, I would like to acknowledge the love and support of my son, Dave Cole, during 2005, a very difficult year for me, when writing was, by necessity, sporadic.

A number of people have informed the ideas in this book. Of these, many have been kind enough to read various drafts and parts of the book, and to make useful suggestions. I am very grateful to the following for their help: Pat Ainley; Dennis Beach; Angela Clark; Viv Ellis; Julia Finnimore; Rosalyn George; David Gillborn; Dave Hill; Jane Kelly; Bruno Kyhan; Samuel Lee; Corinna Lotz, Alpesh Maisuria; Keith Mercer; Susi Nielsen; João Paraskeva; Scott Poynting; Lindsay Prior; Glenn Rikowski; Rodolfo D. Torres; Satnam Virdee; Paul Warmington; Mandy Williams and Terry Wrigley. It goes without saying that any shortcomings in the book are mine, and mine alone.

Last but not least, I would like to thank Anna Clarkson for her general support and for her forbearance in the light of the late delivery of the manuscript.

1 Introduction

Personal and political reflections on a life in education

This book is the result of a lifetime's interest in politics, not so much party politics, although this has always been of interest to me, but more so political theory. Given the fact that, apart from two years of manual (and clerical) work, I have been in the education system since I was a child, my interest understandably has been in the interface between political theory and educational theory. Having had the fortune to travel, as part of my work, to most parts of the world (see below), this interest has always been an international one. My lifetime's experiences have served to constantly reinforce my heartfelt belief that the world in which we live cannot be even remotely understood without reference to the capitalist system, and specifically the ongoing and relentless struggle between the two main social classes.

I was born in 1946, during the post-war Labour government of Clement Attlee (1945–1951). In order to foreclose the possibility of social revolution at the time, the ruling class was prepared to offer a series of major reforms, thus the period saw sweeping reforms that had begun with the Beveridge Report of 1942 (Beveridge, 2004), which had promised major changes in welfare. Attlee's government created a national insurance system, the National Health Service and embarked on a massive programme of nationalisation. Given the political volatility of the period after the Second World War, the creation of the British welfare state may be seen as a compromise between capital and labour. While, for all progressive people, the British welfare state was a major achievement (indeed an economic and political consensus was forged which would last until Callaghan's 1976 Ruskin College speech, and the onset of the Thatcher government of 1979), the changes were not untainted by the legacy of British imperialism. Thus the argument deployed in favour of introducing child allowances, in the Beveridge Report, was that 'with its present rate of reproduction the British race cannot continue, means of reversing the recent course of the birth rate must be found' (paragraph 413) (see Cole and Virdee, 2006, p. 48). Conflating racism with sexism, the Report assigned to women the role of baby-machines in the service of capitalism and British hegemony. Women were told: 'in the next thirty years housewives as Mothers have vital work to do in ensuring the adequate continuance of the British Race and British Ideals in the world' (paragraph 117) (see Cole and Virdee, 2006, pp. 48–49). Growing up in Bristol, a key pivot of the slave trade in the eighteenth and early nineteenth centuries, imperialism and racism has always been central to my consciousness, and so these systems of exploitation and oppression are of no surprise to me.

My school years

These years saw the return to power of the Conservatives under Sir Winston Churchill (1951–1955), and continued under the Conservative administrations of Sir Anthony Eden (1955–1957), Harold Macmillan (1957–1963) and Sir Alec Douglas-Home (1963–1964). During the early part of this period the Labour Party moved to the right, and at the Party conference in 1953, the right-wing of the Party won almost every vote of importance, including the defeat of land nationalisation (Benn, 1996, p. 35). My memories from this period are the Cold War and the H-bomb (the threat of nuclear war literally terrified me), the launch of the first sputnik (heralding the start of the era of modern mass communications), the Suez crisis, anti-colonial struggle, the Soviet invasion of Hungary, and, as the growing consumer culture of the 1950s replaced the austerity of post-war Britain, Prime Minister Harold Macmillan claiming in 1957 that most Britons had 'never had it so good'. In the same speech, Macmillan took the opportunity to attack the 'doctrinaire nightmare' of socialism and its policies of nationalisation and central planning (BBC, 2006a).

In 1959 the Labour Party leader, Hugh Gaitskill, attempted to get rid of clause IV, section 4 of the Labour Party Constitution which aimed to 'extend democratic power and secure for the people the full fruits of their industry, and the most equitable distribution thereof, that may be possible on the basis of the common ownership of the means of production, distribution and exchange'. This essentially socialist core of Labour Party ideology was finally ditched in 1995 by anti-socialist (New) Labour leader, Tony Blair (see below and Chapter 7).

My earliest remembrances of the class war are discussions between my uncle (a charge-hand at Rolls Royce) and my father (a clerk at the Cooperative Wholesale Society). My uncle's experience on the shop floor had radicalised him more than my dad. I remember my dad calling my uncle a 'bloody communist'.[1] I also remember at Bristol Grammar School, when I was in the fourth stream out of five, the straw boater (allowed during the summer) of a 'middle class' boy (the vast majority of us in the bottom stream wore caps), being stamped on and thrown out of the window. I have fond memories of meeting my mother after school in the department store where she worked in the windowless basement for most of her working life. I recall a number of years later in 1970, when the Equal Pay Act was introduced, making it 'unlawful for employers to discriminate between men and women in terms of their pay and conditions where they are doing the same or similar work; work rated as equivalent; or work of equal value' (Women and Equality Unit, 2004), my mum told me how the management had redefined the roles of the men, so that they could continue to get more wages. She was always acutely aware of gender as well as social class, ever since her own family, not having enough money to send both her and her brother to school, had taken her out of school to make way for him.

Briefly a manual worker

When I left school I worked first of all as a porter in a supermarket and, after that, as a labourer in a tobacco factory. I remember unloading a truck outside of Sainsbury's, when the driver clenched his fist and proclaimed, 'we're in brother!'. It was 1964, and Harold Wilson was returned with a very small majority, amid tremendous excitement and enthusiasm, with a Labour government promising a new (socialist) Britain, forged in the white heat of technology. In 1966, Wilson was re-elected with a governable majority, and almost immediately faced a National Seaman's strike, aimed to secure higher wages and to reduce the working week from 56 to 40 hours. It was widely supported by union members and caused great disruption to shipping. The political importance of the strike was enormous, interfering with trade, and adversely affecting the UK balance of payments, provoking a run on the pound and threatening to undermine the government's attempts to keep wage increases below 3.5 per cent. Wilson was strongly critical of the strike, alleging that it had been taken over by 'communists' aiming to bring down his administration. Around this time, I had moved out of the world of manual labour and was working in an insurance company in St. James's, London as a Kalamazoo reconciliation clerk. I did not know what that was then and do not know now, but I do know that the class structure of British society existed *in extremis* in that company. The bosses wore bowler hats, called us by our second names ('let's face it, Cole, you're not really up to reconciling accounts are you? We'll give you something simpler'), and told the workers to extinguish their cigarettes, as they walked passed us smoking cigars. In 1969, the Labour government produced the White Paper, *In Place Of Strife* (foreshadowing the anti-trade union legislation of the Thatcher years. Amongst its numerous proposals were plans to force unions to call a ballot before a strike was held. *In Place Of Strife* was was eventually defeated in response to union anger and other Left protest.[2]

Back into schools

By the time the Conservative government of Edward Heath (1970–1974) was installed, I had re-entered the education system as a student teacher, the prelude to a 35-year ongoing career in education. The Heath government was determined to return state industries to private ownership and to get rid of 'lame duck' firms. This resulted in a 16-month ultimately successful work-in (1971–1972) by the Upper Clyde Shipbuilders in Glasgow.

At this time I had begun a five-year stint working in inner London schools, where, primarily because I was male, I was rapidly promoted; actually becoming Acting Deputy Head for a term during my fourth year of teaching. All my teaching in schools was in inner city London. In my last year, I taught in Ladbroke

Grove. At the beginning of the year I was told that the young people in my class (almost all of African-Caribbean origin in the final year of primary school) would get nowhere educationally. These young people and I were delighted, though not surprised, when we got some of their poems published in *West Indian World*, a popular adult weekly at that time. One of the many things that sticks in my mind is a girl of Dominican origin in my class telling me that there were too many rats in her flat, and about the white man who drove round every Friday in his Rolls Royce to collect the rent.

On May Day, 1973, 1.6 million workers staged a strike in support of the TUC's call for a 'day of national protest and stoppage' in protest at the government's pay restraint policy and price rises. This action followed numerous strikes in the first few months of the New Year. In February 290,000 civil servants and 47,000 gas workers called strikes against the government's pay freeze as did 7,000 London dockers on 2 April.

Active in the National Union of Teachers, I can recall with great joy, one evening after attending a union meeting watching the early evening news in a local pub, and noting that every single item featured some industrial dispute or other. The Heath government proclaimed a state of emergency in 1973, following a ban on overtime by electricity and coal workers and, in the following year, to conserve electricity, introduced the three-day week in industry.

My dad died just before I spent a year doing an MA degree at Sussex University, under the tutelage of Marxist sociologist, Tom Bottomore and Stephen Ball (now one of Britain's leading sociologists of education). My father's death was an event from which I have never recovered. His life experiences had moved him decidedly to the Left, and, just before his death in 1975, he was selling *Socialist Worker*, weekly newspaper of the Marxist Socialist Workers' Party, in the works canteen.

Working in higher education

From 1976 until 2005, I worked as a lecturer in education at Brighton Polytechnic/ University of Brighton. My early years there witnessed the Labour government of James Callaghan (1976–1979) (Harold Wilson had been returned to power briefly in 1974). Callaghan's speech at Ruskin College in 1976 signalled the need to align schooling closely to the needs of industry, thus going beyond the sphere of education and sowing the seeds of 'New Labour', with its essentially neo-liberal agenda.

Following the so-called 'winter of discontent' which saw the British working class strike and take to the streets in an impressive show of trade union militancy, the Thatcher governments of 1979–1990 brought with them the end of the post-war consensus, a wholesale commitment to neo-liberalism and major attempts to smash the unions, particularly the miners, whose strike lasted nearly a year (1984–1985). It was this period and the subsequent John Major Conservative government (1990–1997) that consolidated, as a composite entity, my roles as a teacher, trade union activist in Natfhe (the National Association of Teachers in

Further and Higher Education) and Marxist writer. It was also this period that witnessed a large degree of government surveillance of teacher education, of which I personally was on the receiving end (Cole, 2004a). Partly as a response to this, The Hillcole Group of Radical Left Educators was founded in 1989 by myself and Dave Hill at the Institute for Education Policy Studies. It was a group of socialist practitioners and academics in education in Britain, whose aim was 'to improve the quality of schooling and teacher education; to confront the assaults by the radical right on the quality of education; and to influence policy and decision making on educational matters' (Hill, 2004a). The Group published 11 pamphlets and two books, aimed at countering the arguments of the then influential Radical Right Hillgate Group, and all analysing education from a Marxist perspective.

One of the beauties of Marxism is that, in its very essence, it is a very *practical* as well as a theoretical endeavour. Although having been on numerous marches and demonstrations, it was experiences of joyous solidarity on picket lines, formed by my union at the entrance to the Polytechnic/University, which more than anything else enthused me on a personal level. This was most momentous when action was in conjunction with members of the other union, Unison.

My first book *Blind Alley* (co-edited with Bob Skelton), was published in 1980 (Cole and Skelton, 1980).[3] I made a decision that I would never publish anything that did not reflect my politics. Subsequent writing has been in the area of issues of equality (and education) (mainly racism), and Marxism, poststructuralism, postmodernism, transmodernism and Critical Race Theory.

Despite never being promoted at Brighton Polytechnic/University of Brighton, something I still feel angry about, my time there did enable me to engage a number of students and staff with equality issues. It also enabled me to travel extensively overseas to teach and to present at conferences. During these trips, the multifarious manifestations and experiences of global capitalism (apartheid in the US, and in 'post-apartheid' South Africa; the barrios in Brazil; the grinding poverty in India are particularly unforgettable) all solidified my Marxist perspective on life.

In the run-up to the 1997 election victory of New Labour, I recall numerous conversations with socialists, with the basic theme of 'let's get Labour back in' and they'll then be able to show their true (socialist) colours. I never believed this and, as history will bear witness, the Blair governments have shown a fervent commitment to Thatcherite policies (see Chapter 7). In many ways, especially with respect to education policy, Blair has gone further than Thatcher ever dared.

Although this book is decisively informed by party politics, it is not *about* party politics. Instead, it aims to critically document the ongoing developments in educational theory, which have occurred since I had the luxury, on entering higher education in 1976, to keep abreast with theoretical developments. Specifically, the book explores the contribution of Marxism, poststructuralism, postmodernism, transmodernism and Critical Race Theory (CRT) to educational theory. I first read Marx in my early years at Brighton Polytechnic (*Capital* reading groups were popular at the time) and have more recently embarked on a study of the other *isms*, which are the subject matter of this book. Marxism was hegemonic to the discipline of the Sociology of Education in the 1970s and

1980s (see Chapter 3). However, in recent years, its influence in academia has been overshadowed by developments in poststructuralism and postmodernism, particularly in the UK, the US and Australasia. In the US, CRT has also had an enduring history, and, as we shall see in Chapter 9, is beginning to be influential in the UK. In South America, transmodernism was developed by Enrique Dussel, and has been popularised in educational theory in the US by David Geoffrey Smith. Transmodernism has also been exalted by the influential transatlantic writer, Paul Gilroy (2004) (see Chapter 6). It is the aim of this book to consider these developments in the light of the rise, fall and rise again of Marxism within educational theory. It is vital that these theories are addressed because, like Marxism, they lay claims to social change and social justice, and because of their influence in education and beyond.

Outline of the book

In order to consider and understand Marxism, poststructuralism, postmodernism, transmodernism and CRT in Educational Theory, it is first necessary to deal with each school of thought per se, as well as to locate them within educational theory. At this point, first let me make two things clear. First, my brief is the contribution of these issues to *educational theory*. A wealth of material concerning these issues has been produced that is not connected to educational theory, and my arguments in this book do not pertain to these writings. Second, my aim is the pursuit of *dialogue*, with all those with a belief in social justice and social change, and it is my hope that this book will encourage and contribute to the promotion of such dialogue.

The book is divided into two parts. The first part considers origins and addresses socialism and Marxist theory, Marxist theory and education, and Nietzsche, poststructuralism and postmodernism respectively.

The second part of the book begins with a Marxist critique of poststructuralism and postmodernism in educational theory, and their connections to social change and social justice. In this second part, I also consider the challenge of transmodernism. In addition, I address globalisation, neo-liberalism and environmental destruction, before turning to a discussion of postmodern, transmodern and Marxist perspectives on the New Imperialism. Next I critique a couple of the central ideas of CRT, using contemporary racist Britain as a case study. Educational implications are discussed throughout. The final chapter of the book addresses some popular misconceptions about Marxism and provides a Marxist response.

Part 1: origins

The second chapter opens with an outline of the origins of socialist thought, beginning with some antecedents to utopian socialism, before a consideration of the contributions to socialist theory of three key utopian socialists, Henri de Saint-Simon, Charles Fourier and Robert Owen. I then go on to examine Karl

Marx and Frederick Engels' critique of utopian socialism, and the Marxist conceptualisation of 'scientific socialism'.

In the third chapter, I begin by sketching the views of utopian socialists on education. I then go on to briefly examine some of the thoughts on education of Karl Marx and Frederick Engels. I also assess two major Marxist contributions to educational theory, Louis Althusser's *ISA* essay, and Sam Bowles and Herb Gintis's book, *Schooling in Capitalist America.* I next address the responses to Bowles and Gintis's book. I conclude with some suggestions for the future of Marxist educational theory, based on the work of Glenn Rikowski.

The fourth chapter begins with a brief discussion of some of the defining features of the terms, modernity and modernism. I then go on to examine some of Friedrich Nietzsche's key critiques of modernity, before assessing his influence on the thinking of leading poststructuralists, Michel Foucault and Jacques Derrida. Next I consider the meanings of postmodernity and postmodernism, focusing on the work of Jean-Francois Lyotard and Jean Baudrillard. This includes an assessment of their indebtedness to Nietzsche.

Part 2: issues

In the fifth chapter, I make some brief comments on the educational ideas of Nietzsche, on those of the poststructuralists, Foucault and Derrida, and those of the postmodernists, Lyotard and Baudrillard. Next I take a snapshot of the current state of global capitalism. The bulk of the chapter considers claims by prominent poststructuralists/postmodernists within educational theory, Elizabeth Atkinson, Patti Lather and Judith Baxter, that poststructuralism/postmodernism can be forces for social change and social justice.

Having rejected these claims I assess, in Chapter 6, the contribution of transmodernism within educational theory in the pursuit of social change and social justice. I begin by looking at the origins of the concept of transmodernism, and suggest what are, for me, its defining features. I go on to examine the transmodern critique of modernity, of modernism and of postmodernism. The next part of the chapter consists of a Marxist critique of transmodernism, focusing on the work of David Geoffrey Smith. I assess his writings on: liberating the oppressor; the rejection of totalising synthesis; the complicity of modernists in the oppression of the South; analogic reasoning; and the tensions between rethought liberal democracy and democratic socialism. I then make some critical comments on the transmodern interpretation of Marxism and social change. I conclude with a consideration of the political and economic choices presented by transmodernism and Marxism, respectively, and the role of the educator.

Chapter 7 begins with a sketch of the all-pervasive concept of globalisation. Many capitalist world leaders insist that globalisation is a benign world movement. Typical among them is ex-British Prime Minister, Tony Blair. I thus go on to examine his claims that globalisation can be a force for good. Next I outline a Marxist analysis of globalisation. After that, I address the issue of environmental destruction, looking at the destruction of resources; unhealthy food; genetic modification and at climate change. I conclude with a discussion of neo-liberal global capitalism, the destruction of the environment and education.

In Chapter 8, I analyse and critique a postmodern interpretation of the 'New Imperialism', before examining the US reality, including how globalisation is used to justify imperialism. I conclude with analyses of imperialism from trans-modern and Marxist perspectives respectively. This includes a discussion of the transmodern concept of 'enfraudening', and of the Marxist concept of 'racialisa-tion'. I conclude that an analysis of imperialism, old and new, should be at the heart of the curriculum.

Chapter 9 begins with a Marxist critique of two central tenets of Critical Race Theory (CRT). I then go on to formulate my own preferred definition of the concept of racism, a wide definition, which I attempt to defend against those who argue for a narrower one. I then go on to look at contemporary racist Britain. Concentrating on British Imperialism and its legacy, I utilise the Marxist concept of racialisation, discussed in Chapter 8, to try to understand continuing anti-black racism, Islamophobia and the newer phenomenon of xeno-racism. Racialisation, it is argued, has more purchase in explaining manifestations of racism in Britain today than CRT. In the final part of the chapter, I consider the implications for education.

In the final chapter of the book, I address some of the common objections to Marxism, and attempt to respond to them. Those considered are:

- how is the Marxist vision of socialism different from capitalism and why is it better;
- Marxism is contrary to human nature because we are all basically selfish and greedy and competitive;
- some people are naturally lazy and won't work;
- why shouldn't those who have worked hard get more benefits in life;
- Marxism can't work because it always leads to totalitarianism;
- someone will always want to be 'boss' and there will always be natural 'leaders' and 'followers';
- it is impossible to plan centrally in such a hugely diverse and complex world;
- someone has to do the drudge jobs, and how could that be sorted out in a socialist world;
- socialism means a lower standard of life for all;
- socialism will be dull, dreary and uniform and we will all have less choice;
- a social revolution will necessarily involve violence and death on a massive scale;
- the working class won't create the revolution because they are reactionary;
- Marxists just wait for the revolution rather than address the issues of the here and now;
- Marxism is a nice idea, but it will never happen.

To counter the charge that Marxists just wait for the revolution rather than address the issues of the here and now, I provide a URL link, detailing the platform of *Respect – the Unity Coalition*, an increasingly influential organisation within British party politics.

To conclude this first chapter, I would like to address the issue of the title of the book. *Marxism and Eductional Theory: Origins and Issues* reflects a concern with what are for me the major issues currently of concern in educational *theory*. While the book deals in depth with social class issues and with racism, it does not address per se the issues of gender, sexuality and disability. For a thorough consideration of these key issues written from Marxist and other Left socialist perspectives, see the companion volume, *Education, Equality and Human Rights: Issues of Gender, 'Race', Sexuality, Disability and Social Class* (Cole, ed., 2006), which deals with the issues both per se and with respect to education. It should be stressed that oppression based on identities other than class is now acknowledged in recent and current Marxist analysis and practice.

Part I

Origins

2   Socialism and Marxist theory

In this chapter, I begin by outlining some antecedents of utopian socialism, before considering the contributions to socialist theory of three key utopian socialists, Henri de Saint-Simon, Charles Fourier and Robert Owen. I then go on to examine Karl Marx and Frederick Engels' critique of utopian socialism, and the Marxist conceptualisation of 'scientific socialism'.

Introduction

It is a general perception that socialism was born in the nineteenth century in Britain and France. The word was first used publicly in English in 1827 in connection with the Owenite movement (see below); and in French, in 1835, with respect to the Saint-Simonians (Berki, 1975, p. 12) (see below). In a sense, at least in its modern form, this birth-date is accurate. However, the common ownership, cooperation and collective activity that socialism entails are not new to humankind. In fact, as Marx and Engels argued, in very early history most, if not all, societies held common property in the soil and were grouped according to kindred.

The ideas behind socialism have surely been in existence as long as there have been class-based societies.[1] For example, in the Old Testament of the Bible, the prophet, Amos, born in the eighth century BC, showed nothing but contempt for those who 'lie upon beds of ivory ... [and] drink wine in bowls ... [and] make the poor of the land to fail' (*Holy Bible*, Amos 6 and 8). The future, he felt, lay in a new kind of society where the people would 'build the waste cities' from the old perished order, and 'plant vineyards, and drink the wine thereof ... [and] make gardens, and eat the fruit of them' (ibid., Amos 9). In the New Testament, the Apostles 'had all things common ... sold their possessions and goods and parted them to all *men*, as every man had need' (*Holy Bible*, The Acts 44–45).[2]

In the ancient world, slave rebellions were quite common. Probably the most famous is that led by Spartacus against the Roman Empire, which began in 73 BC. However, while there was a vain hope to build an ideal city commonwealth, and while a fierce spirit of egalitarian democracy was unleashed, this was not socialism. Whenever those in revolt spoke, it was on behalf of the 'populus', by which they meant those who had political rights and the vote – the 'citizens' and nothing approaching the majority of the inhabitants (Crick, 1987, p. 2).

In empires that succeeded Rome, such as the Byzantine Empire (AD 330–1453), there were similar attacks on the ruling class. In the fourteenth century, there was a major peasants' revolt in Britain and rebellions in Germany in the sixteenth century (Paczuska, 1986, pp. 9–14).

Not only have there always been insurrections against the ruling class, there have also been visions of how things could be. As Bernard Crick puts it: 'From the beginning of written records we find evidence of revolts of the poor against the rich, of oppressed peoples against ruling elites, and of dreams of a perfectly just and usually egalitarian human order' (1987, p. 1). Perhaps the most ambitious attempt at describing how societies could be run in a non-exploitative way is Sir Thomas More's book, *Utopia*, published in 1516. The word 'utopia' has origins in Greek and Latin and means literally, 'a place that does not exist'. However, the usual meaning is 'a place to be desired' (Hodgson, 1999, p. 4). Running to some 423 pages, *Utopia* is written as a contrast to England at the time. On an imaginary island, the citizens pool the products of their labour and draw what they need from the common storehouse; and there is peace and security. The people of *Utopia*, unlike the unhappy English, understand that the scramble for wealth is the source of the problem (MacKenzie, 1967, pp. 21–22). As More argues, through the mouth of a Portuguese explorer, Raphael Hythloday: 'where possessions are private, where money is the measure of all things, it is hard and almost impossible that the commonwealth should have just government and enjoy prosperity' (cited in MacKenzie, 1967, p. 21). Negative aspects of More's utopia include a perception of women as second-class citizens, the presence of slaves and a lack of freedom of movement.

During the English Revolution in the 1640s, the 'Levellers' and the 'Diggers' both presented threats to the gentry. By 1648, the rank-and-file of the parliamentary armies had swung over to support the Levellers, who sought to carry the new democratic ideas to their logical conclusion, and to attack all forms of privilege. While they concentrated on political reform, there is an inherent socialism (albeit a nationalistic socialism) implicit in their doctrine. As MacKenzie (1967, p. 23) states: 'they found their golden age in Saxon England, before the Norman Conquest had placed a privileged and alien hierarchy in power and driven its rightful owners from their communal enjoyment of the soil of England' The leader of the Diggers movement, Gerrard Winstanley, actually anticipated modern socialist ideas in his book, *Law of Freedom* (1652) which advocated agrarian communism (Cole, 1971, p. 9):

> The earth is to be planted, and the fruits reaped and carried into barns and store-houses, by the assistance of every family. And if any man or family want corn or other provision they may go to the store-houses and fetch without money. ... If any want food or victuals, they may either go to the butchers' shops, and receive what they want without money; or else go to the flocks of sheep or herds of cattle, and take and kill what meat is needful for their families, without buying and selling. And the reason why all the

riches of the earth are a common stock is this, because the earth, and the labours thereupon, are managed by common assistance of every family, without buying and selling.

(Winstanley, 1652)

Utopian socialism

My aim in this chapter, however, is not to recount in detail these historical struggles and imagined utopias, but rather to examine, *with particular respect to their contribution to Marxism*, the ideas of three prominent modern utopian socialists, Henri de Saint-Simon, Charles Fourier and Robert Owen.

It is not until the eighteenth century that there begin ideas of cumulative social change. Prior to that, the belief was that the future would resemble the past. As Crick (1987, p. 3) puts it:

One regime was good, another bad, life was happy or unfortunate; our children's generation may be more fortunate than ours, but the next might swing back again. Cyclical theories were common, the wheel of fortune kept on turning on a fixed axis.

Henri de Saint-Simon

Claude-Henri de Rouvroy, Comte de Saint-Simon (1760–1825) was not yet 30 when the French Revolution (1789–1799) began. This revolution was, of course, a bourgeois or middle-class revolution. An impoverished aristocrat turned commoner, Saint-Simon assumed the name 'Citoyan Bonhomme', and took part in revolutionary events, on the side of the revolution (Berki, 1975, pp. 43–44). For Saint-Simon, the antagonism was between 'industrial forces' (defined as manufacturers, merchants and bankers, as well as wage-workers) and 'idlers' (defined as the old aristocracy who took no part in production or distribution but merely lived off others):

Man is lazy by nature. ... He only works, therefore, according to his needs and desires. ... But there is surrounding society ... a throng of parasites who, although they have the same needs and desires as the others, have not been able to overcome the natural laziness common to all men, and who, although they produce nothing, consume or seek to consume as though they did produce. These men use force to live off the work of the rest, either off what they are given or what they can take. In short, they are idlers, that is, thieves.

(Saint-Simon, 1817)

The liberation of humanity was to come about when the bourgeoisie (manufacturers, merchants and bankers) transformed themselves into 'public officials' who, holding a commanding and economically privileged position vis-à-vis the working class, would pave the way forward for this liberation. The bankers especially were to be central in this:

> Thus, the industrials can and should be considered as having an organisation and forming a corporation: And in fact all the farmers and other manufacturers are linked together by the class of merchants; and all the merchants have their own common agents in the bankers; so that the bankers can and should be considered as the general agents of industry. ... In this situation the chief banking houses of Paris are called upon to direct the political action of the industrials.
>
> (Saint-Simon, 1975 [1817], p. 212)

Saint-Simon believed that 'all men ought to work' (Engels, 1977 [1892], p. 399), and that the state had an obligation to find work for all its citizens, who, in turn, were obliged to work for the common good. Saint-Simon's favoured society was not intended to be democratic or egalitarian. Wages would be allotted to each, according to their respective contributions to that common good (Crick, 1987, p. 33). Later in life, Saint-Simon sought to combat the selfishness in the spirit of the age, by what he referred to as 'New Christianity', linking together the scientists, artists and industrialists to make them 'the managing directors of the human race' (Saint-Simon, cited in Berki, p. 45). The aim of 'New Christianity' was the well-being of the poor.

While Saint-Simon's 'New Christianity' was 'rigidly hierarchic' (Engels, 1977 [1892], p. 399), he was adamant that:

> The new Christian organisation will base both temporal and spiritual institutions on that principle that *all men should treat one another as brothers*. It will direct all institutions, whatever their nature, towards increasing the ... *moral and physical condition of the poorest class* [emphasis original].
>
> (Saint-Simon, 1975 [1817], pp. 291, 303)

Elsewhere, Saint-Simon also referred to the promotion of 'the moral, *intellectual* and physical improvement of poorest and most numerous classes' (cited in Crick, 1987, p. 32; my emphasis).

Saint-Simon's vision was thus of a state of harmony between capital and labour: an elitist vision of a centralised and planned industrial society administered for the common good and looking to the future. As Crick (1987, p. 33) points out, it is 'a picture of a capitalist society without a free-market [and] with a collective capacity to organise and steer the economy for the common good'. Like Marxism, the theory underlying Saint-Simon's utopia is of stages of human development. However, these stages are not related to class struggle as in Marxism, but rather to advances in knowledge. For Saint-Simon, economic change was the outcome of scientific discovery. The roots of human progress are in the advance of knowledge. Accordingly, it is the great discoverers who are the supreme makers of history (Cole, 1971, p. 49) rather than the oppressed masses as in Marxism:

> The improvement of scientific theory was Descarte's chief concern. ... For the sake of scientific progress, the happiness of humanity, and the glory of the French nation, the Institute [of France] [previously the French Academies] must work to improve theory. It must resume the approach of Descartes.
>
> (Saint-Simon, 1975 [1817], p. 86)

What is of greatest significance in Saint-Simon's thoughts for the subsequent development of Marxism is his recognition of class struggle but, in his case, the bourgeois struggle against the aristocracy. Thus Saint-Simon writes of the 'struggle between the King and the great vassals, between the chiefs of industrial enterprises and the nobles ... the direct action of the industrials against the nobles' (Saint-Simon, 1975 [1817], p. 246). He also refers to 'the two classes [that] existed in the nation ... before the ... industrials ... those who commanded and those who obeyed' (Saint-Simon, 1975 [1817], p. 247). As Engels (1977 [1892], pp. 399–400) notes, to recognise the French Revolution as a class war was 'a most pregnant discovery'.

Charles Fourier

Born to a middle-class merchant family which lost most of its possessions during the French Revolution, François-Marie-Charles Fourier (1772–1837) was particularly scathing about the hypocrisy of the bourgeoisie after the revolution, particular with respect to commercial corruption (Engels, 1977 [1892], p. 400). He once remarked that commerce had made virtue less lucrative than vice (MacKenzie, 1967, p. 27), and that his own fate was doomed, as he put it, by 'participating in the deceitful activities of merchants and brutalizing myself in the performance of degrading tasks'. (Fourier, cited in Kreis, 2006, p. 4). 'Under a true organization of Commerce', he argued, 'property would be abolished, the Mercantile classes become agents for trade of industrial goods and Commerce would then be the servant of Society' (Fourier, 1820, p. 1). Fourier disliked large-scale production, mechanisation, and centralisation in all their forms (Cole, 1971, p. 62). Indeed, he believed that all manual labour was arduous and irksome, whether in the factory, workshop or field, and that the plight of the workers was intolerably dehumanising. He was of the opinion, however, that it was possible to make all work into play, to make it pleasurable and desirable and deeply satisfying, both physically and mentally. This was to be a feature of the later work of Marx and Engels (Kreis, 2006, p. 4).

Fourier was a strong advocate of communities (phalanxes) where labour would be more attractive, a source of constant joy, rather than sweat and toil:

> We shall see people engaged in attractive occupations, giving no thoughts to material wants, free from all pecuniary cares and anxieties.

As women and children all work, there will be no idlers, all will earn more than they consume. Universal happiness and gaiety will reign. A unity of interests and views will arise. ... Elegance and luxury will be had by all.

(Fourier, 1820, p. 2)

He was quite meticulous about the specific and gendered roles children and infants might have in the phalanxes:

The thing to be done is to separate the smallest peas for the sweetened ragout, the medium ones for the bacon ragout, and the largest for the soup. The child of thirty-five months first selects the little ones which are most difficult to pick out; she sends all the large and medium ones to the next hollow, where the child of thirty months shoves those that seem large to the third hollow, returns the little ones to the first, and drops the medium grains into the basket. The infant of twenty-five months, placed at the third hollow, has an easy task; he returns some medium grains to the second, and gathers the large ones into his basket.

(Fourier, cited in Kreis, 2006, p. 7)

The phalanxes, which would enable people to work in multiple occupations, should have an ideal size of 1,600–1,800 people, cultivating about 5,000 acres of land (Cole, 1971, pp. 65–66). Fourier believed that we should strive to eliminate all tedious or unpleasant jobs, learning, if possible, to do without the products derived from such labour, with productive teams competing with one another to produce the most delicious peaches or the best pair of shoes (Kreis, 2006, pp. 4–5) (see Chapter 10, pp. 132–133 of this book for a discussion of drudge jobs and unnecessary labour). For Fourier, the need to compete would satisfy a natural passion, since he believed we are, by nature, competitive. However, the harmful aspects of competitive commerce in civilization would not be reproduced because production would be based on the overall good of society, rather than individual profit in the market (Kreis, 2006, p. 5). In Fourier's phalanxes, rich and poor would all enjoy that which he described as 'trifling work' (cited in Kreis, 2006, p. 7), as well as the work of the artisans. The 'workers' would include the children of the rich, nearly all of who would be 'enamoured of various very plebeian occupations, such as those of the mason, the carpenter, the smith, the saddler' (cited in Kreis, 2004, p. 7).

Fourier believed in communal living. As he put it:

Let a man provide himself with fine viands, fine wines, with the intention of enjoying them alone, of giving himself up to gormandizing by himself, and he exposes himself to well-merited gibes. But if this man gathers a select company in his house, where one may enjoy at the same time the pleasure of the senses by good cheer, and the pleasure of the soul by companionship, he will be lauded, because these banquets will be a composite and not a simple pleasure.

(Fourier, cited in Kreis, 2004, p. 3)

However, the communal living in the phalanxes would be segregated. Although 'meals will be in common but there will be at least three different tables with different prices and children will have their own tables, separate from the adults' (Fourier, 1820, p. 2). In addition in these communities, apartments were to be adaptable to different tastes, requirements and *levels of income* (Cole, 1971, p. 66). Fourier did not believe in economic equality, nor had he any objection to unearned income derived from the possession of capital. Indeed he constantly appealed to capitalists to come forward to finance his envisaged communities. Equality, he believed, was inconsistent with human nature, which dictates that we have a natural desire to be rewarded according to our work (Cole, 1971, p. 67). Human nature, Fourier believed, was created by God and organised society should respect that and not try to fight it (Kreis, 2006, p. 4).

Fourier's communities may seem relatively unimportant in the industrialised and finance-dominated capitalisms of the twentieth and twenty-first centuries. However, the importance of his work lies in his critique of bourgeois morality.

Fourier believed in combining the passions, such as the sharing of a good meal in good company, while conspiring to arrange a sexual orgy with the couple at the next table. Fourier was an ardent advocate of sexual liberation and a staunch defender of sexual preferences, not accepted by religion or society in his time. He believed that the only sexual activity that could be forbidden is that which involved pain or force. He accepted sadism and masochism among consenting partners as well as sodomy, lesbianism, homosexuality, pederasty, bestiality, fetishism and sex between close relatives (Kreis, 2006, p. 5). While I would view pederasty, bestiality and incest as inherently problematic, Fourier's ideas were certainly ahead of his time.

Fourier considered the position of women in his society as a form of slavery, and believed that the existing family structure was partly responsible for the subjugation of women, the family turning people exclusively inward to spouse and children, rather than outward to society. He thus rejected patriarchy and familial conditions in the phalanx (Kreis, 2006, p. 5). Fourier was the first to declare that in any given society, the degree of women's emancipation is a measure of the general emancipation of the society (Engels, 1977 [1892], p. 400).[3] Fourier believed that pleasure in work was a natural endowment of women as well as men, and wished that women should have equal freedom with men in choosing their jobs. Indeed, he looked forward to complete sex equality in the new order (Cole, 1971, p. 69).

It is easy to see how Fourier's ideas have informed sexual liberation in the late twentieth and early twenty-first centuries, including its impact on education. As Kreis (2006, p. 5) concludes, Fourier's 'quickness to see oppression no matter how veiled, and his penetrating concern with character formations and problems, links him to modern educational theory'.

For Engels (1977 [1892], p. 401), however, Fourier's greatest contribution to socialism is his dialectical conception of history.[4] Thus, Fourier sees societies as having moved through four stages: savagery; barbarism; the patriarchate; and civilisation. The last stage is the modern bourgeois society in which he lived. However, whereas Marxists employ dialectical thinking in a progressive way (see later in this chapter for a discussion), Fourier's dialectic view of history ends in the ultimate destruction of the human race. The moral bankruptcy and hypocrisy inherent in the bourgeoisie in the aftermath of the French Revolution exemplifies a stage in this process of destruction (Engels, 1977 [1892], p. 401).

Robert Owen

Robert Owen (1771–1858) came to prominence when he acquired the New Lanark cotton mills in 1800. That Owen was a philanthropic capitalist is witnessed by the fact that he worked his employees only ten and a half hours, compared to this competitors' thirteen or fourteen; paid full wages when a crisis in cotton stopped work for four months; and founded infant schools in New Lanark (Engels, 1977 [1892], p. 402). Believing that everyone is capable of goodness and excellence, he was driven by the need for two great changes: the abandonment of unregulated brutal competition between capitalist employers and the eradication of false beliefs about the formation of character (Cole, 1971, p. 88). Owen put forward his views on the evils commerce in his *Report to the County of Lanark*:

> Commerce … has made man ignorantly, individually selfish; placed him in opposition to his fellows; engendered fraud and deceit; blindly urged him forward to create, but deprived him of the wisdom to enjoy. In striving to take advantage of others, he has overreached himself. … From this principle of individual interest have arisen all the divisions of mankind, the endless errors and mischief of class, sect, party, and of national antipathies, creating the angry and malevolent passions, and all the crimes and misery with which the human race has been hitherto afflicted.
>
> (Owen, 1820)

Owen was concerned about these evils brought on by the Industrial Revolution and deeply revolted by the accompanying poverty, and gradually became convinced that human character was the product of the environments and social systems in which people grow up, rather than character being the fault of the individual (a position which was to become a central tenet of Marxism – see Chapter 10, pp. 129–130). As Owen put it:

> I … gradually came to the conclusion that man could not make his own organization, or any of its qualities, and that these qualities were, according to their nature, more or less influenced by the circumstances which occurred in the life of each, over which the individual had no other control than these

combined circumstances gave him, but over which society had an over-whelming influence.

(cited in Silver, 1969, p. 47)

Thus, his two major enemies were laissez-faire economics[5] and the Christian churches for their view that our characters are of our own making. Fourier, as we have seen, argued that human nature was derived from God.

In *Report to the County of Lanark* (1820), Owen put forward his views on the *labour theory of value* (LTV), soon to become the economic foundation stone of the writings of Marx, suggesting that labour should supersede money as the standard for measuring the relative values of different commodities (Cole, 1971, pp. 94–95) (for a discussion of Marx's LTV, see below, pp. 24–25). However, Owen's 'communism' was based upon a business foundation, the outcome of commercial calculation. Thus in 1823, he proposed the relief of the distress in Ireland by communist colonies, and drew up complete estimates of costs of funding them, yearly expenditure and probable revenue (Engels, 1977 [1892], p. 403). A year later, Owen left England in order to see what could be done in what he felt was the comparatively uncorrupted atmosphere of the US. Here he bought the community village of New Harmony in Indiana (Cole, 1971, p. 96), in an attempt to set up a self-governing community. However, the experiment was racked by sectarianism (ibid., p. 100) and, in 1829, Owen returned to England.

On his return, he found that that a number of workers had taken up his ideas. His support increased after the Reform Act of 1832. This Act, which extended the right to vote from the landed gentry to the more prosperous middle classes (prop-ertied males paying an annual rent of £10), embittered the working class and, by 1833 Owen's ideas had a firm hold in the trade unions, which were springing up all over the country. Owen himself established the Grand National Consolidated Trades Union, which, at its height, had over half a million members (MacKenzie, 1967, pp. 34–35). His ideas also inspired a number of cooperative enterprises and, in 1844, the Rochdale Equitable Pioneers set up the modern cooperative movement (ibid., p. 3) which is still flourishing in Britain today.

For Engels, Owen's great significance in the development of socialism (the word itself, according to MacKenzie (1967, p. 35), was first used in an Owenite paper) was his advocacy of 'communism', albeit business-based, his commit-ment to the working class and his advocacy of cooperatives. As Engels (1977 [1892], p. 404) puts it, 'every social movement, every real advance in England on behalf of the workers links itself on to the name of Robert Owen'.

The Marxist critique of utopian socialism and the development of 'scientific socialism'

To summarise: for Engels, Saint-Simon's major contribution to Marxism was his recognition of class struggle; Fourier's was dialectical thinking; and Owen's bequest was his dedication to workers' welfare. What these utopian socialists all had in common was that, unlike Marxists, who advocate the revolutionary emancipation of the working class in order to change society, the utopian social-ists were concerned with liberating all humanity without such revolutionary changes. As Marx and Engels (1977a [1847], p. 60) point out, Saint-Simon, Fourier and Owen all recognised the class antagonisms in existing societies, but viewed the working class as 'a class without any historical initiative'. This is pri-marily because of the 'undeveloped state' of the proletariat[6] at the time (Marx and Engels, 1977a [1847]). For the utopian socialists, change was to come about by 'peaceful means', by 'small experiments' and by 'force of example' (ibid.). Marx and Engels, on the other hand, 'openly declare that their ends can be attained only by the forcible overthrow of all existing social conditions' (ibid., p. 63).[7]

Although Marx denounced utopian socialism, he never actually referred to his own ideas as 'scientific socialism'. It was, in fact, Engels (1977 [1892], p. 404) who, believing utopian socialism to be 'a mish-mash' of 'absolute truth, reason, and justice' based on 'subjective understandings' associated with various schools of utopian socialist thought, argued that 'to make a science of socialism, it had first to be placed upon a real basis' (ibid., p. 405) (his and Marx's concep-tion of 'utopia' accords with its original meaning, 'a place that does not exist'). This 'real basis' is the *materialist conception of history* (ibid., p. 411) and the aforementioned *labour theory of value* (the basis of *surplus value*). As Engels (1962 [1877], p. 43) argues: 'These two great discoveries, the materialist con-ception of history and the revelation of the secret of capitalistic production through surplus value, we owe to Marx. With these discoveries socialism became a science'.

The materialist conception of history

The materialist conception of history 'starts from the proposition that the pro-duction of the means to support human life and, next to production, the exchange of things produced, is the basis of all social structure' (Engels, 1977 [1892], p. 411). All past history, with the exception of its most early stages – primitive communism – the original hunter-gatherer society of humanity – is, according to Marx and Engels, the history of class struggles. These warring classes are always the products of the respective modes of production, of the *economic* conditions of their time. Thus, slaves were in class struggle with their masters in the historical epoch of slavery; feudal serfs with their lords in times of feudalism; and in the era of capitalism, workers are engaged in a class struggle with capitalists. Like slavery and feudalism, capitalism is viewed merely as a *stage* in human development. Marxists see such stages as containing a number of *contradictions*, which resolve themselves dialectically. Thus, when these contradictions become too great, a given stage gives way to another. For example, just as the privileges which feudal lords held and the hereditary basis of subordinating serf to lord in the feudal societies contradicted the need for 'free' labour power in emerging capitalism ('free' in the sense that workers were not needed to be indentured to the capitalists; they were, of course, forced to sell

their labour power in order to survive), present day capitalism contains contradictions which Marxists believe, given the right circumstances, will eventually
lead to its demise. Engels describes the unfolding of modes of production
through mediaeval society (individual production on a small scale), through the
capitalist revolution (the transformation of production from individual to social
means) and beyond (ibid., p. 428).

Capitalism has an inbuilt tendency to constantly expand. As Marx and Engels
put it in *The Communist Manifesto*, when describing its development:

> The markets kept ever growing, the demand ever rising. ... The place of
> manufacture was taken by the giant, Modern Industry, the place of the indus-
> trial middle class, by industrial millionaires. ... Modern industry has estab-
> lished the world-market. The need of a constantly expanding market for its
> products chases the bourgeoisie over the whole surface of the globe. It must
> nestle everywhere, settle everywhere, establish connexions everywhere ... In
> one word, it creates a world after its own image.
>
> (Marx and Engels, 1977a [1847], pp. 37–39)

This expansion takes three main forms: first, spatially (globalisation), as capital
occupies all known sociophysical space (including outside the planet) – this is
extension; second, capital expands as the differentiated form of the commodity,
creating new commodities – this is *differentiation*; third, it expands through
intensification of its own production processes (Rikowski, 2001, p. 14). Capitalism is thus a thoroughly dynamic system.

In its inherent need to extract more and more surplus value, capital is also out
of control. As Rikowski has argued:

> Capital moves, but not of its own accord: the mental and physical cap-
> abilities of workers (labour-power) enable these movements through their
> expression in labour. Our labour enables the movements of capital and its
> transformations (e.g. surplus value into various forms of capital). The social
> universe of capital then is a universe of constant movement; it incorporates
> and generates a restlessness unparalleled in human history. ... It is set on a
> trajectory, the 'trajectory of production' ... powered not simply by value but
> by the 'constant *expansion* of surplus value'. [It is a movement] 'independ-
> ent of human control'. ... It is a movement out of control.
>
> (Rikowski, 2001, p. 10; surplus value is discussed in the next section)

The anarchy of capitalist production creates the material conditions for the proletarian revolution (the transformation of the socialised means of production
from the hands of the bourgeoisie into public property) (Engels, 1977 [1892],
p. 428). While, for Marxists, proletarian revolution is not *inevitable*, it is always
on the cards. As Tom Hickey (2006) explains, capitalism has an inbuilt tendency
to generate conflict, and is thus *permanently* vulnerable to challenge from the
working class. As he puts it:

The objective interests of the bourgeoisie and the proletariat are incompatible, and therefore generate not a tendency to permanent hostility and open warfare but a permanent tendency toward them. The system is thus prone to economic class conflict, and, given the cyclical instability of its economy, subject to periodic political and economic crises. It is at these moments that the possibility exists for social revolution.

(Hickey, 2006, p. 192)

The labour theory of value

An understanding of the source of this incompatibility and permanent tendency toward hostility can be facilitated by Marx's *labour theory of value* (LTV). The LTV explains most concisely why capitalism is objectively a system of exploitation, whether the exploited realise it or not, or indeed, whether they believe it to be an issue of importance for them or not. The LTV also provides a *solution* to this exploitation. It thus provides *dialectical* praxis – the authentic union of theory and practice.

According to the LTV, the interests of capitalists and workers are diametrically opposed, since a benefit to the former (profits) is a cost to the latter (Hickey, 2002, p. 168). Marx argued that workers' labour is embodied in the goods that they produce. The finished products are appropriated (taken away) by the capitalists and eventually sold at a profit. However, the worker is paid only a fraction of the value s/he creates in labour; the wage does not represent the *total* value s/he creates. We *appear* to be paid for every single second we work. However, underneath this appearance, this fetishism, the working day (like under serfdom) is split in two: into socially necessary labour (and the wage represents this) and surplus labour, labour that is not reflected in the wage. Greatly oversimplifying matters, let us assume that a capitalist employs a worker to make a table. Let us say that the value of the basic materials is £100, and that after these basic materials have had labour embodied in them (i.e. have become a table) that table has a value of £500. Let us further assume that in the time it takes to make the table £20 of overheads are used up. What happens to the £400 surplus value that the worker has created? The worker is paid, say, £100 and the remaining £300 are appropriated, taken away, by the capitalist. After overheads are paid, the capitalist still has £280 *surplus* that he or she can reinvest to create more surplus. To continue the example, with this £280 surplus the capitalist can buy £200 worth of basic materials, and employ two workers, and after these basic materials have had labour embodied in them (e.g. have become two tables) those tables have a value of £1,000. Assuming overheads increase to £30, and two workers are each paid £100, the capitalist is now left with £770 surplus which can be thrown back into production to create yet more surplus value, and so on and so on. If the capitalist continues to employ workers, say seven, the surplus would be over £6,000. It is thus easy to see how surplus value multiplies and how capitalists' surplus (which is converted into profit) is, in truth, nothing more than accumulated surplus value, really the 'property' of the worker but appropriated from that worker.[8]

While the value of the raw materials and of the depreciating machinery is simply passed on to the commodity in production, labour power is a peculiar, indeed unique commodity, in that it creates new value. 'The magical quality of labour-power's ... value for ... capital is therefore critical' (Rikowski, 2001, p. 11). 'Labour-power creates more value (profit) in its consumption than it possesses itself, and than it costs' (Marx, 1966 [1894], p. 351). Unlike, for example, the value of a given commodity, which can only be realised in the market as itself, labour creates a new value, a value greater than itself, a value that previously did not exist. It is for this reason that labour power is so important for the capitalist in the quest for capital accumulation.

It is in the interest of the capitalist or capitalists (nowadays, capitalists may, of course, consist of a number of shareholders, for example, rather than outright owners of businesses) to maximise profits and this entails (in order to create the greatest amount of new value) keeping workers' wages as low as is 'acceptable' or tolerated in any given country or historical period, without provoking effective strikes or other forms of resistance. Therefore, the capitalist mode of production is, in essence, a system of exploitation of one class (the working class) by another (the capitalist class).

Whereas class conflict is endemic to, and ineradicable and perpetual within the capitalist system, it does not always, or even typically, take the form of open conflict or expressed hostility (Hickey, 2002, p. 168). Fortunately for the working class however, capitalism, as argued above, is prone to cyclical instability and subject to periodic political and economic crises. As also argued above, at these moments, the possibility exists for social revolution. Revolution can only come about when the working class, in addition to being a 'class-in-itself' (an *objective* fact because of the shared exploitation inherent as a result of the LTV) becomes 'a class-for-itself' (Marx, 1976a [1885]). By this, Marx meant a class with a *subjective* awareness of its social class position, that is to say, a class with 'class consciousness' – including its awareness of its exploitation and its transcendence of 'false consciousness'.

Marx argued that, if and when the working class has become a 'class-for-itself', it has the potential to seize control of the means of production, the economy and take political power. Seizure of the economy would constitute such a social revolution (Hill and Cole, 2001, p. 147). This, of course, is not an easy option but, for Marxists, it is the working class that is most likely to be at the forefront of such a revolution.

As Michael Slott has put it with great clarity:

> Marxists have understood perfectly well that there are many obstacles to the working class becoming a universal agent for socialism. At the same time, Marxists have argued that, because of the particular interests, collective power, and creative capacities that are generated by workers' structural position in society, the working class is more likely to be at the core of any movement of social transformation.
>
> (2002, p. 419)[9]

For Marx, socialism (as we have seen – see Chapter 1, note 1 – a stage before communism – that mode of existence when the state would wither away and we would live communally) is a world system in which 'we shall have an association, in which the free development of each is the condition for the free development of all' (Marx and Engels, 1977a [1847], p. 53). Such a society would be democratic (as such, socialism as envisaged by Marx should be distanced from the *undemocratic* regimes of the former Soviet bloc) and classless, and the means of production would be in the hands of the many, not the few. Goods and services would be produced for need and not for profit.

Marx explains his vision of 'the higher phase of communist society' (Marx, *Critique of the Gotha Programme*, 1875, cited in Bottomore and Rubel, 1978, p. 263) that would come after the temporary phase of socialism:

> In the higher phase of communist society, when the enslaving subordination of the individual to the division of labour, and with it the antithesis between mental and physical labour, has vanished; when labour is no longer merely a means of life but has become life's principal need; when the productive forces have also increased with the all-round development of the individual, and all the springs of co-operative wealth flow more abundantly – only then will it be possible completely to transcend the narrow outlook of the bourgeois right, and only then will society be able to inscribe on its banners: From each according to his ability, to each according to his needs.
>
> (cited in ibid.)

In a communist world, the 'original goodness' of humanity is realised, and 'the private interest of each' coincides 'with the general interest of humanity' (Marx and Engels, *The Holy Family*, 1845, cited in ibid., p. 249). This can only be achieved with the overthrow of capitalism. As Hickey (2006) explains:

> Crises provide the opportunity for transition from the oppressive and exploitative, competitive and alienating conditions of the order of capital to a realm of human freedom in which humanity as a whole, through a radically democratic structure, engages collectively in satisfying its needs, ordering its priorities, and constructing new needs and aspirations to strive for, and challenges to overcome.

Clearly Marx's vision of communism is fundamentally different from that of Owen, which was based on a business foundation. It also differs in essence from the countries of the former Soviet bloc. It is ironic that the West falsely designated these states 'communist'. In reality (despite the fact that many had a number of positive features – full employment, housing for all, free public and social services, safety for women to walk the streets at night and so on) they were undemocratic dictatorships with special privileges for an elite and drudgery for the many. These Eastern European societies were not real socialist states, and were also far removed from Marx's vision of communism. As we have seen

(Chapter 1, note 1), they have been described as 'state capitalist' rather than socialist or communist.

An understanding of the essence and thrust of scientific socialism is a necessary prerequisite in the struggle for true socialism and ultimately communism. For Engels (1977 [1892], p. 428) the proletarian revolution:

> frees the means of production from the character of capital they have thus far borne, and gives their socialised character complete freedom to work itself out ... To thoroughly comprehend the historical conditions and thus the very nature of this act, to impart to the now oppressed proletarian class a full knowledge of the conditions and of the meaning of the momentous act it is called upon to accomplish... is the task of the theoretical expression of the proletarian movement, scientific socialism.

Education, according to Louis Althusser (1971), is the primary *ideological state apparatus* that militates against a proper comprehension of the oppressive nature of capitalist society. Education can also be a means of facilitating an understanding of this oppression, an awareness of how it might be eradicated, and of what might replace it. It is *Marxist theory and education*, which is the focus of the next chapter.

3 Marxist theory and education

In this chapter, I begin with a brief sketch of the views of utopian socialists on education. I then go on to briefly examine some of the thoughts on education of Karl Marx and Frederick Engels. Next I assess the contribution of the twentieth century's most influential Marxist educationists, Louis Althusser and Sam Bowles and Herb Gintis, and the responses to their work. I conclude with some suggestions as to the future of Marxist educational theory, based on the work of Glenn Rikowski.

Introduction

The views on education of the utopian socialists understandably reflect their general views on society. Accordingly, their suggestions are gradualist and reformist rather than revolutionary.[1]

Thus, Saint-Simon, in tandem with his overall views on the need for a hegemony of the middle classes, rather than of either the aristocracy or the workers, believed that education should be elitist and under the control of those noted for 'the superiority of their enlightenment' (Taylor, 1993a, p. 16). For Saint-Simon, this meant scientists rather than the clergy. As Taylor (1993a, p. 17) concludes: 'Saint-Simon's views on education were developed upon the assumption that the workers would be content to receive guidance from a scientific elite, and that they had no desire to challenge the relatively new capitalist class'. Believing that the French proletariat had higher levels of intelligence and foresight than the proletariat of other European countries, Saint-Simon's aim was to convince influential sections of society that the education system needed to adapt to the rise of industrialism (ibid., p. 18).

Charles Fourier's educational views were also conducive to the maintenance of class cohesion. He was intent on eradicating the divisions between mental and manual work with the aim of serving the interests of the community rather than the affectations of a particular class (Taylor, 1993b, p. 15). His position on education was also consistent with his libertarian position on society in general. Predating the views of the 'free-schoolers',[2] Fourier believed that children should be free to pursue their own interests and even to remain ignorant (ibid., p. 15), and that study in the schools should occupy a subordinate place with respect to labour in the gardens and workshops (Fourier, 1820). Unlike Saint-Simon's dedication to a rigid hierarchy favouring the new industrial and scientific elites rather than the old aristocracy, Fourier's preferred education system was more anarchistic. Refusing to defer to the world of scholarship and academic attainment, which he contemptuously referred to as 'civilised education' (ibid., p. 15), he aimed to mould society to fit the variety of human characteristics (Taylor, 1994a, p. 20). As Taylor (ibid., p. 19) puts it, 'whereas civilised education aimed to cultivate the mind, Fourier's harmonian education dealt with the senses and social virtues before the intellect'. In Fourier's words:

> Harmonian education starts from practice, leading then to theory. Children learn first to refine their senses, next start practising various crafts to which they are attracted. Only after mastering various practical skills are they taught to read and write.
>
> (Fourier, 1830)

For Robert Owen, the function of education was to decrease the distance between the classes by raising the level of all, in order to promote social harmony (Taylor, 1994b, p. 21). Owen warned that industrialism might degrade the workers if their tasks became too specialised and repetitive, so hoped that education could broaden young workers' capabilities (ibid., p. 20). Like Saint-Simon, Owen's education system was elitist: children should be taught what is 'necessary' for them to know. This would depend on the 'rank of life in which they are likely to be placed' (ibid.). Workers, according to Owen, rather than being left to mind the machines without mental effort or rational reflection, should be educated with the right habits, information, manners and dispositions to benefit the capitalist class and to be well governed (ibid.). The longer-term aim was 'a peaceful transition to socialism' (Taylor, 1994c, p. 20). Unlike the Marxist conception of scientific socialism, however, this transition was to be achieved without the overthrow of the capitalist system.

Marx and Engels and education

Speaking to the General Council of the First International in August 1868, Marx stated: 'on the one hand a change of social circumstances was required to establish a proper system of education, on the other hand a proper system of education was required to bring about a change of social circumstances' (cited in Price, 1977, p. 69). Marx also noted that 'we must therefore commence where we were' (cited in ibid.). As Price (1977, p. 69) concludes, 'all this implies that the major concern of education should be ... the development of socialist consciousness'.

As we have seen in Chapter 2, for Marx and Engels the transformation of society is to come about through class struggle, and class action, rather than as a result of the spread of enlightened opinion throughout society; thus education did not figure prominently in their work, at least in the sense of being educated formally in institutions.[3]

What Marx and Engels did argue was that workers were educated very much by their experiences of labour under capitalism. Marx, in fact, believed that, from the age of nine, education in schools should be combined with labour. Marx and Engels felt that combining education with labour would increase general awareness of the (exploitative) nature of capitalism.[4]

Marx noted that, on the one hand, the bourgeoisie fail to offer real education and, instead, education is used to spread bourgeois moral principles (Marx, 1847, cited in Taylor, 1995, p. 19), while, on the other hand, Engels (1975 [1845], p. 243) argued that 'an educated proletariat will not be disposed to remain in the oppressed condition in which our present proletariat finds itself', and thus believed that education could contribute to increased awareness. For Marxist educationists, therefore, there are two interrelated issues which are of importance with respect to education under capitalism: first how and to what extent does institutionalised education reproduce capitalism; second, in which ways might education in capitalist societies undermine capitalism.[5]

Education and the reproduction of capitalism

Louis Althusser on education

It is first necessary to understand the role of education in capitalist society. Louis Althusser (1971) differentiates between what he calls the *Repressive State Apparatuses* (*RSAs*) (government, administration, army, police, courts, prisons) and the *Ideological State Apparatuses* (*ISAs*) (religion, education, family, law, politics, trade unions, communication, culture). The *RSAs* operate primarily by force and control. This can be by making illegal the forces and organisations (and their tactics) that threaten the capitalist status quo and the rate of profit. Thus, for example, restrictions are placed on strike action and trade union activities. More extreme versions of *RSA* action include heavy intimidatory policing and other forms of state-sanctioned political repression and violence by the police and armed forces (Hill, 2001a, p. 106; see also Hill, 2001b, 2004b, 2005b). While the *ISAs* operate primarily through ideology, it needs to be pointed out that the two state apparatuses function both by violence and by ideology. It is worth quoting Althusser at length:

> What distinguishes the ISAs from the (Repressive) State Apparatus is the following basic difference: the Repressive State Apparatus functions 'by violence', whereas the Ideological State Apparatuses' *function* '*by ideology*'. I can clarify matters by correcting this distinction. I shall say rather that every State Apparatus, whether Repressive or Ideological, 'functions' both by violence and by ideology, but with one very important distinction which makes it imperative not to confuse the Ideological State Apparatuses with the (Repressive) State Apparatus. This is the fact that the (Repressive)

State Apparatus functions massively and predominantly *by repression* (including physical repression), while functioning secondarily by ideology. (There is no such thing as a purely repressive apparatus.) For example, the Army and the Police also function by ideology both to ensure their own cohesion and reproduction, and in the 'values' they propound externally. In the same way, but inversely, it is essential to say that for their part the Ideological State Apparatuses function massively and predominantly *by ideology*, but they also function secondarily by repression, even if ultimately, but only ultimately, this is very attenuated and concealed, even symbolic. (There is no such thing as a purely ideological apparatus.) Thus Schools and Churches use suitable methods of punishment, expulsion, selection, etc., to 'discipline' not only their shepherds, but also their flocks. The same is true of the Family. ... The same is true of the cultural IS Apparatus (censorship, among other things), etc.

(Althusser, 1971, pp. 144–145)

The ruling class, and governments in whose interests they act, tend to prefer, in normal circumstances, to operate via *ISAs*. Changing the school curriculum to make it more in line with the requirements of capital, for example, is less messy than sending in the riot police or the troops; and it is deemed to be more legitimate by the populace (Hill, 2001a, p. 106). For Althusser, whereas the religious *ISA* (system of different churches) used historically to be the major *ISA*, 'the ISA which has been installed in the dominant position in mature capitalist social formations ... is the *educational ideological apparatus* ... [it is] number one' (Althusser, 1971, p. 153). Althusser argued that schools are particularly important for inculcating the dominant ideology, since no other *ISA* requires compulsory attendance of all children eight hours a day for five days a week. Althusser suggested that what children learn at school is 'know-how' – wrapped in the ruling ideology of the ruling class. As Madan Sarup (1983, p. 13) put it: 'in this system each mass of children ejected en route is practically provided with the ideology which suits the role it has to fulfil in class society'. One of the advantages to the ruling class of the educational *ISA* is that, while given its high profile in party political rhetoric, education, in everyday usage, is no longer perceived as neutral in a party political sense, it is certainly not thought of as an agent of cultural and economic reproduction.[6]

The Bowles and Gintis moment and its legacy

Bowles and Gintis' (1976) book, *Schooling in Capitalist America* (*SCA*) rose to prominence in Britain in the wake of an Open University sociology of education module, *Schooling and Society*. This remarkable course needs to be situated historically.[7]

In the early 1970s, prior to the publication of *SCA*, many radical sociologists of education became seduced by the New Sociology of Education (*NSE*) (e.g. Young, 1971). Its promise was to reveal the political character of educational knowledge, which was perceived as a construct of 'underlying meanings'. The task of *NSE* was to explore the construction of these meanings. Methodologically ethnographic (concerned with interaction at the classroom level), its concern was with individual actors rather than social structures (Cole, 1988a, p. 7). *NSE* was a radical departure from traditional sociological concerns with functionalist explanations (how schools and other institutions 'function' to maintain cohesion in societies). However, as Robert Moore (1988, p. 52) points out, it represented radicalism within sociology of education, rather than political radicalism. It was not so much that *NSE* rejected political radicalism: rather it was unable to make the connections upon which a political radical analysis depended, and, in this sense it was fundamentally flawed (Cole, 1988a, p. 7). While *NSE* recognised the centrality of notions of power and control, it was unable to make the link between the micro level (the school and the classroom) where meanings, including power relations were thought to be constructed, defined and redefined; and the macro level (the capitalist economy where economic power, ownership and control ultimately resided) (ibid.). For many, the publication of *SCA* was a major breakthrough: an analysis, which made the capitalist economy central to an understanding of processes in schools.

The correspondence principle

The key concept in *SCA* is 'the correspondence principle' – the reproduction of social relations of production is facilitated through a structural correspondence between the social relations of education and those of production. 'To reproduce the social relations of production', Bowles and Gintis (1976, p. 130) argue, 'the education system must try to teach people to be properly subordinate and render them sufficiently fragmented in consciousness to preclude their getting together to shape their material existence'. Specifically, according to *The Correspondence Principle*, 'the educational system helps integrate youth into the economic system ... through a *structural correspondence* between its social relations and those of production' (ibid., p. 131; my emphasis). It is worth quoting Bowles and Gintis (ibid.) at length:

> The structure of social relations in education not only inures the student to the discipline of the work place, but develops the types of personal demeanor, modes of self-presentation, self-image, and social-class identifications which are the crucial ingredients of job adequacy. Specifically, the social relations of education – the relationships between administrators and teachers, teachers and students, students and students, and students and their work – replicate the hierarchical division of labor. Hierarchical relations are reflected in the vertical authority lines from administrators to teachers to students. Alienated labor is reflected in the student's lack of control over his or her education, the alienation of the student from the curriculum content, and the motivation of school work through a system of grades and other external rewards rather

than the student's integration with either the process (learning) or the outcome (knowledge) of the educational 'production process'. Fragmentation in work is reflected in the institutionalized and often destructive competition among students through continual and ostensibly meritocratic ranking and evaluation. By attuning young people to a set of social relationships similar to those of the work place, schooling attempts to gear the development of personal needs to its requirements.

Largely because of *SCA*'s endorsement by the Open University – a very influential body at the time (*SCA* was an Open University set book), *SCA* had a very wide influence, including becoming a central feature of sociology A-level in schools. *SCA* has been a major progressive force, and the critique of *SCA*, which follows, therefore, should be read not as an attempt to undermine the positive political impact of the book. Instead, it should be viewed as comradely criticism, designed to move forward Marxist theory, and Marxist analysis of schooling and education.

In the Classical Age of Marxist Educational Theory,[8] most of the critiques of Bowles and Gintis were from within the Marxist tradition. One of the most influential was Paul Willis's (1977) *Learning to Labour*. Willis, in fact, turns the correspondence principle on its head. Schooling, for Willis, delivers 'the lads' as compliant factory workers by *failing* to manipulate the personalities of pupils to produce ideal workers (Cole, 1983, p. 474). Anxious to leave school at the earliest opportunity, 'the lads' actually prepare themselves, through their cultural rebellions (having a 'laff' at the school's expense), through their sexism and racism, for the macho and racist world of shop floor life.

Education and the undermining of capitalism

Madan Sarup (1978, pp. 172–184; see also Apple, 1979, 1982; Giroux, 1981, 1983) makes a number of neo-Marxist[9] criticisms of *SCA*. In particular, he criticises *SCA* for its functionalism and determinism. Although Bowles and Gintis have a Marxist commitment to overthrowing capitalism, Sarup suggests that their view of society is functionalist and economic determinist. In other words, the impression one gets from reading *SCA* is that everything is 'sewn up' and totally resistant to change – schooling produces the workforce that capitalism requires and there is not much that can be done about it. This interpretation was confirmed by my teaching in the 1980s. As I put it at the time (Cole, 1983, p. 473):

> Some of my student teachers have even looked upon the [correspondence] principle as reassuring in its promise of stability and the maintenance of the status quo, while others, with a more radical mind, have despaired at the seeming lack of space for individual and collective action.

While this determinist reading of *SCA* must always be considered alongside the two final chapters of the book where Bowles and Gintis address 'Educational

Alternatives' (which they debunk) and 'Education, Socialism and Revolution' (where they end the book with a plea for the revolutionary transformation of the US economy), these problems of functionalism and determinism remain. Understandably, commentators concentrated on the central theme of *SCA, The Correspondence Principle*. Glenn Rikowski's (1997a, pp. 551–574) has outlined five interlinked 'debilitating problematics' with Bowles and Gintis's thesis, and the Marxist educational theory that it spawned. I will deal with each in turn.

The first is the *base/superstructure* model, where the economic base *determines* the superstructure (e.g. the political, legal and, in this case, the schooling system). As Rikowski (1997a, p. 556) points out, such determinism leaves no theoretical space for class struggle and engenders fatalism. As I have argued above, while this critique is valid, it needs to be considered in the light of the last two chapters of *SCA*.

Rikowski's second problematic, which leads on from this, is that the correspondence principle's essential functionalism militates against Marxism. While Marxism is, like functionalism, also centrally concerned with how societies function, Marxism is not just a theory *of* society, but also a theory against society; a theory which moves *beyond* presently existing society, in the pursuit of a socialist future (ibid., p. 557). This is also a valid point, but also needs considering alongside the last two chapters of *SCA*.[10]

Rikowski's third point is that, in order to escape the *base/superstructure* dilemma, a number of commentators (e.g. Apple, 1982; Carnoy and Levin, 1985) have drawn on relative autonomy theory, derived from the work of Louis Althusser and others, where there is a degree of autonomy or separateness between the requirements of the capitalist economy (the base) and what happens at the superstructural level of society (education, the political system, etc.). Relative autonomy theorists talk about determination 'in the last instance'. This was seen to offer the best of both worlds: a weak form of determination; and a space for resistance (Rikowski, 1997a, p. 558). Problems with relative autonomy theory are determining when 'the last instance' actually arrives; and the tendency for relative autonomy to slide into complete autonomy, thus deserting the Marxist project altogether (see Hill, 2001b, 2005b).[11]

Fourth, the seeming lack of space for resistance in *SCA* led a number of commentators (e.g. Willis, 1977; Apple, 1982) to concentrate on the ways in which pupils/students *resist* capitalist schooling. The problem with these writings on resistance, however, is the unspecificity of the term, which, Rikowski (1997a, p. 561) argues, thus renders it redundant. *Resistance*, in the work of the resistance theorists, has included, for example, fucking, fighting, farting, fiddling, anti-intellectualism, racism and sexism (Rikowski, 1997a, p. 561).

Rikowski's (1997a) fifth and final point is the dichotomy between *education for autonomy* and *social revolution*, his argument being that there is a danger that, at the expense of enhancing the individual's capacity for independent thinking, we may lose sight of Marxism's stress on social revolution, as discussed above. I have to disagree with Rikowski here. While this dichotomy may be true of other (Marxist) writings in the 1970s and 1980s, in the final two chapters of

SCA, Bowles and Gintis make it perfectly clear, as I have indicated, that their overriding concern is with social revolution. As they end their book:

> the political challenge facing us [cannot] be met through the spontaneous efforts of individuals or groups working in isolation. The development and articulation of the vision of a socialist alternative, as much as the ability to meet today's concrete human needs requires a mass based party able to aid in the daily struggles of working people throughout the United States and committed to a revolutionary transformation of the U.S. economy.
>
> (Bowles and Gintis, 1976, p. 288)

Marx's prescription for education under capitalism was an education that aimed at a critical analysis of capitalist society, through combining work with education (Rikowski, 2004b). Given the fact that most students now have to engage in unskilled manual labour as well as study in order to obtain a first degree at university, at this level at least, the connections between education and work may be easier to make.

Rikowski's solution to the dilemmas of the correspondence principle and its legacy is to dissolve *Marxist sociology of education* altogether and to make the concept of *labour power* the starting point for an analysis of the relationship between schooling and capitalism. It is well known that the starting point of Marx's major work, *Capital,* is an analysis of commodities (as flagged in Chapter 2, commodities are things that can be sold), the accumulation of which underpins the capitalist mode of production (Marx, 1965 [1887], p. 35).

Citing Marx (1969 [1863], p. 167), Rikowski (2000, p. 20) makes it clear that there are two classes of commodities: first, labour power; second, commodities distinct from labour power. Labour power is the individual's power to work in order to produce surplus value and is an *internal commodity*. Those commodities which are *external* to people include physical objects (such as the products of workers' labour), but also services and intellectual property (e.g. knowledge). Labour power is unique in that it is the only commodity, which produces a value greater than itself (when workers engage in capitalist production, they get paid less than the value they produce, the surplus being appropriated or hived off by the capitalist) (see pp. 24–25 of Chapter 2 for a discussion of the labour theory of value). What characterises the capitalist mode of production is that education and training socially produces labour power. In capitalist society, labour power takes the form of human capital – the capacity of workers to work and, therefore to produce surplus value.

With increasing globalisation, in order to compete with other capitalists, capitalists need labour power with more human capital than their competitors. The 'intentionality and social drive to reduce education and training to the social production of labour power in capitalism', as Rikowski (2000, p. 23) argues, therefore grows 'stronger with time'. This growth in strength is apparent in the global drive to privatise schooling, both in order to increase profits from the schooling process itself (e.g. Hill 2004c, 2004d, 2006b; Hill and Kumar, 2008; Hill *et al.,*

2008), and in the attempt to massively increase capitalist control over the form and content of schooling (e.g. Cole, 2007a).[12]

Despite this intense drive by capital, because of a fatal flaw in this development, Rikowski (2004b) is optimistic about the possibility of education as a force for opposing this process. As he argues:

> The significance of a politics of human resistance is that labour-power, as a phenomenon is *capital's weakest link*, in a double sense. First, the transformation of labour-power into labour in the labour process by labourers creates value and surplus-value, the latter being the first form of capital. The whole system depends on labour-power. Secondly, labour-power is an aspect of personhood, and hence under the sway of a will potentially hostile to the social domination of capital in education, and indeed the whole of social life. Thus, an anti-capitalist education of the future might embrace a politics of human resistance to the capitalisation of humanity through education and training being implicated in the social production of labour-power. Education and training would be at the forefront in the politics of human resistance.

I have some reservations about education and training being *at the forefront* of resistance to global capitalism. As I argued earlier in this chapter, following Marx and Slott, it is the working class who are likely to be at the forefront.[13] However, there would be general agreement among Marxists that it can play an important role in such resistance. I suppose it depends what Rikowski means by 'forefront'.

SCA and the correspondence principle were indeed revolutionary moments in the sociology of education. While a focus on the capitalist economy, provided by the correspondence principle, is welcome (and while Marxists must laud Bowles and Gintis's (1976) uncompromising commitment to social revolution); my view, following Rikowski (1997a, 2000), is that we should dissolve Marxist sociology of education altogether and build and develop an understanding of the schooling/capitalist economy relation around the material concept of labour power – to return to Marx in order to develop a Marxist educational theory for the twenty-first century. The need for a return to Marx is not limited to this chapter, but is the theme of this book. In the next chapter I look at Nietzsche and the origins of poststructuralism and postmodernism, in order to assess, in Chapter 5, the contribution of poststructuralism and postmodernism, on the one hand, and Marxism, on the other, to social change and social justice.

4   Nietzsche, poststructuralism and postmodernism

In this chapter I begin with a brief discussion of some of the defining features of the terms, modernity and modernism. I then go on to examine some of Friedrich Nietzsche's key critiques of modernity, before assessing his influence on the thinking of leading poststructuralists, Michel Foucault and Jacques Derrida. Next I consider the meanings of postmodernity and postmodernism, focusing on the work of Jean-Francois Lyotard and Jean Baudrillard. This includes an assessment of their indebtedness to Nietzsche.

Introduction

Modernity and modernism

In order to assess the contribution of Friedrich Nietzsche to poststructuralism and postmodernism, it is first necessary to understand what is meant by and to define their historical precedents, *modernity* and *modernism*. Before doing this, however, it needs to be established that whereas modernity is a state of being, modernism refers to the social, cultural, aesthetic and political *movements* associated with modernity. Of these movements, it is the political ones that are of interest here.

Modernity entails, most notably, the decline of feudalism and the ascendancy of modern industrial capitalism, and all that accompanied it, including the growth of the modern proletariat. Modernity witnessed the rise of the nation state, bureaucracy, urbanisation and secularisation. It is very much associated with the *Enlightenment*. A Europe-wide phenomenon associated with the eighteenth century, the Enlightenment witnessed, in the name of the public exaltation of *reason*, an attack on the authority of tradition, especially in terms of church and state.

Modernity is related to scientific logic and discovery, to 'modern literature', modern art and classical music; with the growth of printing, and *the increasing economic and social power of the bourgeoisie.*

Modern*ism* refers to an acceptance of the ideals of modernity and the Enlightenment, to a belief in rationality over superstition. Modernism is about progress and evolution, rather than cyclical versions of history or beliefs in 'the end of history'. Marxism is a product of modernism.[1]

Friedrich Nietzsche and the critique of modernity

Late nineteenth century Europe had sustained a belief in the Enlightenment ideals of historical progress. However, as these societies entered into what Eric Hobsbawm (1994) has referred to as the *Age of Extremes*, ushered in by the First World War, this faith in such progress became difficult to maintain (Callinicos, 2003, p. 115). One of the fiercest critics of this evolutionary optimism was Friedrich Nietzsche, son of a Prussian Lutheran pastor, born in 1844. Nietzsche, whose ideas are widely acknowledged to underpin the subsequent development of both poststructuralism and postmodernism, developed a critique of modernity that is peculiar in that it combines naturalism (a belief that humankind is part of nature) with anti-naturalism (where human beings are seen as distinct from other species). Thus he believed both in the human subject as an incoherent cluster of biological drives *and* as possessing the will to power (Callinicos, 2003, p. 115). Nietzsche was contemptuous of European bourgeois society, once referring to the 'France of taste' (Nietzsche 1982 [1887], p. 382) who have in common, plugging 'their ears against the raging stupidity and the noisy twaddle of the democratic bourgeois' (ibid.). The various catchwords of the day: *progress, evolution, democracy, nationalism, socialism* are all dismissed by him as mere shibboleths. For Nietzsche, the pursuit of the ideas of the French Revolution – *Liberty, Equality, Fraternity* had produced universal mediocrity (Callinicos, 2003, p. 115). Post-revolutionary Europe epitomised, for him, a nihilism, in which everything is devalued (Callinicos, 2003, p. 118.). In accordance with his preferred tactic of critique through the presentation of *difference* and his favoured historical method of beginning with the present and going backward in time until a difference is located (Sarup, 1988, p. 63), Nietzsche contrasts the present state of affairs ('no herdsman and one herd') (Nietzsche, 1969 [1883–1885], p. 46) with aristocratic society:

> a society that believes in the long ladder of an order of rank and differences in value between man and man, and that needs slavery in some sense or other. Without that *pathos of distance* which grows out of the ingrained difference between strata – when the ruling caste constantly looks afar and looks down upon subjects and instruments and just as constantly practices obedience and command, keeping down and keeping at a distance – that other, more mysterious pathos could not have grown up either – the craving for an ever new widening of distances within the soul itself, the development of ever higher, rarer, more remote, further-stretching, more comprehensive states – in brief, simply the enhancement of the type 'man', the continual 'self-overcoming of man', to use a moral formula in a supra-moral sense.
>
> (Nietzsche, 1982 [1887], p. 391)

For Nietzsche, 'every enhancement of the type "man" has so far been the work of an aristocratic society – and it will be so again and again' (Nietzsche, 1982

[1887], p. 391). Nietzsche sought a revaluation of values, in which select individuals could once again affirm themselves and life (Callinicos, 2003, p. 118). Life, according to Nietzsche, is an endless struggle for domination among competing centres of power: 'this world is the will to power and nothing else besides' (Nietzsche, 1968 [1906], cited in Callinicos, 2003, p. 119). In this 'will to power', the human subject has no coherence or unity, other than to influence and dominate others (Callinicos, 2003, p. 119). As Callinicos (ibid.) puts it:

> nature in its entirety – the human world as well as the interactions of physical bodies and the development of living organisms – is thus the continuous process of transformation arising from the endless struggle among a multiplicity of rival centres of power.

Nietzsche was particularly interested in the elevation of particular individuals, a small exceptional élite. Indeed, it was Nietzsche's 'one great intention', according to Rikowski (1997b, p. 8, following Waite, 1996), to render the human world into two for all time: the élite (the enlightened ones) on the one hand, and, on the other, the masses or 'herd' (those who toil to create the material conditions for the emergence and flourishing of this élite), an eternal rift in humankind. Nietzsche subscribed to a cyclical notion of time, whose essence was the *eternal recurrence of the same* (cited in Rikowski, 1997b, p. 12). Thus, in Waite's (1996, p. 14) words: this would ' "break humanity in two" by keeping slaves out of the know, elites in the know – a polarization that is increasingly global' (cited in Rikowski, 1997b, p. 12). This polarisation has increased on an unprecedented scale in the late twentieth and early twenty-first centuries, as a brutal neo-liberal and hierarchical world capitalist system plunders the developing world (see Chapters 7 and 8); tempered only by the needs, on the one hand, to provide the 'herd' with the knowledge that is necessary to keep profits flowing, and, on the other, by the ever-diminishing restraints of technology.

Nietzsche rejected all-encompassing theories of history and theodicies, and viewed claims about the truthfulness and emancipatory thrust of scientific knowledge as masks for power (Antonio, 1998, p. 26). The world is constituted by a set of shifting relations of force, where there is 'no limit to the way in which the world can be interpreted' (Nietzsche, 1968 [1906], cited in Callinicos, 2003, p. 119). Reality is inherently plural. All knowledge is relative. Objective truth is impossible and every centre of force, not only humankind, construes all the rest of the world from its own viewpoint (ibid., pp. 119 and 120). Thus knowledge is not some kind of external reality or its producer neutrally motivated purely by cognitive or ethical aims. All knowledge, for Nietzsche, is open to suspicion, challenge and discussion, with the borders between 'facts' and 'interpretations' ambiguous and subject to contestation. In Nietzsche's view, philosophy and science cannot be autonomous sources of values (Antonio, 1998, p. 26). There is no single, physical reality beyond our interpretations. There are only perspectives (Sarup, 1988, p. 50). As Nietzsche (1964 [1873]) claims: 'What, therefore, is truth? A mobile army of metaphors, metonymies, anthromorphisms: truths are illusions of which one has forgotten that they are illusions'. As Antonio (1998, p. 26) argues, this perspectivism 'frames a partial, uncertain, plural, contextual, experimental approach to knowledge that anticipated postmodern positions', where all major explanations of society, all metanarratives become redundant.

The will to power is not only social and political, but aesthetic too. For Nietzsche, art achieves greatness. 'Becoming what one is' means turning one's life into a work of art. As Callinicos (2003, p. 122) explains:

> The force of his rejection of modernity lies in its not being undertaken in the name of an idealized past. Nietzsche replaced the vista of historical progress evoked by the Enlightenment ... with the grim panorama of an endless struggle for domination, and at the same time he offered the artistic life – or life as a work of art – as the best way of responding to this situation.

Nietzsche saw his own life as such a response, in the process of becoming the higher type of humankind. His views on education were characteristically élitist. Nietzsche argued that the educated man [*sic*] is one who knows a great deal more than the average, and who is constantly increasing knowledge in an orderly logical fashion (Mencken, undated, p. 1). This man is one who is above the mass, both in his thirst for knowledge and in his capacity for differentiating truth from falsity (ibid., p. 3). However, Nietzsche believed that the education he witnessed in his day was mediocre, and that 'school teachers ... are probably the most ignorant and stupid class of men in the whole group of mental workers' (ibid., p. 1).

Nietzsche did not see the formation of the 'highest exemplars' of humanity as purely a cultural process, achieved through education, experience and debate. His view was that particular human types are also cultivated through 'breeding', and thus transmitted genetically (Callinicos, 2003, pp. 120–121). Education, for Nietzsche, should be about a continuation of the process of breeding, both breeding and education being part of producing beings capable of surviving in the struggle for existence (Mencken, undated, p. 2). According to Waite (1996, cited in Rikowski, 1997b, p. 10) the capitalism of Nietzsche's day was not sufficiently geared towards the 'breeding' of such cultural colossi.

Poststructuralism

In the rest of this chapter, I will consider Nietzsche's legacy to both poststructuralism and postmodernism. Poststructuralism has two interrelated forms. One form is primarily associated with the work of Michel Foucault, and examines the relationship between discourse and power; in particular, the notion that power is everywhere and not just located centrally.

The other form of poststructuralism is to do with the role of language in forming individual subjectivity. Thus, whereas *structuralists* aimed to discover uniform linguistic patterns that gave order and coherence to human existence, *post*structuralists highlight the unstable patterns of linguistic and therefore subjective and social order. Whereas structuralism was a *constructive* project, intent on identifying linguistic and social order, poststructuralism is concerned with *deconstruction* (Seidman, 1998, p. 221). The aim is to demonstrate that all claims to ground an order to society, to knowledge, or morality in something beyond traditions or communities is unwarranted and, following Nietzsche, concealed a will to power (ibid., p. 222). Deconstruction is pre-eminently associated with the work of Jacques Derrida.

Michel Foucault and the diffusion of power

Whereas the Nazis took from Nietzsche the idea of the will to power (which was seen as the drive of nations and exceptional individuals to dominate) along with biological racism, and life as an eternal struggle, the poststructuralists, such as Michel Foucault (1926–1984), drew on the notion of history as the interplay of forms of domination (Callinicos, 2003, p. 121). According to Foucault (1977a, p. 151), therefore:

> humanity does not gradually progress from combat to combat until it arrives at universal reciprocity where the rule of law finally replaces warfare; humanity installs each of its violences in a system of rules and thus proceeds from domination to domination.

Foucault's major studies (Foucault 1972, 1977b, 1979, 2001 [1964]) examined a number of human sciences. However, his intention was not to determine whether these disciplines are true or to chart their progress, but to assess the extent of institutional power and control exercised by various institutions. It is the power/knowledge configuration that was his concern (Seidman, 1998, p. 236). Foucault acknowledged his debt to Nietzsche rather than Marx in an interview:

> It was Nietzsche who specified the power relation as the general focus, shall we say, of philosophical discourse – whereas for Marx it was the production relation. Nietzsche is the philosopher of power, a philosopher who managed to think power without having to confine himself within a political theory in order to do so.
>
> (Gordon, 1980, p. 53)

Marx and Engels had developed a model of exploitation and emancipation (scientific socialism) that clearly located the source of this domination and exploitation (the capitalist system and its accompanying mode of production); and the source of this emancipation and the liberation of humankind (the working class). Foucault, however, following Nietzsche, replaced this model with one that advocated a number of power/discourse formations. Since there is no *system as a*

whole and no central power, the would-be revolutionary is rendered paralysed
and redundant. Unlike Althusser (see Chapter 3, pp. 30–31), Foucault did not
believe that power existed in a unified state apparatus. Power does not reside in
some primary central location or locations: 'power is everywhere ... power is not
an institution, nor a structure, nor a possession. It is a name we give to a complex
strategic situation in a particular society' (Foucault, 1979, p. 93). According, to
Foucault, we should focus on how discourses are produced and how they nor-
malise individuals (Sarup, 1983, p. 98).

Foucault had little to say about class consciousness or class interest, since he
did not believe in class struggle: 'one should not assume a massive and primal
condition of domination, a binary structure with "dominators" on the one side
and "dominated" on the other, but rather a multiform production of relations of
domination' (Foucault, 1980, p. 142).

The only forms of political action, therefore, are local, diffused and strategic.
Struggle cannot be totalised (a theme to be taken up with a vengeance by the
postmodernists: see Chapter 5). Related to this is Foucault's belief that there are
no grand theories of society (another central tenet of postmodernism see
Chapter 5). As Sarup (1988, p. 106) argues with respect to Nietzsche's perspectivism and rejection of a progressive and dialectic role for history:

> some of the Nietzschean themes in Foucault's thought are the basis of his
> anti-Marxist position. He insists that any general theory should be
> renounced and that life cannot be grasped from a single perspective.
> Believing that truth and power are linked, he adopts a relativist position;
> modern society is not necessarily better than past ones. We are not pro-
> gressing from the dark to the light. Foucault attacks Marxists because they
> believe that they have deciphered the secret of history. For him history is
> discontinuous and Marxism is a global totalitarian theory which is out of
> date.

In fact, Marxist dialectics are replaced by Foucault with the Nietzschean tactic
of critique through the presentation of *difference*. Nietzsche, as we have seen,
begins with the present and goes backward in time until a difference is located.
The Nietzschean historian then proceeds forward again, tracing the transformation and taking care to preserve the discontinuities as well as the connections (Sarup, 1988, p. 63). The gap between the past and the present underlines
the principle of difference.

As Sarup (ibid., p. 64) explains genealogical analysis (derived from Nietzsche, and adopted by Foucault)[2] differs from traditional or 'total' forms of
historical analysis in that whereas the latter inserts events into grand
exploratory frameworks and linear processes, celebrates great moments and
individuals and seeks a point of origin, genealogy turns away from the spectacular, looks to singular events, and concentrates on the discredited, the
neglected, and a whole range of phenomena that have been denied a history. In
Sarup's words:

According to Foucault there has been an insurrection of subjugated knowledges, of a whole set of knowledges that have been disqualified as inadequate – naïve knowledges located low down on the hierarchy, beneath the required level of scientificity … Genealogies focus on local, discontinuous, disqualified, illegitimate knowledges against the claims of a unitary body of theory which would filter, hierarchize and order them in the name of some true knowledge.

(Sarup, 1988, p. 64)

Foucault is interested in the union of scholarly knowledge and local memories to establish a historical knowledge of struggles and to use this tactically in the present. While Marxists support all such local struggles (see Chapter 5), the problem with Foucault's genealogical approach is that, in rejecting the pursuit of *the origin* (for Marxists, exploitative systems and their respective modes of production) in favour of a conception of historical beginnings as lowly, complex and contingent, 'there can be no constants, no essences, no immobile forms of interrupted continuities structuring the past' (Sarup, 1988, p. 64). If history has no longer a structure, then chance and contingency can assume a far greater importance (Callinicos, 2003, p. 275). Thus, for Foucault (1983, p. 207):

History … is meaningful to the extent that [it] serves to show how that-which-is has not always been; i.e., that the things which seem most evident to us are always formed in the confluence of encounters and chances, during the course of a precarious and fragile history.

For Foucault, as we have seen, power is diffuse. He argued that forms of power in society are imbued with social and psychological knowledge, but also that these forms of knowledge are permeated by power relations. The exercise of power over the populace and the accumulation of knowledge are thus two sides of the same coin (Sarup, 1983, pp. 93–94). As Foucault (1977b, p. 27) puts it: 'Power and knowledge directly imply one another. … There is no power relation without the correlative constitution of a field of knowledge, nor any knowledge that does not presuppose and constitute at the same time power relations'. For Foucault, truth does not exist outside power, still less in opposition to it, each society having its own regime of truth (what can be said and what must be left unsaid) (Sarup, 1983, p. 97).

Foucault (1977b) shows how the techniques of discipline and observation incorporated in the new prison are derived from centuries of practice in other spheres, notably in the army, and in education. For Foucault, discipline takes place in cells. Thus, in schools, borders slept in cells under constant supervision, while in the daytime, their activities were dictated by a cellular system of grades, according to age and 'ability', the chief mechanism of control being the timetable. As Sarup (1983, p. 94) points out, children in schools are 'supervised, hierarchized, rewarded and punished'. As Sarup (1983, pp. 94–95) concludes, 'the techniques of hierarchical observation and normalizing judgement combine in the examination'.

While the oppositional implications of all these systemic attempts at conformity are anti-authoritarianism in schools and elsewhere, there is little, given Foucault's rejection of connections with material processes, that can be gleaned for solutions to the problem of power. As Sarup (1983, p. 102) concludes, noting this defect:

> [Foucault] ignores the fact that the exercise of power depends on material conditions existing independently of it. One of the main problems of Foucault's work is that discourses/practices seem to be virtually independent of the production process, of class struggle, of politics ... schools emerge as structures of statements. Power appears as a function not of classes, not of the state, but of discourse itself. Indeed, Foucault says that his own work is to be regarded as 'a discourse about discourse'. Wherever Foucault looks, he finds nothing but discourse.

Jacques Derrida, discourse and deconstruction

The legacy of Jacques Derrida (1930–2004) also relates to analyses of discourse. In addition, Derrida developed the concept of deconstruction. He disputed the structuralist assertion that meanings are fixed, and proposed that, on the contrary, meanings are unstable, multivocal and constantly changing. Thus, for example, while the binary opposition man/woman may seem stable and universal, it carries various meanings depending on national context, social class, 'race', age, sexuality, disability and so on. Derrida interpreted the meanings of signifiers – words and sounds – as being in a state of continuous flux and contestation, holding that, following Nietzsche, whenever a linguistic or social order is said to be fixed, or meanings to be unambiguous and stable, that this disclosure is less to do with truth, and more to do with power: 'the capacity of a social group to impose its will on others by freezing linguistic and cultural meanings' (Seidman, 1998, p. 222). Deconstruction is defined by Steven Seidman (ibid.) as linguistic and political subversion: 'Poststructuralism is a kind of permanent rebellion against authority, that of science and philosophy but also the church and the state. Its strategy of linguistic and political subversion is called "deconstruction". In particular, Derrida exerted his critical energies towards undermining the hierarchical dualities central to Western culture: speech/writing; presence/absence; meaning/form; soul/body; masculine/feminine; man/woman; literal/metaphorical; nature/culture; positive/negative; transcendental/empirical; and cause/effect (Seidman, 1998, pp. 222 and 223).

Derrida's main debt to Nietzsche is systematic distrust of metaphysics (the branch of philosophy concerned with explaining the nature of the world) and a deep suspicion of the values of 'truth' and 'meaning' (Sarup, 1988, p. 49). The text is central to deconstructionist analysis. Sarup (1988, pp. 3–4) has explained succinctly the importance of the text for poststructuralists:

> while structuralism sees truth as being 'behind' or 'within' a text, poststructuralism stresses the interaction of reader and text as a productivity.

In other words, reading has lost its status as a passive consumption of a product to become a performance.

Indeed, for deconstructionists, in Derrida's (1976, p. 158) words, 'there is nothing outside the text'. By this, Derrida meant that there are no cultural practices that are not defined by frameworks that are 'caught up in conflicting networks of power, violence and domination' (Baker, 1995, p. 129). Richard Rorty (1982, p. 141) has used the term 'textualism' to describe the Derridean notion that the world, rather than existing independently of the ways we talk about it, is constructed in discourse. The most common metaphor used to understand the process of deconstruction is that of the palimpsist; reading texts is akin to the X-raying of pictures, which discover, under the epidermis of the last painting, another hidden one (Sarup, 1988, p. 55). Derrida applies this to the written text. In practical terms, this involves reading texts in a radically new way. There must be an awareness of the discrepancy between its meaning and the assertion of the author (ibid., p. 57). For both Nietzsche and Derrida, life is about being a source of meaning. However, in Parrish's words 'Derrida argues that we should come as close as possible to respecting the face of each other as a sovereign face, and Nietzsche claims that because life is about being a source of meaning we should each embrace our own will to power and reject that of each other' (Parrish, 2006a, p. 36).

Moreover, for Derrida, deconstruction enables human beings to be as non-violent as possible. By stripping way 'law's pretension to be other than politics' (Nietzsche, 1982 [1887]), deconstruction, according to Derrida, shows that dominant positions are bound by discourse to their purveyors rather than being universal or incontestable. Indeed, deconstruction constantly overcomes dominant discourses in the name of justice (Parrish, 2006b). What is more, as we shall see in Chapter 5, for Derrida, construction *is* justice.

Sarup (1988, p. 115) has summarised the poststructuralist debt to Nietzsche. First, the poststructuralists share an antipathy to any 'system'; second, they reject the Marxist view of history as progress; third, they are highly critical of the trend towards conformity; fourth, there is an obsession with the subjective and the 'small story'.

Postmodernity and postmodernism

Just as with modernity and modernism, a distinction needs to be made between postmoder*nity* and postmoder*nism*, with the former referring to a perceived state of being and the latter, the movement associated with this perception.

In order to conceptualise *postmodernity*, it is necessary to introduce the concept of *metanarrative* or *grand narrative*. This means the attempt to make sense of the totality of human history (Callinicos, 2003, p. 2). 'Postmoder*nity* represents the collapse of these grand narratives, the abandonment of any attempt to cast the entire historical process into a single interpretive scheme' (ibid.). Marxism is the major grand narrative or metanarrative, rejected by Jean-François Lyotard. As we shall see shortly, Lyotard defines postmodern*ism* as a rejection of the metanarrative. Elizabeth Atkinson (2002, p. 74) has amplified the implications of Lyotard's definition in her definition of postmodernism:

- resistance towards certainty and resolution;
- rejection of fixed notions of reality, knowledge or method;
- acceptance of complexity, of lack of clarity, and of multiplicity;
- acknowledgement of subjectivity, contradiction and irony;
- irreverence for traditions of philosophy or morality;
- deliberate intent to unsettle assumptions and presuppositions;
- refusal to accept boundaries or hierarchies in ways of thinking; and,
- disruption of binaries which define things either/or.[3]

Jean-François Lyotard and the nature of knowledge

In his younger days, Lyotard (1924–1998) was active in the trade union movement, and, for some 15 years, in the small Marxist group, *Socialisme ou Barbarie*. Lyotard took part in the revolutionary events of May 1968, while a Professor of Philosophy at Vincennes University (Sarup, 1988, p. 106; Seidman, 1998, p. 225). However, in a subsequent succession of books (Lyotard, 1971, 1973, 1974), he quickly developed some ideas for a post-Marxist critical social theory. Lyotard rejected not only Marx, but also key aspects of the modern Enlightenment. Its quest for truth, he argued, was allied to the establishment of social hierarchy and oppression. As he argued:

> the desire for a unitary and totalizing truth lends itself to the unitary and totalizing practice of the system's managers ... in countries with liberal or advanced liberal management, the struggles and their instruments have been transformed into regulators of the system; in communist countries, the totalizing model and its totalitarian effect have made a comeback.
>
> (Lyotard, 2004, pp. 12–13)

Lyotard's solution was a critical postmodern knowledge that dismantles foundations, disrupts hierarchies and speaks on behalf of the oppressed (Seidman, 1998, p. 225). In *The Postmodern Condition: A Report on Knowledge* (2004) Lyotard makes a distinction between modern and postmodern knowledge. In the book, he sketches a series of broad historical changes in the nature of knowledge. Thus, in pre-modern societies, narrative types of knowledge (telling a story) prevailed. The 'popular stories' (Lyotard, 2004, p. 19) had a plot, a linear sequence of events, a definite beginning and end, and tales of good and evil that were intended to shape social behaviour. Narratives were considered knowledge, not because they corresponded to 'facts', but because they conformed to social rules, which fixed who has the right to speak, to whom and when. As such, they carried authority (Seidman, 1998, pp. 225–226). As Lyotard (2004, p. 23) explains:

narratives ... determine criteria of competence and/or illustrate how they are to be applied. They thus define what has the right to be said and done in the culture in question, and since they are themselves a part of that culture, they are legitimated by the simple fact that they do what they do.

Modernity is characterised by an assault on narrative knowledge. Narratives, such as religion and myth, are accordingly dismissed as ignorance and superstition, and as indications of a primitive society. In place of storytelling and myth-making (which is poetic and evocative), comes science that is claimed to yield objective truths. Whereas pre-modern narrative is self-legitimating, so long as the story and the storyteller conform to social norms and mores, science requires external legitimation (Seidman, 1998, pp. 225–226). Modern science also appeals to narratives for this legitimation, but to a different type of narrative, to what Lyotard refers to as *metanarratives*, grand theories about society. The post-modern condition is characterised by Lyotard as the decline of the legitimating power of metanarratives. Indeed, for Lyotard, this is the defining characteristic of postmodernism: 'I define postmodern as incredulity toward metanarratives' (Lyotard, 2004, p. xxiv). He contrasts the postmodern with the modern, the latter being:

> any science that legitimates itself with reference to a metadiscourse ... making an explicit appeal to some grand narrative, such as the dialectics of Spirit, the hermeneutics of meaning, the emancipation of the rational or working subject, or the creation of wealth.
>
> (ibid., pp. xxiii–xxiv)

Postmodernism abandons absolute standards, universal categories and grand theories in favour of local, contextualised and pragmatic conceptual strategies. Following Wittgenstein (2001) Lyotard (2004, p. 10) describes social life as a series of 'language games'. This refers to a set of linguistic practices, all marked by their own rules, conventions and aims. Lyotard uses the analogy of a game of chess:

> each of the various categories of utterance can be defined in terms of rules specifying their properties and the uses to which they can be put – in exactly the same way as the game of chess is defined by a set of rules determining the properties of each of the pieces, in other words, the proper way to move them.

Thus science is a language game whose aim is truth; aesthetics is a game of judgements of beauty and considerations of spatial form, colour and dimension, rather than truth. Society is conceived as a multiplicity of language games. Nothing can be reduced to a universal logic, such as class struggle or traditional feminist struggle against patriarchy (Seidman, 1998, p. 228).[4]

On the contrary, struggles which take place in institutional spheres around issues of identity, such as social class, 'race', nationality, gender, sexuality and disability are irreducible to each other and cannot be subsumed under one banner. Postmodern society for Lyotard is a kind of generalised revolt by marginalised and excluded groups against centralising tendencies. Derrida's deconstructive assault on textual authority is thus applied by Lyotard to the sphere of knowledge and society. As Seidman (1998, p. 228) concludes: 'the quest for intellectual foundations, objectivity, certainty, and universal truths is abandoned. In place of grand theories, Lyotard described and advocated a postmodern condition featuring the proliferation of multiple, conflicting discourses'. The nature of knowledge is central to the thoughts of Lyotard. Like Foucault, Lyotard believes that knowledge and power are two aspects of the same question: 'Knowledge in the form of an informational commodity indispensable to productive power is already, and will continue to be, a major – perhaps *the* major – stake in the worldwide competition for power'. (Lyotard, 2004, p. 5). He argues that during the last 40 years, the leading sciences and technologies have become increasingly concerned with language, with computerised knowledge becoming the principle *force of production*. The re-composition of the workforce in the 'developed countries' exemplifies this, with progressively fewer people working in factories and on the land, and more and more in offices on computers. It is conceivable, Lyotard suggests, that nation states will fight for control of information, just as they battled for control over territories in the past (Lyotard, 2004, p. 5).

Jean Baudrillard and the political economy of the sign

Jean Baudrillard (1929–) also describes the perceived shift from modern to postmodern in more global social and historical terms. Having started out with the intention of revising Marxism (e.g. Baudrillard, 1968, 1970, 1972), Baudrillard ultimately turned against it. In fact, he inverted Marxism. Whereas Marx conceived of history as driven by natural human need and labour, Baudrillard believed that society was structured by symbolic or linguistic meanings. Whereas Marx outlined stages of successive socioeconomic formations (see Chapter 2, pp. 22–24), Baudrillard proposed a history of the 'political economy of the sign'. As he put it (Baudrillard, 1981, p. 148): 'the object of this political economy, that is, its simplest component, its nuclear element – that which precisely the commodity was for Marx – is no longer today properly either commodity or sign, but indissolubly both'. By this he meant that it was the sign that had changed through history. Signs are words, sounds, images that organise the social universe by giving people or things a social identity and location (Seidman, 1998, p. 229). Thus in pre-modern societies, signs had clear referents and context-specific meanings. These societies were organised around 'symbolic exchange' where communication was immediate, direct and reciprocal. There were no mediating structures such as the market or the mass media. Symbolic exchanges were not defined by their instrumental purpose. In acts such as gift giving, religious rituals and festivities, exchange directly affirmed social status and social order (Seidman, 1998, p. 229).

Baudrillard goes on to argue that from the early modern period to the post-modern, the structure and role of the sign changes in two ways. First, the relationship between the sign and reality is disturbed; second, the sign forms a 'code' that standardises both meanings and social responses. Signs were once considered to have a more or less clear relation to an object or to reality (ibid.). Modern culture was organised around a series of distinctions between truth and falsity, essence and appearance, reality and illusion and so on (ibid., pp. 229–230). By the Second World War, according to Baudrillard, these binary oppositions had begun to collapse. In particular, the line between sign and reality and word and world had become blurred. As postmodernity dawned, signs created their own universe of meaning without any clear relation to the real world of objects and events (ibid., p. 230). For Baudrillard, history seemed to be coming to an end as current realities were overwhelmed by a sign system that was destroying any semblance of order, truth, reality and, in the light of the failure of the Paris uprisings of 1968, of political resistance (ibid.). In Seidman's (ibid.) words, for Baudrillard, the social world has come to resemble a flattened, monotone mass levelled by the spiralling weight of signs, meanings and information. We have entered, says Baudrillard, the age of the *simulacrum*. Simulacra are signs that function as copies of real objects or events. In postmodernity, they can be images of originals, which never actually existed, Disneyland/Disneyworld being archetypal examples of simulacra. Whereas modernity is characterised by explosions of new divisions (e.g. popular and 'high' culture), postmodernity features *implosion*, where boundaries collapse and the modern politics of oppression and revolt give way to a postmodern politics of seduction and surrender (ibid., p. 231). Power is not lodged in a specific class, or capitalism or the state, but is diffuse and saturates the social field. In place of modern social theory, Baudrillard urges 'fatal theory', where resistance must take the form of a deliberate passivity, a refusal to be absorbed into the imploded universe of signs and meanings, which will eventually lead to the collapse of the system under its own dead symbolic discharge (ibid., pp. 231–232).

Seidman (1998, p. 232) summarises the contribution of Lyotard and Baudrillard to postmodernism:

> [they] take poststructuralism in a social theoretical direction. The aim of deconstructing textual order is directed to the social field. Thus, Lyotard offers a sketch of the rise of postmodern cultural legitimations of knowledge and authority. Baudrillard proposes a sweeping outline of the passing of an era of Western modernity.

What poststructuralists and postmodernists have in common is a rejection of any notion of order and coherence in society, and a refusal to accept binary oppositions. As we have seen, according to poststructuralists/postmodernists, societies are not polarised, for example, in terms of social class or gender. Thus mass struggle is off the agenda. For Marxists, the important point to make is that this rejection of such struggle ultimately plays into the hands of those whose interests lie in the maintenance of national and global systems of exploitation and oppression. With respect to Nietzsche, it is worth stating here that, while capitalism has always been a global phenomenon (see Chapter 7 for a discussion), twenty-first century global capitalism has become much more hierarchical than at the time Nietzsche was writing. In addition, global technology is harnessed by herdsmen and herdswomen to exploit workers worldwide in ways unimagined in the nineteenth century.

While poststructuralists/postmodernists reject the possibility of an ordered socialist society or world, claims are made that poststructuralism/postmodernism can be forces for social change and social justice. In the next chapter, I will evaluate these claims, concentrating on the arguments of three prominent post-structural/postmodern educational theorists.

Part II

Issues

5 Poststructuralism and postmodernism in educational theory
Social change and social justice

In this chapter I begin by making some brief comments on the influence of the ideas of Nietzsche, of those of the poststructuralists, Foucault and Derrida, and of the postmodernists, Lyotard and Baudrillard on the work of poststructuralist/postmodernist educational theorists, Elizabeth Atkinson, Patti Lather and Judith Baxter. Next I take a snapshot of the current state of global capitalism. I then look at attempts in Britain and the US to argue the case, within educational theory, that postmodernism and poststructuralism can be forces for social change and social justice. Concentrating on Atkinson, Lather and Baxter, I argue that such claims are illusory. I make the case that Marxism is a more viable option in the pursuit of social change and social justice.

Introduction

Postmodernism has a high profile in educational theory, and in many ways, along with poststructuralism, it may be viewed as the dominant paradigm in this field in the UK, and in the US.[1] I will begin this chapter by assessing the influence of the poststructural/postmodern thinkers discussed in Chapter 4, on the feminist poststructuralism/postmodernism of UK educational theorists Elizabeth Atkinson and Judith Baxter and on US theorist, Patti Lather.

In general terms, Foucault has had a major influence on post-Marxist feminists. First, his notion of the diffusion of power allows for a consideration of male power and accompanying violence in the domestic sphere. Second, his rejection of binary struggle has encouraged feminists to examine women's multiple identities. Third, this has been further facilitated by Foucault's discussion of subjugated knowledges, and the way in which, delegitimised by the mainstream, such knowledges have taken on insurrectionary forms.

While, as we have seen, discourse is a central concern of poststructuralists as a whole, discourse for Derrida is intimately connected to deconstruction. The meaning of the *sign* is unstable, multivocal and changing. For example, while the binary opposition woman/man may, at first, seem fixed and universal, it carries a variety of meanings, according to numerous different contexts. As Seidman (1998, p. 222) puts it:

one discourse may construct women as maternal, emotional, passive, and desexualized; another discourse projects women as erotic and powerful … [thus] Derrida's break from structuralism is more than a matter of amending its view of signs; it is about the politics of language and knowledge.

Deconstruction, as we shall see below, is a central political and linguistic tool of the major feminist postmodernist/poststructuralist educational theorists: Elizabeth Atkinson, Patti Lather and Judith Baxter, addressed in the main part of this chapter. Another Derridean concept drawn upon by Atkinson and Lather is the *ordeal of the undecidable*, while Baxter employs Derrida's notion of *supplementarity*. I will deal with each concept in turn.

The ordeal of the undecidable is linked to deconstruction. As Edgoose (1997) explains, deconstruction is the process of transition between the written, universal law and the many particularities that are the voices of Others.[2] Law, in its universal language, cannot be made to converse at once with all Others, each in their idiomatic languages. Thus, a synthesis of caring justice (*juste*) and law (*droit*) is not possible. Both need each other, as Derrida argues, yet there is always – necessarily – a gap between them. Law (*droit*) can never reach caring justice (*juste*) despite its constant striving. Thus caring justice cannot be simply the product of a legal machine, but must stem from a fresh and complete re-engineering of that machine. It demands both lineage and rupture.

There must be a decision between the continuous and the discontinuous, or between different singular Others. As Derrida warns us (1990, p. 963, cited in Edgoose, 1997):

> A decision that didn't go through the ordeal of the undecidable would not be a free decision, it would only be the programmable application or unfolding of a calculable process. It might be legal; it would not be caring [*juste*]. … And once the ordeal of the undecidable is past (if that is possible), the decision has again followed a rule or given itself a rule, invented it or reinvented, reaffirmed it, it is no longer *presently* fully caring [*juste*].

Richard Parrish (2006a, p. 8) explains:

> any claim – any discursive position – is a universal claim that in order to be universal must continually re-found itself. Any position, even the position that universal positions are impossible, is a universal claim and is therefore considered iterable universally. This universal iterability denies in its structure the legitimacy of counter-claims made by others, thus denying that others are really faces, independent sources of meaning that are capable of their own independent speech.

The Derridean concept of *supplementarity* is also linked to deconstruction. Explaining 'supplementarity', Zavarzadeh comments that the politics of deconstruction, 'in which the "margin" rearticulates the "center" by "supplementing" it ... constructs semiotic "power" for the economically exploited "marginal"' (2002, p. 4). However, as he goes on, 'this is merely an idealist discursive freedom in lieu of the material emancipation that the "center" has refused the marginal' (ibid.).

With respect to Lyotard, it is his definition of postmodernism as 'incredulity toward metanarratives' that encapsulates his work. Thus Patti Lather is most sceptical of 'the right story', while Elizabeth Atkinson calls into question the 'discovery of some sort of truth' and 'single projects for social justice' and Judith Baxter stresses the anti-essentialism of feminist poststructuralist discourse analysis (FPDA). All also make use of notions of 'language games' of 'multiple discourses' and all see Marxism as hierarchical and oppressive (see below).

Baudrillard's archetypal postmodern belief in the collapse of binary opposition, that history is coming to an end as current realities are overwhelmed by a sign system that was destroying any semblance of order, truth or reality is, as we shall see, apparent throughout the work of Atkinson, Lather and Baxter.

Postmodernism and poststructuralism in educational theory have been subject to sustained critique in recent years from Marxist educators (e.g. Green, 1994; Cole and Hill, 2002; Cole *et al.*, 1997, 2001; Hill *et al.*, 2002b; McLaren and Farahmandpur, 2002a, 2002b; Cole, 2003a, 2004b, 2005a). Leading British postmodern educational theorist, Elizabeth Atkinson (2002) addresses herself to some recent writings on educational theory from within the Marxist tradition: specifically Marxist critiques of postmodernism (and, in particular, some of the work of Dave Hill, Jane Kelly, Peter McLaren, Glenn Rikowski and myself; namely, Cole and Hill, 1995; Cole *et al.*, 1997; Hill *et al.*, 1999; Kelly *et al.*, 1999). Atkinson concentrates on our claims that one of the greatest problems with postmodernism is that it lacks an agenda for social change and social justice. Her argument is that, 'through the acceptance of uncertainty, the acknowledgement of diversity and the refusal to see concepts such as "justice" or "society" as fixed or as governed by unassailable "truths"' (Atkinson, 2002, p. 73), postmodernism, far from lacking such an agenda, is, in fact, a powerful force for social change.[3]

Arguing in a similar vein, in a critique of an article by Peter McLaren (1998),[4] Lather suggests that the progressive potential of feminist postmodernist/poststructuralist analysis lies in its rejection of 'economistic Marxism' in favour of 'a praxis of not being so sure' (derived from Jacques Derrida's 'ordeal of the undecidable').

Both Atkinson and Lather are associated with what has been described by Lather (1991) as 'resistance postmodernism'. Lather contrasts this with what she labels 'postmodernism of reaction' (ibid.). 'Postmodernism of reaction', described as neo-Nietzschean, is, Lather claims, concerned with the collapse of meaning, with nihilism, and with cynicism. The conception of the individual is of a fractured schizoid consumer, existing in what Lather describes as 'a cultural whirlpool of Baudrillardian simulacra' (Lather 1991, pp. 160–161). This vortex is captured perfectly by Jean Baudrillard:

[Postmodernism] is a game with the vestiges of what has been destroyed. ... We must move in it, as though it were a kind of circular gravity ... I have the impression with postmodernism that there is an attempt to rediscover a certain pleasure in the irony of things, in the game of things. Right now one can tumble into total hopelessness – all the definitions, everything, it's all been done. What can one do? What can one become? And postmodernity is the attempt – perhaps it's desperate, I don't know – to reach a point where one can live with what is left. It is more a survival among the remnants than anything else (Laughter).

(Baudrillard, 1984, in Gane, 1993, p. 95)

Lather (1991) defines 'postmodernism of resistance', on the other hand, as participatory and dialogic, encompassing pluralistic structures of authority. It is non-dualistic and anti-hierarchical and celebrates multiple sites from which the word is spoken (Lather, 1991, p. 160). 'Postmodernism of resistance' is claimed to be fundamentally theoretically different from 'postmodernism of reaction' and to be a challenge to the status quo. Judith Baxter (see below) makes the claim that 'feminist post-structural analysis',[5] is an effective tool *both* to deconstruct cultural processes responsible for oppression *and* to ultimately promote social transformation.

My argument is that the 'two postmodernisms', despite *some* progressive and radical potential for 'resistance postmodernism', are in fact one and that postmodernism is, in essence, reactionary (for an extended analysis of the 'two postmodernisms', see, for example, Cole and Hill, 2002). Atkinson (2003) has attempted to link 'postmodernism of reaction', also known as 'ludic postmodernism', to 'postmodernism of resistance'. As she puts it, postmodernism can act as a form of resistance by pitting its 'ludic … playful … ironic … restless, shape-shifting dance … against the ludicrous' (p. 5). She concludes by stating that she wants fun and resistance combined:

I want more than Carnival … once a year. I want to hear the voices from the margins; to ask the questions which arise from uncertainty, hybridity and multiplicity. I want to speak the unspeakable and have awful thoughts. I want to ask the questions that open up the trouble.

(2003, p. 12; for a critique of Atkinson's (2003)
arguments, see Cole, 2004b)

My view is that neither postmodernism (however described) nor 'feminist post-structural analysis' are conducive to the pursuit of social change or social justice and that, in the context of global capitalism today, Marxism provides a more viable option in that pursuit.

Global capitalism today

I would like to begin with a few recent and current facts about the state of globalised capitalism in the US, the UK and the 'developing world'. As far as the US is concerned, the poverty rate rose from 11.3 per cent in 2000 to 13.1 per cent in

2004, while the number of poor increased also by 5.4 million to 37 million (US Census Bureau, 30 August 2005). In 2001, the top 1 per cent of households owned 33.4 per cent of all privately held wealth, and the next 19 per cent had 51 per cent, which means that just 20 per cent of the people owned a remarkable 84 per cent, leaving only 16 per cent of the wealth for the bottom 80 per cent. In terms of financial wealth, the top 1 per cent of households had an even greater share: 39.7 per cent (Domhoff, 2006).

In the UK, the latest figures show that the wealthiest 1 per cent own 23 per cent of wealth, while the wealthiest 50 per cent own 94 per cent (Babb *et al.*, 2006, p. 84). With respect to income in the UK, the bottom fifth of people earn less than 8 per cent of disposable income and the top fifth over 40 per cent (Department for Work and Pensions, 2004/2005, supplementary table, A3, p. 105). There are more than 100,000 millionaires, and more than 40 billionaires in the UK today (Kealey, 2006, p. 22). Meanwhile, London has the highest rate of child poverty of any region in the UK. Forty-four per cent of children live in households where income, after housing costs, is half the national average, compared with 25 per cent in the southeast and 34 per cent in the UK as a whole.

Morgan and Short (2005) have pointed out that more than one in four London children live in a household where no one works, compared with 18 per cent in the whole of the UK. More than one-third (38 per cent) of children living in London are poor – approximately 700,000 children. In Outer London, the level of child poverty is close to the national average at 30 per cent, but in Inner London, the child poverty rate is an astonishing 54 per cent. This compares with a national rate of 29 per cent. Recent government and independent reports show disturbing trends in the living conditions of Londoners. Within the UK, London has the widest gulf between rich and poor.

The cost of housing in the capital, rising by more than 250 per cent in the last decade, is putting further economic strain on millions of working people living there. Adam Sampson, the director of Shelter, said, 'In a country increasingly obsessed by house prices, the growing inequality in housing is marginalising a whole section of society'. Children born this century, he added, would be 'more financially unequal than at any time since the Victorian era' (cited in Mogan and Short, 2005).

As far as the 'developing world' is concerned, for two decades poverty in Africa and Latin America has increased, both in absolute and relative terms. Nearly half the world's population are living on less than £1.40 a day and for every £1 of aid going into poor countries, multinationals take £1.50 of profits out (World Development Movement, 2006). The turning over of vast tracts of land to grow one crop for multinationals often results in ecological degradation, with those having to migrate to the towns living in slum conditions and working excessive hours in unstable jobs (Harman, 2000). At the end of the twentieth century, there were about 100 million abused and hungry 'street kids' in the world's major cities, slavery had re-emerged, and some two million girls from the age of five to 15 were being drawn into the global prostitution market. Approximately, 100 million human beings did not have adequate shelter and 830 million people were not 'food secure', i.e. hungry (Mojab, 2001, p. 118). Six thousand children die every day because of unclean water (World Development Movement, 2006), and up to 11 million children will die in 2006, simply because they were born poor (Save the Children, 2006).

In fact, the world is becoming polarised into central and peripheral economies, with the gap between rich and poor, between the powerful and the powerless, growing so large that, by the late 1990s, the 300 largest corporations in the world accounted for 70 per cent of foreign direct investment and 25 per cent of world capital assets (Bagdikan, 1998, cited in McLaren, 2000, p. xxiv). At the start of the twenty-first century, the combined assets of the 225 richest people was roughly equal to the annual incomes of the poorest 47 per cent of the world's population (Heintz and Folbre, 2000, cited in McLaren and Farahmandpur, 2001, p. 345) and eight companies earned more than half the world's population (World Development Movement, 2001).

Today, 125 million children cannot go to school and 110 million children, young people and adults have to leave school before they have completely acquired the basic skills of reading and writing. At the same time, the global education market is estimated to be worth more than 3,000 billion euros (National Union of Education, Research and Culture, General Confederation of Labour, France, 2002, p. 4).

The ordeal of the undecidable

If postmodernism and poststructuralism can be forces for social change and social justice, then one would assume that they could in some way redress these global injustices. Atkinson (2002) begins her arguments by advocating Stronach and MacLure's (1997) concept of the postmodernist as 'a responsible anarchist'. They, in turn, borrowed this 'anarchic position' from Schurmann (1990) in an attempt to argue that the 'acceptance of disorder should not be mistaken for passivity or acquiescence' (Stronach and MacLure, 1997, p. 98). Responsible anarchism involves 'standing against the fantasies of grand narratives, recoverable pasts, and predictable futures' (Atkinson, 2002, pp. 73–74). I will take these three propositions in turn.[6] First, as I will argue later, I believe grand narrative (Marxism), albeit amenable to critical interrogation, is essential in the promotion of social justice. Second, as far as 'recoverable pasts' are concerned, I would suggest that, while it is not possible nor necessarily desirable to return to the past per se, there have been events in the past from which we can learn as we plan for the future (e.g. Marx and Engels, 1977b [1872], pp. 31–32).[7] Third, with respect to 'predictable futures', Marxists do not *predict* the future but merely have a vision of how societies *could* be run.[8]

Atkinson then challenges the view that 'it is essential to choose one theoretical perspective or course of action over another' (2002, p. 75). This is derived, *inter alia*, from the work of Jacques Derrida, including his 'ordeal of the undecidable'. This has been developed by Patti Lather in her attempt to counter what she refers to as Marxists' 'insistence on the "right story"'. Lather attempts to link Derrida with Marx by reminding us that in her book, *Getting Smart*, she ended the section on 'postmarxism' with Foucault's prophecy that 'it is clear, even if one admits that Marx will disappear for now, that he will reappear one day' (Foucault, cited in Lather, 1991, p. 45). However, she rejects what she sees as Marxists' 'discourse of mastery/transparency/rationalism and repositioning of economistic Marxism as the "master discourse of the left"' (Lather, 2001, p. 187). Rather than return to historical materialism (the belief that the development of material goods necessary to human existence is the primary force which determines social life), Lather's interest is in 'a praxis of not being so sure' (ibid., p. 184), 'a praxis in excess of binary or dialectical logic' (ibid., p. 189) a 'post-dialectical praxis', which is about: 'ontological stammering, concepts with a lower ontological weight, a praxis without guaranteed subjects or objects, oriented towards the as yet incompletely thinkable conditions and potentials of given arrangement' (ibid., p. 189). In fact, Lather's adoption of such a 'praxis' does not reposition Marxism; it leaves its domain entirely (see Chapter 2 for a discussion of dialectical praxis in the context of the labour theory of value). For Lather, nothing is certain or decided. The 'ordeal of the undecidable' has 'obligations to openness, passage and nonmastery'; 'questions are constantly moving' and one 'one cannot define, finish, close' (Lather, 2001, p. 184). Citing Derrida, Lather asserts that undecidability is 'a constant ethical-political reminder' 'that moral and political responsibility can only occur in the not knowing, the not being sure' (Lather, 2001, p. 187).

Her academic efforts are informed by Alison Jones (1999), who, reminiscent of Baudrillard's discussion of the end of political resistance, and general hopelessness in a world flattened by signs (see Chapter 4, pp. 48–50) concludes 'with a call for a "politics of disappointment", a practice of "failure, loss, confusion, unease, limitation for dominant ethnic groups"' (Lather, 2001, p. 191). Lather and Jones are claiming to be anti-colonialist in supporting Maori students in their wish to break up into 'discussion groups based on ethnic sameness' (ibid., p. 190). While it is *always* vital to challenge the colonialism and racism of dominant groups, it is not clear how Jones' list of negative politics and practices (disappointment, failure, loss, confusion, unease and limitation) is helpful in such a quest. In addition, since Lather believes that all 'oppositional knowledge is drawn into the order against which it intends to rebel' (1998, p. 493), it is difficult to see what possible progressive potential is entailed in hers and Jones' anti-colonialism or indeed in Lather's overall project. Are these Maori students destined to be drawn into the dominant order (colonialism)? In the meantime, is 'undecidability' all poststructuralist or postmodernist teachers have to offer them? In fact, all that Lather provides, by way of conclusion, is an assertion that there are 'forces already active in the present' and that we will 'move toward an experience of the promise that is unforeseeable from the perspective of our present conceptual frameworks', in the pursuit of 'a future that must remain to come' (ibid., p. 192).

Any defender of social injustice would surely be delighted to hear that Patti Lather who, like so many of her poststructuralist/postmodernist contemporaries, was arguing in the 1980s that 'feminism and Marxism need each other' (Lather,

1984, p. 49) and that 'the revolution is within each and every one of us and it will come about' (ibid., p. 58), now posits the contradictory position that the future is an open book, with some progressive potential, and in which all opposition is drawn into the dominant order. This is neither conducive to progressive social change nor social justice.

Truth and social justice

Citing Jane Flax, and consistent with her pluralist views on theory and action, Atkinson argues that postmodernism calls into question 'the discovery of some sort of truth which can tell us how to act in the world in ways that benefit or are for the (at least ultimate) good of all' (2002, p. 75). This is reminiscent of Derrida's assertion that 'truth is plural' (1979, p. 103) (see Chapter 4, pp. 44–45), the implication being that the 'truth' of the exploiter is equally valid to the 'truth' of the exploited. For Derrida, 'difference' is in each and not between the two. While I would agree that knowing the 'truth' is not a question of describing some 'true' ontological essence, it is also not a function of an endless round of language games as some would lead us to believe (e.g. Lyotard, 2004). A Marxist analysis of truth rejects both plurality and ontological essentialism in favour of 'a dialectical understanding of the dynamic relations between superstructure and base; between ideology ... and the workings of the forces of production and the historical relations of production' (Ebert, 1996, p. 47; for an analysis, see Allman, 1999, p. 136).

Referring specifically to the *concept* of 'justice', Atkinson states that 'postmodern theorists ... invite us to consider concepts such as "justice" as "effects of power"' (2002, p. 75). 'Social justice agendas', she implies, need to be deconstructed in order to reveal 'their own underlying assumptions and beliefs' (ibid.). No Marxist would, of course, disagree with this (something which Atkinson acknowledges (ibid.)). The underlying assumptions and beliefs in the concept of 'justice' as employed by, for example, George W. Bush or Tony Blair is very different from that employed by, say, Noam Chomsky or John Pilger.

It needs to be pointed out at this stage that whether or not Marx had a theory of justice has been an issue of great controversy and has generated an enormous literature, particularly among North American philosophers.[9] The crux of the matter is that, as Callinicos has put it, on some occasions Marx eschews ethical judgements and, on others, apparently makes them (1989, p. 13). This was because he was confused about justice (Cohen, 1983), or to put it another way, 'Marx did think capitalism was unjust but he did not think he thought so' (Geras, 1983, p. 245; see also Cohen, 1983; Pennock and Chapman, 1983; Lukes, 1982; Callinicos, 2000). His materialist conception of history entailed a relative, rather than a universal, account of ethics, since morality was seen as reflective of the prevailing mode of production. He was also unable to contextualise his own morality. As Callinicos explains:

> Marx's erroneous meta-ethical theory prevented him from seeing universal moral principles as anything but the expression of historically specific class

interests and therefore from recognizing the basis on which he himself condemned capitalist exploitation.

(2000, p. 28)

Callinicos gives several clear examples of Marx's inherent belief in some universal principle of justice: 'the burning anger with he describes the condition of the working class'; 'the ostensibly egalitarian "needs principle"', 'from each according to his abilities, to each according to his needs!' (*Critique of the Gotha Programme*); his description of capitalist exploitation as the 'the theft of alien labour time' (the *Grundrisse*) which, since Marx makes it clear that this does not violate capitalist property laws, must, as Callinicos points out, imply an appeal to some transhistorical principle of justice (Callinicos, 2000, p. 28); his moral position on the collective ownership of land (*Capital Vol. 3*) (ibid., p. 29) and his implication that treating unequals equally is unjust (*Critique of the Gotha Programme*) (ibid., p. 82).

Whatever Marx's relationship to the *concept* of justice, the important point for Marxists is that Marx's vision of a socialist society allows us to look beyond the multiple injustices of global capitalism. As Geras has put it, 'the largest paradox here is that Marx, despite everything, displayed a greater commitment to the creation of a just society than many more overtly interested in analysis of what justice is' (1983, p. 267).[10]

Callinicos is quite unambiguous as to his *own* views on the relationship of capitalism to social justice. Recalling what is distinctive about Marx's account of capitalist exploitation, namely that the *appearance* of a free exchange between worker and capitalist is nullified by the unequal distribution of the productive forces (owned solely by the latter), Callinicos argues that 'exploitation is directly unjust ... because workers are illegitimately *compelled* to work for the capitalist', in order to receive a wage. Unlike slavery and serfdom, where illegitimate compulsion is obvious, this *appearance* of freedom is masked by what Marx referred to as 'the dull compulsion of economic relations' (Marx, 1965 [1887], p. 737), whereby workers working for a wage, if not directly coerced, have no viable legal alternative but to perform surplus labour for the capitalist.[11] Furthermore, as Callinicos points out, the exploitative relationship *indirectly* contributes to injustice in the massive polarisation between rich and poor, which is largely the result of excessive extraction of surplus value of workers by capitalists (Callinicos, 2000, p. 68) (see Chapter 2, pp. 24–25 for a discussion of the labour theory of value).

Whereas postmodernists engage in an endless and relatively ahistorical process of deconstruction (see below), Marxists look to history to understand both underlying assumptions with respect to social justice *and solutions to social injustice*. A fundamental premise of Marxism is that from the dissolution of primitive communism to the overthrow of capitalism, there is no social contract that the ruling class or their representatives will enter into with the subordinate class, except as a result of a defeat in struggle or as a tactical and temporary retreat to preserve long-term interests. For example Marx would say that no aristocracy would voluntarily reduce feudal obligations, no capitalist would reduce the length or pace of the working day, except in the face or revolt or other mass action, or to gain a short-term advantage. Allied to this, no peasantry or proletariat has accepted an economic arrangement for long without challenging it. Change will only be brought about by workers' struggles. Accordingly, improvements in the relative position of the working class cannot, for Marxists, be brought about by appeals to any universal sense of justice (Miller, 1989, pp. 209–210). In addition, as Richard Miller points out:

> Even when such a sense exists, no appropriate consensus can be achieved as to whether the demands of justice have in fact been fulfilled. For instance, capitalists, as a class, have always insisted that a proposed reduction of the working day ... would do immeasurable harm to workers by destroying the capitalist economy on whose existence workers' welfare depends.
>
> (1989, p. 210)[12]

Another fundamental premise of Marxism is the notion that the capitalist class is a class whose interests are served by all the major institutions in society. While the role of the state in capitalist societies has been a vigorously debated issue within Marxist theory (for an overview, see Jessop, 1990; for a brief summary, see Hill, 2001b and Cole, 1992, pp. 33–35), there is a consensus among Marxists that 'the state' is a complex of institutions, rather than just central government, and that both apparatuses of the state, the ideological and the repressive (Althusser, 1971, pp. 121–173; see Chapter 3, pp. 30–31 for a discussion) are not neutral but act, to varying degrees, albeit with some disarticulations, in the interests of capitalism.[13] For these reasons, for Marxists, the creation of true social justice within capitalism is not viable. The capitalist state must, therefore, be replaced rather than reformed.

Deconstruction and social change

Whereas for Marxists, the possibility of postmodernism leading to social change is a non sequitur, for Atkinson, postmodernism is 'an inevitable agent for change' in that

> it challenges the educator, the researcher, the social activist or the politician not only to deconstruct the certainties around which they might see as standing in need of change, but also to deconstruct their own certainties as to why they hold this view.
>
> (2002, p. 75)

This sounds fine, but what do these constituencies actually *do* to effect meaningful societal change once their views have been challenged? What is *constructed* after the deconstruction process? Atkinson provides no answer. Nor does Patti Lather (nor, as we shall see, does Judith Baxter). This is because neither postmodernism nor poststructuralism is capable of providing an answer (Hill, 2001b; Rikowski, 2002, pp. 20–25). Deconstruction 'seeks to do justice to all positions … by giving them the chance to be justified, to speak originarily for themselves and be chosen rather that enforced' (Zavarzadeh, 2002, p. 8).

Indeed, for Derrida (1992, pp. 14–15), 'deconstruction *is* justice' (my emphasis). When asked by prominent French philosophical educator, Jean Hyppolite, to explain the direction of his thinking, Derrida replied, 'If I clearly saw ahead of time where I was going, I really don't believe that I should take another step to get there' (cited in Trifonas, 2000). Thus, once the deconstruction process has started, justice is already apparent and not only is there is no discernible direction in which to head, if a direction were to be ascertained, immobility sets it.

In declaring on the first page of the preface of her book *Getting Smart: Feminist Research and Pedagogy With/In the Postmodern*, her 'longtime interest in how to turn critical thought into emancipatory action' (1991, p. xv), Lather is, in fact, wasting her time. After over 200 pages of text, in which indications are made of the need for emancipatory research praxis; in which proclamations are made of how the goals of research should be to understand the maldistribution of power and resources in society, with a view to societal change, we are left wondering how all this is to come about.

Postmodernism cannot provide strategies to *achieve* a different social order and hence, in buttressing capitalist exploitation, it is essentially reactionary. This is precisely what Marxists (and others) mean by the assertion that postmodernism serves to disempower the oppressed.[14]

According to Atkinson, postmodernism 'does not have, and could not have, a "single" project for social justice' (2002, p. 75). Socialism then, if not social change, is thus ruled out in a stroke.[15] Atkinson then rehearses the familiar postmodern position on multiple projects (ibid.).

Despite Atkinson's claims that postmodernism views 'the local as the product of the global and *vice versa*' and that postmodernism should not be interpreted as limiting its scope of enquiry to the local (2002, p. 81), because postmodernism rejects grand metanarratives and since it rejects universal struggle it can, *by definition*, concentrate only on the local. Localised struggle can, of course, be empowering for individuals and certain selected small groups, but postmodernism cannot set out any viable mass strategy or programme for an emancipated future. The importance of local as well as national and international struggle is recognised by Marxists, but the postmodern rejection of mass struggle is ultimately conducive, as I have argued, to the interests of national and global capitalism. Furthermore, 'as regards aims, the concern with autonomy, in terms of organisation', postmodernism comprises 'a tendency towards network forms, and, in terms of mentality, a tendency towards self-limitation' (Pieterse, 1992). While networking can aid in the promotion of solidarity, and in mass petitions, for example (Atkinson, 2001), it cannot replace mass action, in the sense, for example, of a general or major strike; or a significant demonstration or uprising which forces social change. Indeed, the postmodern depiction of mass action as totalitarian negates/renders illicit such action.

Allied to its localism, is postmodernism's non-dualism (Lather, 1991). This does have the advantage of recognising the struggles of groups oppressed on grounds in addition to, or other than, those of class. However, non-dualism prevents the recognition of a major duality in capitalist societies, that of social class (Cole and Hill, 1995, pp. 166–168; 2002; McLaren and Farahmandpur, 1999a; Sanders *et al.*, 1999: Hill *et al.*, 2002a). This has, I believe, profoundly reactionary implications, in that it negates the notion of class struggle.

> Marxism, on the other hand, allows a future both to be envisioned and worked towards. This vision can and has been extended beyond the 'brotherhood of man' concept of early socialists, to include the complex subjectivities of all (subjectivities which the postmodernists are so keen to bring centre stage). Socialism can and should be conceived of as a project where subjective identities, such as gender, 'race', disability, non-exploitative sexual preference and age all have high importance in the struggle for genuine equality.
>
> (Cole and Hill, 1999a, p. 42)

In her attempt to present the case that 'postmodern deconstruction ... is not the same as destruction' (Atkinson, 2002, p. 77), Atkinson cites Judith Butler (1990) who argues that: 'to deconstruct is not to negate or to dismiss, but to call into question and, perhaps most importantly, to open up a term ... to a reusage or redeployment that previously has not been authorized' (cited in Atkinson, 2002, p. 77). This is precisely what Marxism does. The difference is that Marxist concepts such as, for example, the fetishism inherent in capitalist societies, whereby the relationships between things or commodities assume a mystical quality hiding the real (exploitative) relationships between human beings, provide a means of both analysing that society, understanding its exploitative nature *and* pointing in the direction of a non-exploitative society. The Marxist concept of the labour theory of value is a good example (see Chapter 2 for a discussion).

Drawing on a study of girls' and boys' speech and arguing in identical vein to Atkinson and Lather, but in a much more self-effacing, almost apologetic tone, Judith Baxter (2002a) sets out to show how the use of feminist poststructural analysis can 'produce powerful insights about gendered discourse that may in the end lead to significant change' (2002a, p. 5). Baxter is gaining a burgeoning influence on linguistic analysis in Britain (Baxter, 2003; see also Baxter, 2002a, 2002b, 2002c, 2002d, 2004, 2005, 2006a, 2006b, 2007a, b), with her (2003) book, *Positioning Gender in Discourse* having been nominated for the BAAL (British Association for Applied Linguistics) Book Prize in 2004.

Baxter begins her article by suggesting that:

> Feminist post-structuralist discourse analysis is much more than simply an effective tool with which to deconstruct the cultural processes responsible

for constituting structures of oppression. It ... ultimately may prompt social and educational transformation.

(Baxter, 2002a, p. 5)

Acknowledging that poststructuralist enquiry has been described as 'a "fallacy", as nihilistic, cynical, serving a loose philosophy of "anything goes" and even as a "grand narrative" itself' (ibid., p. 8), Baxter presents three reasons why she believes that poststructuralism has 'potentially transformative possibilities' (ibid.). First, poststructuralism is anti-essentialist. It cannot be pinned down. Second, its quest is 'to create spaces to allow the voices of marginalised groups, such as women, the disabled, or the gay community to be heard with ringing clarity' (ibid.). It is not, she claims, 'just about deconstructive critique' (ibid., p. 9).

It must also have a libertarian impulse to release the words of marginalised or minority speakers in order to achieve the richness and diversity of textual play that only emerges from the expression of different and competing points of view.

(ibid., p. 9)

Third, feminist poststructuralist discourse analysis (FPDA), unlike modernist feminism, is capable of describing the complexities of the experiences of numerous women/girls. 'It equips feminist researchers with the thinking to "see through" the ambiguities and confusions of *particular* discursive contexts where women/girls are located as simultaneously powerful and powerless' (ibid.). 'FPDA potentially provides them with a "proper platform" on which to be heard' (ibid.).

After seven and a half pages of discourse analysis, Baxter reiterates her belief in the emancipatory potential of poststructuralism. Emphasising poststructuralism's lack of closure, she argues that it should incorporate Derrida's aforementioned concept of 'supplementarity', 'where no voice is suppressed, displaced by, or privileged over another, but rather, each voice complements, enhances, and at the same time undercuts the other' (ibid., p. 17). Zavarzadeh (2002, p. 4) has dismissed 'supplementarity' as merely a device by which that which is denied workers by the mechanisms of the free market is given back to them in the form of a freedom of 'phrases'. Like other concepts derived from postmodernism, 'supplementarity' acts *ideologically* to disempower the working class.[16]

Citing Alison Jones (1993), Baxter acknowledges that 'the attempt to utilise the more complex ideas of post-structuralism can indeed lead to "a paralysing ambivalence for feminist activists"' (ibid.). However, this is 'not because such ideas produce disillusionment. Rather, it is the difficulty in living up to Derrida's [concept of "supplementarity"] by demonstrating the possibility of such ideas through research practice' (ibid.). 'Might it be in the practice rather than the theory than [*sic*] feminist post-structuralist analysis fails to succeed?' is Baxter's conclusion. We will only know the answer 'when more feminist researchers take up the FPDA cudgels' (ibid., p. 18). So there we have it. According to Baxter, poststructuralism may ultimately promote social and educational transformation because it listens to all voices, and because it deconstructs. However, as she acknowledges, it is unconvincing in practice and can only (possibly) become convincing if more feminist researchers take it up. Of course, no indications are given of how the promotion of transformation might occur. More recently (Baxter, 2006a) has made clearer (one of) her interpretation(s) of 'social and educational transformation'. What she has in mind are more women in the hierarchy of British society, particularly the echelons of British capitalism. Baxter begins by expressing concern that in business world, 'women occupy just 10 per cent of all non-executive positions and 3 per cent of executive directorships' (Aurora, 2002), and that, at the time of her survey, 'there was just one female CEO [Chief Executive Officer] in the UK, one female chairman [*sic*] and one female joint Managing Director working within FTSE 100 companies' (Baxter, 2006a, p. 159). Baxter (2006a, p. 176) concludes that women need to be taught '*how* to deconstruct the gendered power relationships assumed within many social and educational discourses ... [and] will need to learn *how* to talk their way to the top'. Incidentally, we *are* talking about 'the top': 230 of the FTSE 100 directors were paid more than £1 million in 2004 (Kealey, 2006, p. 22).

Conclusion

Atkinson's main argument seems to be that the strength of postmodernism is that it 'comes as something of a shock' (2002, p. 78)[17] and reveals sub-texts and textual silences (ibid.). Well, so does Marxism on both counts. The difference is that with the former, after our shock, there is not much else to do, except at the local level. One of the great strengths of Marxism is that allows us to move beyond appearances and to look beneath the surface *and* to move forward. It allows us to transgress Derrida's 'ordeal of the undecidable', Lather's 'praxis of not being so sure', and Baxter's 'paralysis of practice'.

Postmodernists and poststructuralists are clearly capable of asking questions but, by their own acknowledgement, they have no answers.

The Marxist critique of postmodernism relates to postmodernism's rejection of the metanarrative, such as Marxism (or indeed neo-liberalism); its rejection of duality, thus failing to acknowledge the existence of class struggle; its plural view of truth, such that all accounts have equal worth, rather than privileging some accounts over others (related to this is the concept of multivocality (multiple voices) where everyone's opinion has equal worth); its stress on deconstruction alone, rather than deconstruction and reconstruction; and its concentration of the local at the expense of the national and the global, thus rendering major structural change non-viable.

To this I would reiterate that postmodernism and poststructuralism could be empowering to individuals and to localised groups. But to be politically valid, an analysis must link 'the small picture' to 'the big picture'. Postmodernism and poststructuralism, again by their protagonists' acknowledgement, cannot do this. They are, thus, not merely unable to promote social justice and social change, but, albeit usually by default, act as ideological supports for capitalism, both within nation states and globally.[18]

To recap, Marxism is about dialectical praxis. Such praxis is outside the remit of poststructuralism and postmodernism. Neither is able to address the global social injustices outlined at the beginning of this chapter. By their very essence, poststructuralism and postmodernism are about neither theory nor practice. They fail in both and remain an academic practice, based on deconstruction alone, with no practical implications for social or educational transformation. Indeed, deconstruction without reconstruction typifies the divorce of the academy from the reality of struggle on the ground (Cole and Hill, 1999b; Hill *et al.*, 1999, 2002b). Peter McLaren (2000, pp. xxiv–xxv) has described postmodernists in the most scathing terms: 'For those voguish hellions of the seminar room, post-modernism is the toxic intensity of bohemian nights, where the proscribed, the immiserated, and the wretched of the earth simply get in the way of their fun'. Recently, there has been a further challenge to Marxism from transmodern theory. In the next chapter, therefore, I will look at the origins of trans-modernism to assess the extent to which transmodern ideas are able to offer a further insight into the current state of world capitalism, and to move us a step forward in the struggle for equality and social justice.

6 Transmodernism in educational theory

A step closer to liberation?

This chapter is primarily concerned with the utilisation, by David Geoffrey Smith, of transmodernism *within educational theory*. In it I begin by looking at the origins of the concept of transmodernism and describe what are, for me, its defining features: a rejection of totalising synthesis; a critique of modernity; of Eurocentrism; and of postmodernism; its advocacy of analogic reasoning, and its reverence for indigenous and ancient traditions (its critique of (US) imperialism is dealt with in Chapter 8). The next part of the chapter consists of a Marxist critique of the politics of transmodernism, focusing on: liberating the oppressor; the complicity of modernists in the oppression of the South; and rethought liberal democracy or democratic socialism. I then make some critical comments on the transmodern interpretation of Marxism and social change. I conclude with a consideration of the political and economic choices presented by transmodernism and Marxism, respectively.

Introduction

The founder of the concept of transmodernism[1] is Argentinian philosopher Enrique Dussel. Professor of Ethics at the Universidad Autonóma Metropolitana/ Iztapalapa, Dussel was born in Mendoza in 1934. He is one of the most eloquent and incisive contemporary Left intellectuals; a prolific writer, well known for his dedication to a thorough ongoing and original reading of Marx, and for his numerous publications on various aspects of Marxism. This chapter does not attempt a critique of the works of Dussel as a whole, scholarly endeavours for which I have great respect.[2] Instead, I concentrate on the concept of transmodernism; a concept relatively new to academia in the Northern hemisphere and one which is, I believe, essentially flawed.[3] In the context of the concerns of this book, I am particularly interested in the way in which Dussel's concept of transmodernism has been utilised in *educational theory*, and, in particular, by David Geoffrey Smith.[4] Before I address such theory, however, I will first sketch Dussel's writings on the concept itself. In order to understand transmodernism, it is first necessary to examine Dussel's views on ethics.

Dussel is committed to 'ethical hermeneutics', putting oneself in the position of the oppressed and taking on their interests (Barber, 1998, p. 69); and to a 'philosophy of liberation', particularly attentive to the needs of 'the developing world' (Dallmayr, 2004, p. 8). Transmodernism thus shares common ground with the liberation theology wing of the Catholic Church (for which, incidentally, Dussel believes Marxism continues to have relevance (Hughes, 2004, p. 2)). Dussel is 'interested in the debunking of egocentrism, that is "the insistence on non-totality in the sense of an openness to the ethical demands of the "Other", especially the marginalized and disadvantaged"' (Dallmayr, 2004, p. 8).

Transmodernism has been enthusiastically endorsed by leading cultural theorist Paul Gilroy, who has described it as 'a geopolitical project with a longer reach and more profound consequences than is customarily appreciated' (2004, p. 48; see also p. 10 and p. 58). Gilroy (ibid., pp. 80–81) argues that 'transmodern dissidence is increasingly connected to the emergence of an anticapitalist culture that aims to make resistance to neoliberalism as global as capital has become'.

A number of the features of transmodernism are addressed and developed within the context of educational theory, by David Geoffrey Smith (Smith, 2003). Given transmodernism's 'newness' in the North and, in particular, given the acclaim given to Smith's paper (it won The Canadian Association for Curriculum Studies award for 'The Most Outstanding Publication in Curriculum Studies in Canada in 2003'), it is particularly important that Smith's interpretation of transmodernism receives careful scrutiny. I will accordingly concentrate on Smith's analysis throughout this chapter, while also referring to Dussel.

The defining features of transmodernism

As I understand them, transmodernism's defining features are:

- rejection of totalising synthesis;
- critique of modernity;
- anti-Eurocentrism;
- critique of postmodernism;
- analogic reasoning: reasoning from 'OUTSIDE' the system of global domination;
- reverence for (indigenous and ancient) traditions of religion, culture, philosophy and morality and Analectic Interaction: not so much a way of thinking as a new way of living in relation to Others;
- critique of (US) imperialism.

The transmodern critique of (US) imperialism is dealt with at length in Chapter 8. In this chapter, I will deal, in turn, with each of transmodernism's other defining features.

Rejection of totalising synthesis

Like postmodernism, transmodernism and its attendant 'philosophy of liberation' 'rejects all forms of totalising synthesis' (Dallmayr, 2004, p. 10). Marxism is thus ruled out, as is the naming of democratic socialism as a viable future. This rejection is based on a reified conception of Marxism, as tied to modernism, and as a 'theory of universal truth that can become yet another hammer in the hands of the self-righteous' (Smith, 2003, p. 500). Following Dussel, Smith (2003, p. 497) sees the modernist (and postmodern) agendas as trapped within a mutually self-serving antagonism, and hence helpless to address the massive violence against human well-being perpetrated in the name of a parochial truth claim.

While chronologically and geographically, Marxism is, of course, part of modernism it is, as I argued in Chapter 2, a *living philosophy*, not simply a discourse or a body of (academic) knowledge. It is not a reified concept, but able to adapt to new and changing circumstances. There are two important dimensions to this. First of all, as also argued in Chapter 2, Marxists have learnt major lessons from undemocratic dictatorial 'state socialism', practised in the name of Marxism in the former Stalinist states. Indeed, contemporary Marxists are the first to acknowledge, and indeed delineate, violence perpetrated by Stalinism. Second, while adhering to the maxim 'always totalise' (Peter McLaren, personal correspondence, 2007) and while intent on relating all forms of oppression to the metanarrative of capitalism, modern-day Marxists consistently acknowledge and oppose and combating varying oppressions, in addition to social class. Thus, it is inaccurate to put Marxism in a time warp, which associates it with state oppression and class reductionism.

The ruling class benefits from the rejection of totalising synthesis since, once all metanarratives are rejected, the very real metanarrative of capitalism is aided in the retention of its hegemonic position.

Critique of modernity

Dussel gives the birth date of 'modernity' as 1492, the European 'discovery' and ensuing conquest of the Americas (Dallmayr, 2004, p. 9). While Dussel acknowledges the foreshadowing by some tendencies of the later Middle Ages, he writes:

> [modernity] came to birth in Europe's confrontation with the Other. By controlling, conquering and violating the Other, Europe defined itself as discoverer, conquistador, and colonizer of an alterity likewise constitutive of modernity. Europe never discovered ... this Other as Other but covered over ... the Other as part of the Same: i.e. Europe. Modernity dawned in 1492 and with it the myth of a special kind of sacrificial violence which eventually eclipsed whatever was non-European.
>
> (Dussel, 1995, p. 12)

According to Dussel, Euro-American modernity extends from the late fifteenth century to the present, and is underwritten by a two-sided myth. This is 'the myth of modernity, as Dussel names it, and has for its dominant-surface side the 'myth of emancipative reason'; and for its underside it has the 'myth of sacrificial reason' (Smith, 2003, p. 494). The 'myth of emancipative reason', according to Dussel, is defined not so much by liberty, as it pretends, but by *subjectivity*, or, most importantly, by an elision of liberty into subjectivity. This ensures that self-enclosure, in the sense of a strong personal identity, becomes the character of the modern Western person. It is this basic narcissism ('excessive … interest in oneself and one's physical appearance', Pearsall, 2001, pp. 947–948) that is the source of Western violence, 'because under the assumption of its inherent superiority, the myth of emancipative reason is actually incapable of registering the experience of those falling outside of its own operating paradigm, and most especially those suffering under it' (Smith, 2003, p. 495).[5] Accordingly, the 'myth of sacrificial reason' means that any refusal of the 'myth of emancipative reason', or even ignorance of it, is a cause for subjugation or, in its starkest terms, a just cause for genocide (ibid.).

Genocide, as the practice of modernity's underside, is affected indirectly or directly. Indirectly, it operates out of neglect, resulting in, for example, environmental degradation in the name of progress (see Chapter 7, pp. 90–97 for a discussion), or in ignoring the tragedies of human displacement that inevitably ensue from policies of market deregulation (ibid.) (see Chapter 5, pp. 57–58 on displacement of people). Directly, the myth of sacrifice means 'play it our way' or we will kill you because you stand in the way of what we know to be universally true, and of which truth we are the bearers (ibid., p. 496). US imperialism commenced with the attempted annihilation of indigenous Amerindians, and continues contemporaneously its twenty-first century hegemonic designs (see Chapter 8 for a discussion of current US imperialism, and see also Chapter 8, pp. 104–109 for a critique of 'basic narcissism' as a causal factor of Western violence).

Anti-Eurocentrism

Dialogue should not fall, Dussel argues, into 'the facile optimism of rationalist, abstract universalism that would conflate universality with Eurocentrism' (Dussel, 1995, p. 132). 'What is needed instead is the fostering an alternative or analectical reason open to the traumas of exclusion and oppression' (Dallmayr, 2004, p. 9), an outlook which must 'deny the irrational sacrificial myth of modernity as well as affirm (subsume in a liberating project) the emancipative tendencies of the enlightenment and modernity within a new transmodernity' (Dussel, 1995, p. 132).

Smith argues that the 'critiques or apologies for modernity today are still inexorably Eurocentric' (ibid., p. 497). They fail, he argues, on three counts. First, the work is not located within an understanding of the Euro-American global 'order' (or disorder), the way in which the North is complicit in underdevelopment of the South. Second, the utter violence of that legacy is not acknowledged formally within the West's dominant philosophical paradigms. Third, there is no dialogue between the North and the South (these issues are addressed below).

Critique of postmodernism

Dussel has argued that dialogue should also not 'lapse into the irrationality, incommunicability, or incommensurability of discourses that are typical of many postmoderns' (Dussel, 1995, p. 132). For Dussel (1996, p. 53) the 'myth of sacrificial reason' is irrational. There is, therefore, a need to transcend modernity itself, but also postmodernity. As he puts it, 'our project of liberation can be neither anti- nor pre- nor post-modern, but instead trans-modern'. He offers these further thoughts on postmodernism:

> There are two limitations to postmodernism. First it represents a Eurocentric critique of the included negation, and second, it cannot accomplish the affirmation of those aspects of a culture excluded by European modernity. Postmodernity is critical, but not enough.
>
> (Dussel, 2002, cited in Hughes, 2004, p. 2)

'What moderns and postmoderns have in common', Smith argues, citing Robert Goizueta, is that they 'silence the cries of the victims; the first by ignoring them and the second by relativizing their universal claims' (Smith, 2003, p. 497). While the second claim is true, with respect to postmodernism, neither claim is true with respect to Marxism. Marxists *do not* ignore the cries of victims. Marxists not only listen, but also *act* on the suffering of the victims. Indeed, Marxism's primary project is the *liberation* of those at the receiving end of the ravages of global neo-liberal capital: the international working class.

Smith goes on to address the tension that can be easily observed in the Western academy between the universalistic logic of the sciences and technology and the celebration of particularity by the postmodern humanities, essentially inward-looking, which has 'rendered a collapse of concern for anything beyond what individual experience can express, whether in the name of autobiography, story, nation, tribe, personal therapy, or phenomenology' (Smith, 2003, p. 497).

In restricting modernism to 'the universalistic logic of the sciences and technology', Smith fails to acknowledge the contribution of Marxism both to the ongoing and extremely important (academic) critique of postmodernism (see Chapter 5) and to addressing, explaining *and providing solutions to* the massive violence perpetuated in the name of both neo-liberal global capitalism, commonly claimed to be 'inevitable', and of imperialism (see Chapters 7 and 8). The strength of Marxism is that it provides both critique and solution.

Analogic reasoning: reasoning from 'OUTSIDE' the system of global domination[6]

'Reasoning from *outside* the system of global domination' would appear to be derived from Lenin's interpretation of Marx's dialectical negation of the highest developments in bourgeois thought. It is encapsulated in Lenin's (1901–1902) dictum:

The workers can acquire political consciousness *only from without, i.e.,* only outside of the economic struggle, outside of the sphere of relations between workers and employers. The sphere from which alone it is possible to obtain this knowledge is the sphere of relationships between all classes and the state and the government – the sphere of the interrelations between all classes.

(cited in Slaughter, 1975)

As Cliff Slaughter (1975) explains, here Lenin expresses politically (against those who based themselves on the supposed 'spontaneous' development of socialist consciousness from the experience of the working class), the implications for Marx's writing on working-class consciousness. The working class could only arrive at the necessary consciousness and thereby the unity necessary for social revolution by understanding the full historical implications of its role in production and its capacity for *abolishing class society*. This body of theory could not come from the working class but only 'from the outside, from bourgeois intellectuals' (ibid.). This perspective rests on a particular ontological presupposition: that there is an 'outside' of capital's social universe. It assumes that a group of people – bourgeois intellectuals – can exist socially *qua* intellectuals outside of, and beyond, capital. This needs some justification and, as it stands, appears to present the bourgeois intellectual who dons the revolutionary cloak as a feral, Romantic figure. Moishe Postone (1996), for example, has argued that there is no 'outside' of capital's social universe; there is no 'wild'. Capitalist society is a form of *totality* and totalising of human existence, which incorporates all that it encounters. It has to be imploded from *within*. Furthermore, this position of Lenin/Slaughter appears to fall foul of Marx's Third Thesis in his *Theses on Feuerbach* (Marx, 1976b [1845]). This states that:

The materialist doctrine concerning the changing of circumstances and upbringing forgets that circumstances are changed by men and that it is essential to educate the educator himself. This doctrine must, therefore, divide society into two parts, one of which is superior to society. The coincidence of the changing of circumstances and of human activity or self-changing can be conceived and rationally understood only as *revolutionary practice*.

(Marx, 1976b [1845], p. 121 – original emphasis)

What Lenin's formulation appears to do is to 'divide society into two parts': the bourgeois intellectuals 'in the know' and 'superior' regarding their knowledge of the constitution of capitalist society and 'what should be done'; and the workers 'out of the know', and who are apparently incapable of gaining this knowledge and consciousness by themselves, and are therefore inferior. Thinkers such as Antonio Gramsci and Paulo Freire, following the Marx of the *Theses*, sort to break down this divide between 'superior' revolutionaries and 'the workers' through new organisational and educational forms.

While 'analogic reasoning' appears to be *derived* from Lenin/Slaughter's theorisation of relations between bourgeois intellectuals and the working class, Dussel's *transmodern* 'take' on it is very different from Lenin/Slaughter. Here is Dussel (1995, p. 138) on analogic reasoning:

> The transmodern project achieves with modernity what it could not achieve by itself – a co-realization of solidarity, which is analectic, analogic, hybrid, and *mestizo*, and which bonds center to periphery, woman to man, race to race, ethnic group to ethnic group, class to class, humanity to earth, and occidental to Third World cultures … This new project of transmodernity implies political, economic, ecological, erotic, pedagogic, and religious liberation.

What Dussel seems to be saying is not that workers need to appropriate bourgeois intellectual knowledge in order to change society through class struggle, but that the future society must be born *outside* the class struggle, by a 'co-realization of solidarity'. This is particularly problematic for Marxists, since a central tenet of Marxist analysis is that exploitation (the extraction of surplus value) occurs *within* the system of global domination and must also be resisted within that system. In particular, with respect to the Marxist position on class struggle, the transition for the working class to a *class for itself* (acknowledging its exploitation and willing to challenge the capitalist system), in addition to being a *class in itself* (an *objective* fact because of workers' shared exploitation, explained by the labour theory of value; see Chapter 2) must by definition occur *inside* the system of global domination. Because the ruling class and the working class are objectively antagonistic, no 'co-realization of solidarity' between the classes is possible. Dussel's transcendental approach seeks to *escape* capital's social universe in the realm of thought. In effect, Dussel wishes away the concrete grind of class struggle, exploitation and substantive inequalities. He is a magician of class in yearning for a realm where the classes can melt into some universal and non-conflictual mass of humanity. Dussel's class amalgamation in the realm of 'theory' avoids and evades real class relations and the constitution of capitalist society – and so never works. Marxists aim to *abolish* class society, Dussel's aim is not only to 'bond' genders and ethnicities but also social classes ('the transmodern project … bonds … class to class'); a kind of 'sisterhood and brotherhood of classes'. Dussel invokes wishful thinking on a truly post-historical and heavenly scale in his transmodern project at this juncture.

Reverence for (indigenous and ancient) traditions of religion, culture, philosophy and morality and Analectic Interaction: not so much a new way of thinking as a new way of living in relation to Others

Whereas, as we saw in Chapter 4, p. 46, one of the defining characteristics of postmodernism is 'irreverence for traditions of philosophy or morality', for Smith (2003, p. 500), the agenda of transmodernism is ultimately a moral one, which, in calling 'for a simple acceptance of the impossibility of … a theory [of universal truth]', turns for guidance to Confucianist moral virtue, Buddhist rejection of ego-driven manias, monotheist appreciation of what they are appealing to when they invoke the name of God; and Amerindian traditions of consensus-making, based neither on logic, nor solely on compromise, but on 'sitting together … until that truth is found which can be held in common' (ibid.).

Analectic Interaction involves listening to the voices of 'suffering Others' and interacting democratically with them, in a dialogue that begins with the revelation of the Other as part of a philosophy of liberation of the oppressed. While *analectical interaction* can have progressive implications, it does not, in itself, lead to social change.[7] Whereas for Dussel (Dallmyr, 2004), 'the liberation of the oppressed does not involve a brute struggle for power',[8] for Marxists liberation comes about through such struggle. As I have argued, Marxists believe that social change comes about via a *dialectical* process, whereby progress in societies occurs via thesis, antithesis and synthesis (see Chapter 2).

The politics of transmodernism: a Marxist critique

Like Marxism, transmodernism can provide useful insights into the nature of US imperialism (as in its genesis and long-standing genealogy as noted above) (see also Chapter 8). In addition, as Smith (2003, p. 499) points out, transmodernism goes beyond postmodern deconstruction, and actively seeks out not just Others, 'but … suffering Others'. It is thus theoretically and practically more progressive than postmodernism. However, I believe it is lacking in a number of aspects. In this section, I will consider the following issues, identified by transmodernists as part of their political agenda: liberating the oppressor; the complicity of modernists in the oppression of the South; and rethought liberal democracy or democratic socialism.

Liberating the oppressor

For Dussel, liberating the oppressed encompasses also liberating 'the oppressor from their desire to oppress' thus ultimately appealing to a latent ethical potential (Dallmayr, 2004, p. 9). Marxists do not believe that this is possible. On the contrary, Marxists argue that all progressive gains for the working class have been gained by workers' struggle. As argued in Chapter 2, Marxists believe that, in essence, capitalism is about the relentless extraction of surplus value from workers' labour. It is in the interest of capitalists to maximise profits and this entails (in order to create the greatest amount of new surplus value) keeping workers' wages as low as is 'acceptable' in any given country or historical period, without provoking effective strikes or other forms of resistance. Notwithstanding certain benign tendencies (philanthropic capitalists or certain social democratic governments for example) benefits, which accrue to workers in capitalist societies, have, throughout history, in general, been won by workers' struggle, rather than capitalist latent morality, or basic kindness.

The complicity of modernists in the oppression of the South

With respect to Smith's accusations, referred to above, of 'inexorable Eurocentricity', while these may be true of modernism in general, Marxism is not Eurocentric. That this is the case is attested to by the 'fact that many of the most brilliant, prominent, and effective anticolonial activists have insistently pronounced themselves Marxists' (Bartolovich, 2002, p. 15). While accusations of lack of awareness in the North's complicity in the underdevelopment of the South, of Euro-American genocide, and the lack of dialogue between the North and the South are valid when directed at many 'modernists', they also do not apply to Marxism, particularly *current* Marxist analyses, which do engage with such issues. Top priorities for modern-day Marxists include the way in which the economic situation in the South is a direct result of decisions made in the North, particularly with respect to impoverishment as a result of debt burdens (see Chapter 4, pp. 56–58); the violence and genocide practiced as a result of the economic and political trajectory of neo-liberal capitalism and imperialism (see Chapter 8); and the connections to be made and the lessons to be learned with respect to Left political and economic developments in countries such as Cuba, and in Central and South America.[9]

Rethought liberal democracy or democratic socialism?[10]

Bourgeois democracy is in crisis, given what is happening with respect to the death of truth and media distortion. Smith (2003, p. 488) has dealt with these issues, with respect to the US, at length. He argues that special circumstances, such as 'the condition of contemporary North American culture' require the creation of new language and new terminology. He coins the phrase, 'enfraudening the public sphere' to describe 'not just simple or single acts of deception, cheating or misrepresentation' (which may be described as 'defrauding'), but rather 'a more generalized active conditioning of the public sphere through systemized lying, deception and misrepresentation' (Smith, 2003, pp. 488–489).

Citing Weatherford, 1990, Smith's solution to this enfraudening process, and this appears to be despite transmodernism's aversion to totalising synthesis, is a rethinking of liberal democracy (Smith, 2003, p. 499) and a 'return to the theory of democracy Thomas Paine learned, not from the Greeks or the French, but from the Iroquois on the banks of the Delaware river' (ibid., p. 500). This theory of democracy, itself a form of totalising synthesis, relates to 'consensus making [which] ... arises from "sitting together" until that truth is found which can be held in common' (ibid.). I would argue that this is a utopian vision in the context of current anti-democratic US imperialism and global neo-liberal capitalism, a context critically explored by Smith in his paper. Democratic socialism, based on Marxist principles is, I will suggest, the only viable benevolent future for humankind.[11]

Thomas Paine's rejection of heredity and of a 'House of Commons', which is honest and truthful and serves the best interests of ordinary men and women was, in its time, certainly revolutionary. However, I would argue that the time has passed for the existence of a transparent, open, genuine and truthful form of bourgeois democracy. Paine's wish that governing bodies should truly represent the interests of the people seems strangely anachronistic.

Bourgeois democracy – British style

Rather than 'a search for truth', elections are often characterised by distortions and slurs, pandering to people's baser feelings. This is apparent in Britain in the right-wing popular press, which have a major influence on the outcome of British elections (e.g. MacArthur, 2005). During the run-up to the 2005 General Election, for example, opposition leader Michael Howard 'played the "race" card' by announcing further immigration restriction for asylum-seekers and refugees. Eager to legitimise the racialisation of these groups (categorising people falsely into distinct 'races' – see Chapter 8), the right-wing press featured a large number of references to 'common sense'. For example, political editor of Britain's most popular tabloid, Trevor Kavanagh, wrote an article with huge headlines declaring: 'This isn't racism. It's COMMON SENSE' (the *Sun*, 25 January 2005, pp. 8–9),[12] while, in the same edition, in order to foreclose any consideration of a liberal, let alone Left perspective, columnist Richard Little-john used the phrases 'the Fascist left' and 'the Labour/Liberal/BBC/Guardianistas axis' and informed readers that 'the Left always, always tell lies' (ibid., p. 11) (for an extended analysis of racism, racialisation and common sense, see Chapter 8).

In singling out the Left, Littlejohn was not warning his readers about New Labour, who quickly followed up Howard's intervention by announcing similar policy decisions. During the same pre-election period, New Labour was rebuked for publishing two anti-semitic cartoons on its website: the first portrayed both the Leader of the Opposition, Michael Howard, and the Shadow Home Secretary, Oliver Letwin (both Jewish) as 'flying pigs'; the other, Howard as Fagin (Rees-Mogg, 2005).

There was little in this election campaign that Thomas Paine would recognise as liberal democracy, as anything remotely connected with 'sitting together until that truth is found which can be held in common'. More recently, Smith (2004, p. 644) has appealed to a vision of 'vitalized senses of social democracy as necessary for the future'. Social democracy is epitomised by the British Labour Party in government 1945–1951, 1964–1970 and 1974–1976 (Benn and Chitty, 1996; Hillcole Group, 1997; Hill, 2001c).[13] Following Heffernan (1977), Hill (2001c, p. 14) identifies one of the essential features of social democracy as 'a mixed pseudo-Keynesian economy (an economic mix of public sector and private sector control and provision, together with government reflation during recessions)'.

While Marxists, of course, acknowledge and abhor the recent state of US excesses, and current British political and media manipulations centred around racialisation, their argument is that bourgeois democracy is *always* a numbers game, *always* distorts the truth, and *always* involves manipulation by politicians and by the media. Democratic socialism is a totally different concept to Smith's concept of liberal democracy and his more recent advocacy of social democracy. Unlike consensus-based liberal democracy and social democracy, democratic socialism is not a political bedfellow of the capitalist economy.

Democratic socialism is, by definition, a post-capitalist form of politics. It arises out of the transcendence of class struggle, and thus is a product of *conflict* rather than consensus. Democratic socialism is a much more profoundly *democratic* phenomenon than anything possible under capitalism. As argued in Chapter 2, it amounts to nothing less than a new realm of human freedom.

Thus, I would question Smith's recourse to rethought liberal democracy, or to 'vitalized senses of social democracy'. For similar reasons, I would also reject the arguments of Dussel, who stresses 'co-realization of solidarity' and 'class to class bonding', and those on the Left, who believe in the parliamentary road to democratic socialism since, in capitalist society, the interest of capitalists and workers are diametrically opposed (see Chapter 2, pp. 24–25).

The transmodern interpretation of Marxism and social change

I have three points to make with respect to Marxism and social change: the first relates specifically to Smith's notion that Marxism involves imposition; the second concerns Smith's use of the term '(vulgar) Marxism'; and the third is related to utopianism, specifically to Smith's conception of Marxism as a 'utopian typification', and Dussel's notion of *ex nihilo* multicultural utopia. I will deal with each in turn.

Imposition or majoritarian revolution?

Smith's conception that Marxism involves imposition is implied by his use of the phrase a 'hammer in the hands of the self-righteous' (Smith, 2003, p. 500) and by his assertion that Marxism is 'foist upon us' (Smith, 2004, p. 645). In addition, elsewhere, referring to the 'myth of sacrifice' (the underside of 'the myth of emancipative reason'), Smith (2004, p. 644) states that killing is justified 'as an act of love'. Both capitalism and Marxism, Smith suggests 'are underwritten by this common myth because of their European origins. Hence oceans of blood on both sides in the name of emancipation' (Smith, 2004, pp. 644–645).

This accords with the 'common sense' notion that Marxism has to be imposed because 'people don't want it'. Smith's (2003, p. 500) use of the term 'self-righteous' also implies a morally superior *minority*.

Marxism is not about minority imposition. The establishment of socialism should be a majoritarian project. As argued in Chapter 2, Marx argued that capitalism is subject to periodic political and economic crises. It is at these moments that the possibility exists for social revolution. Such a revolution can only occur, however, when the working class, in addition to being a 'class-in-itself', becomes 'a class-for-itself'. So Marxism is about the action of *the majority* not imposition from a minority, as is implied by Smith. As Marx and Engels state (1976 [1846], p. 56) in *The German Ideology*: 'The proletariat can ... only exist *world-historically* ... its activity ... can only have a "world-historical" existence' (original emphasis).

As Glenn Rikowski points out, this shows that, for Marx and Engels, the struggle for socialism must be majoritarian not just in a national sense, but in a *global* sense, as recognised by the Trotskyite emphasis on permanent, global revolution, as opposed to the (Stalinist) concept of 'socialism in one country'. Socialism is a struggle of the overwhelming majority of people throughout the globe against the forces of, and personal representatives of, capital. For Marx and Engels, the termination of capitalist social relations has to be global (Rikowski's comments on this chapter).

(Vulgar) Marxism

My second point relates to Smith's use of the term '(vulgar) Marxism'. In his 2004 paper, he uses this term on two occasions. First, when he equates Marxism with 'oceans of blood' (see above), Smith actually uses the term '(vulgar) Marxism' (Smith 2004, pp. 644–645).[14] Second, he concludes this paper by stating that we need to 'refuse what both capitalism and (vulgar) Marxism foist upon us' (Smith, 2004, p. 645). In using the term '(vulgar) Marxism' in these contexts, Smith does not seem to be aware of the conventional meaning of the term 'vulgar Marxism'. Vulgar Marxism traditionally refers to economic determinism, where the economic base determines what happens at the other (superstructural) levels of society: the political system, educational system and so on (see Chapter 3, pp. 33–36 for a discussion). As Robert M. Young (1998) puts it:

> The defining feature of Marxist approaches to the history of science is that the history of scientific ideas, of research priorities, of concepts of nature and of the parameters of discoveries are all rooted in historical forces which are, in the last instance, socio-economic. There are variations in how literally this is taken and various Marxist-inspired and Marxist-related positions define the interrelations among science and other historical forces more or less loosely. There is a continuum of positions. The most orthodox provides one-to-one correlations between the socio-economic base and the intellectual superstructure. This is referred to as economism or vulgar Marxism.

However, as Engels (1890) put it, economic determinism was never part of Marxism:

> According to the materialist conception of history the determining element in history is ultimately the production and reproduction in real life. More than this neither Marx nor I have ever asserted. If therefore somebody twists this into the statement that the economic element is the only determining one, he transforms it into a meaningless, abstract and absurd phrase.

Smith's use of '(vulgar) Marxism' does not seem to be connected to notions of the base/superstructure relationship (a widely debated topic in Marxist theory), and, like his use of Marxism per se, seems more to do with Stalinism and 'minority imposition' than conventional understandings of vulgar Marxism. Indeed, Smith's analysis does not show cognisance of developments in Marxism post-Stalinism.

Utopianism and blueprints for the future

My third point relates to Smith's conception of Marxism as a 'utopian typification' (Smith, 2004, p. 645). It is a common misunderstanding that Marxists believe in 'an ideal world'; in a utopia, in a blueprint for the future. How often has one heard in response to the argument of Marxists, the 'common sense' reply: 'it sounds all right in theory, but it won't work in practice'? (see the concluding chapter – Chapter 10 – for an extended discussion). Marxists are actually anti-utopia. Utopianism is, in fact, the province of utopian socialists, rather than Marxists, as argued in Chapter 2. Utopian socialism, as we saw, conventionally refers to the eighteenth/nineteenth century writings of Henri de Saint-Simon, Charles Fourier and Robert Owen.

However, transmodernism, in appealing to the latent morality of the oppressor, in advocating change *outside* the class struggle, in creating a new world *ex nihilo*, and in championing the need along with gender and ethnic solidarity, for 'class to class co-realization of solidarity' (see above) transmodernism is also utopian. In fact, Dussel himself has *described* 'transmodernity' as a utopic vision of multiculturality that could replace postmodernity (Hughes, 2004, p. 2). Liberation does not involve, as we have seen, according to Dussel, a brute struggle for power, which it is felt would merely replace one type of oppression by another. Instead, in line with 'ethical hermeneutics', Dussel's aim is not only to liberate the oppressed and excluded, but also to liberate the oppressor from their desire to oppress. Dussel has suggested that transmodernism accomplishes that which postmodernism cannot, namely it offers an affirmation of the excluded exteriority of a colonial civilisation (Hughes, 2004, p. 2). Dussel argues that 'the *imaginaire* of ancient cultures remains intact' (Hughes, 2004, p. 2), but that the future multicultural utopia that emerges in transmodernity would represent creation from nothing, *ex nihilo*. This utopia would be rebuilt from the excluded aspects of colonial cultures or those parts of the culture that had previously been denied value (Hughes, 2004, p. 2).[15] With respect to a Marxist vision of the future, 'we are ... locked', as Gibson and Rikowski (2004) point out, 'into capitalist society, and our capacity to visualise anything beyond it, such as socialist society ... is impossible'. Furthermore, the trajectory of socialism cannot be decided a priori.[16]

Rikowski (2004b, pp. 559–560) gives four other (inter-related) reasons why Marxists do not have blueprints for the future. First, Marx held that the struggle for socialism must be based on the self-activity of the working class: the workers themselves must *make history*. Thus, he was reluctant to provide a blueprint for socialist society, since this would contradict and negate workers' practical solutions to the movement from capitalist to socialist society. Second, the practice of lone thinkers projecting the 'society of the future' runs against the *collective, democratic* and *experimental* and *experiential* nature of the socialist project. Third, those setting themselves up as 'experts' for generating blueprints for socialism – whether they are leaders of Left political parties, academic Marxists or Marxists writing outside of academia – would amount to establishing themselves as an elite of people 'in the know' with respect to what socialism was and could be. Rikowski cites Marx's aforementioned *Theses on Feuerbach*, where Marx stresses the need for the educator to be educated and signals the dangers of having a two-tier society, with one superior to the other. For Marx, such elitism had no place in the socialist movement.

Fourth, Rikowski continues, Marx was keen to emphasise the creativity and spontaneity of the drive towards socialism, and to chart and assess the practical experiments of workers in this endeavour. He cites, by way of example, the Paris Commune of 1871, the course of which was enthusiastically followed by Marx who wrote about the way workers' power was manifested in novel and exciting ways. Any notion of a definitive model for socialism, Rikowski goes on, would inhibit the creative, energising and exciting moments of the struggle for an alternative society (ibid.).

Thus, Rikowski (2004b, p. 560) concludes, Marxism is not about specifying typifications for future societies. Moreover, there is no final destination. 'The social drive to form a truly human society is infinite, just as capital's social drives (to create value, to enhance human labour-power) are also infinite' (ibid.).

In describing Marxism as *imposition*; in linking it with Stalinism; and in equating it with utopia, Smith seriously misrepresents the Marxist project.

Political and economic choices and the role of the educator

Smith has summarised the difficulties facing the educator in the present conjuncture. As he puts it, following Carl Jung (1989, p. 89), 'children pay much less attention to what adults actually say than they do to the imponderables in the surrounding atmosphere'. One of the most disturbing aspects of current US aggression, he continues, is 'the complete disregard it shows for its lived effects in the lives of ordinary citizens, perhaps especially young people' (Smith, 2003, p. 498). For Smith (ibid.) this heralds 'a pedagogical crisis for teachers'. How can teachers enact democratic pedagogy when US politics is imbricated in the opposite direction? (ibid.). It is worth citing Smith at length:

> If unilateralism and monological decision-making mark the character of political leadership, what becomes, for teachers and students, of the relationship between thought and action, of my belief as a teacher that what I and others may plan for tomorrow may bear an expectation of being brought into effect? If bullying, both domestically and internationally, is legitimized publicly (albeit euphemistically), how as a teacher can I counsel my students against what has become one of the greatest scourges in the contemporary

schoolyard? If lying, duplicity and deliberate misrepresentation are acceptable strategies by which to operate in the name of Truth, what is the basis upon which any human relations may be trusted? ... Children [learn] early that exploiting others for personal gain is 'the way to go'.

(Smith, 2003, p. 498)

So what choices do we have? As we have seen, Dussel, has advocated 'a utopic vision of multiculturality' created from nothing, but built from existing indigenous cultures. Such a proposition has recently been expressed by Bolivian peasants' leader Felipe Quispe who, critiquing Marxism as being a product of European and white thought (see pp. 69–70 of this chapter for a rebuttal of this proposition), has called for a separate nation for the indigenous Aymaran people (Maunder, 2006, p. 13). As Jonathan Maunder (ibid.) argues, creating an Aymaran nation, separate from Bolivian capitalism, is not a viable proposal since it would mean leaving behind the vast wealth created by the Bolivian workers and peasants. Moreover, the Bolivian ruling class, like any ruling class, 'would use their power and organisation to crush such an attempt to create a space liberated from their rule' (Maunder, 2006, p. 13).

Another choice is, with Smith, to seek out 'suffering others' (which, I have argued is more progressive than postmodernism). However his suggestion of rethinking bourgeois democracy: attempting to make capitalism more humane, a project epitomised by the aforementioned social democratic project of the British Labour Party in government from 1945 until the 1970s, is a most unlikely option. Given its rapacious and predatory nature and, in particular, given the advances made by capital since the 1980s neo-liberal revolution (see Chapter 7, pp. 87–90 for a discussion), it is most unlikely that capitalism will retreat to its pre-1980s mixed economy position (where the economy was run by both state – railways, utilities etc. – and business).

My argument is not that capitalism cannot in theory be made more democratic or humane. The point is that, in the words of Kevin Watkins of Oxfam, 'industrialised countries ... have collectively reneged on every commitment made' (*Guardian*, 12 November 2001, p. 22). In fact, organisations such as the World Trade Organization (WTO),[17] the World Bank and the International Monetary Fund (IMF) are constitutionally destined to fail in any attempt at addressing the marginalisation of 'the developing world'. The WTO can only set maximum standards for global trade, rather than the minimum standards that might restrain big corporations, while the World Bank and the IMF, entirely controlled by the creditor nations, exist to police the poor world's debt on their behalf. Rather than recognise these inherent defects, their backers blame the poor countries themselves. Peter Sutherland, former head of the WTO, has asserted that it is 'indisputable that the real problem with the economies that have failed [is] their own domestic governments', while Maria Cattui, who runs the International Chamber of Commerce, insisted that the 'fault lies most of all at home with the countries concerned' (Monbiot, 2001, p. 17).

Any possible gain for poor and dispossessed workers in the developing countries and elsewhere as a result of increasing global political awareness, including the Commission for Africa initiative (www.commissionforafrica.org) by British ex-Prime Minister Tony Blair, ex-Chancellor Gordon Brown and ex-Secretary of State for International Development, Hilary Benn, while supported by Marxists, is likely to be minimalist and short-lived.

The current state of world capitalism has led Ellen Meiksins Wood (1995) to conclude that the lesson that we may be obliged to draw from our current economic and political condition is that a humane, 'social', truly democratic and equitable capitalism is more unrealistically utopian than socialism.

So, if I am right that neither an *ex nihilo* utopia or a 'utopic multiculturality' (Dussel) nor a return to a more democratic and humane capitalism, a 'rethought liberal democracy' (Smith) are likely to happen, the only choices available are to continue down the path of neo-liberal capitalism and imperialism or, worse, fascism; or to challenge capitalism itself. The suggestion by Smith (2004, p. 645) that, in our teaching, we can harness Taoism and Buddhis to refuse capitalism and US imperialism (Smith, 2003, p. 500) seems a most vague hope, particularly in a country like the US, where evangelical theo-conservatism is hegemonic.[18] Smith (2003, p. 501) concludes his article by stressing that 'unless the rules of engagement for human procedure can be rethought in ways that are more equitable, fair and just, what lies ahead may be unthinkable'. As we have seen, unlike poststructuralism/postmodernism which have no rules of procedure, transmodernists adhere to the contradictory position of rejecting totalisation, while adhering to a set of principles with transformative potential. While rejecting theories of universal truth as impossible, and hence (wrongly) implicitly equating such theories with Marxism, and rejecting Marxism itself, Smith (2003, p. 500) goes on to set out his own agenda for change. Despite his denial of romanticism, he espouses a romanticised moralism based on Confucious, Buddha and Amerindian philosophy (Smith, 2003, p. 500). Thus his attempts to teach to end capitalist exploitation are limited in that Smith concentrates on the specifically religious and spiritual roots of capitalist theory, on the basis that he does not think much progress will be made in critiques of capitalism until it is 'desacralized' (personal correspondence). This connects to the transmodern reverence for pre-capitalist religion, culture, philosophy and morality. As Smith argues, what is needed is something like the World Council of Churches' declaration of South African Apartheid as a heresy to be applied to capitalism in order to desacralise and hence delegitimise it. Given the above-noted entrenchment of theo-conservatism, this is a worthy aim, but unlikely to happen.

While Smith's prescription amounts to a fine moral sentiment,[19] given what Dallmayr (2004, p. 11) describes as 'the intoxicating effects of global rule' and the 'corresponding levels of total depravity and corruption among the rulers' (a depravity being constantly revealed in the form of torture and other abuse of Iraqi and Afghanistani detainees by US troops, in Iraq and Guantanamo Bay respectively – see Chapter 8) it remains a utopian *dream*, as does Dussel's vision of class bonding in utopic multiculturality. For Marxists, the logic of the brute force of neo-liberal imperialism must be met, as we have seen, with the logic of the dialectic and with the brute (though hopefully not necessarily excessively violent) force of organised workers.[20] Having examined, in this chapter, the conceptual issues pertaining to transmodernism, primarily, though not exclusively in the context of educational theory, as expounded by David Geoffrey Smith, I turn in the next chapter, to a consideration of the burning issues of globalisation, neo-liberalism and environmental destruction, and their implications for education, before turning, in Chapter 8, to the 'New Imperialism', and the need for an analysis of imperialisms to be at the heart of the curriculum. In that chapter, after examining and critiquing a postmodern perspective on the 'New Imperialism', I return to transmodernism and David Geoffrey Smith in an evaluation of postmodernism's take on imperialism.

7 Globalisation, neo-liberalism and environmental destruction

In this chapter, I begin by providing a sketch of the all-pervasive concept of globalisation. I go on to examine New Labour's claim that globalisation can be a force for good. Next I examine globalisation and neo-liberalism. After that, I address the issue of environmental destruction, focusing on the destruction of resources; unhealthy food; genetic modification and climate change. I conclude with a consideration of the implications for education.

Introduction

There is a burgeoning consensus both inside and outside academia that *the most pressing* issue of the twenty-first century is environmental destruction and, in particular, global warming. My view is that, for Marxists, environmental destruction and global warming must be central considerations in all theoretical and practical endeavours (which for Marxists are linked dialectically) but that such issues cannot be understood without a thorough consideration of processes of globalisation and neo-liberalism. In this chapter, therefore, I will begin by analysing the nature of these two concepts, before moving on to a consideration of environmental destruction in the context of global neo-liberal capitalism. I will argue that examinations of globalisation, neo-liberalism and environmental destruction need to be core elements in the curriculum.

Globalisation became one of the orthodoxies of the 1990s and continues to hold sway into the twenty-first century.[1] It is proclaimed in the speeches of virtually all mainstream politicians, in the financial pages of newspapers and in company reports; it is common currency in corporation newsletters and shop stewards' meetings (Harman, 1996, p. 3). Its premises are that in the face of global competition, capitals are increasingly constrained to compete on the world market. Its argument is that, in this new epoch, these capitals can only do this in so far as they become multinational corporations and operate on a world scale, outside the confines of nation states. The argument continues: this diminishes the role of the nation state, the implication being that there is little, if anything, that can be done about it. Capitalists and their allies insist that, since globalisation is a fact of life, it is incumbent on workers, given this globalised market, to be flexible in their approach to what they do and for how long they do it, to accept lower wages and to concur with the restructuring and diminution of welfare states. The adoption of neo-liberalism has given a major boost to globalisation, both de facto and ideologically.

New Labour and globalisation as a force for good

Marxists are particularly interested in the way such arguments about globalisation are used ideologically to further the interests of capitalists and their political supporters (for an analysis, see Cole, 1998, 2005d), of the way in which it is used to mystify the populace as a whole and to stifle action by the Left in particular (e.g. Murphy, 1995; Gibson-Graham, 1996; Harman, 1996; Meiksins, Wood, 1998).

In this section, I sketch the views of New Labour on globalisation. They are of interest in the context of the overall themes of this book in that New Labour claims that globalisation can be a force for social justice.

Blair's rhetoric provides a prime example of the ideological justification for globalised neo-liberal capitalism. For Blair, globalisation is part of the natural order: 'I hear people say we have to stop and debate globalisation. You might as well debate whether autumn should follow summer' (Speech to the Labour Party Conference, 2005).

Moreover, there is a major current in Blairite rhetoric, which seeks to connect *modernisation* with these capitalist requirements. Modernisation is a key component in New Labour oratory, and the conduit through which New Labour justifies ideologically the policy of continuing alignment to the needs of the global market (Cole, 1998, p. 323, Cole, 2005d). Modernisation means embracing global neo-liberal capitalism. Modernisation means a final break with 'Old Labour' and an end to any speculation that the Blair Government might recommit to social democratic, let alone socialist values as New Labour's core guiding ideology. Blair is, in fact, quite open about this break. The problem, for Blair, is not that trade has become too global, but that 'there's too little of it' (*Guardian*, 3 October 2001, p. 4). At the TUC Conference in 2005, Blair effectively told trade union leaders to get real and face globalisation or cease to exist. He urged them to find solutions 'based on reality' (Carlin and Hope, 2005) and stressed the necessity for 'fundamental modernisation' (ibid.). In a pre-2005 Labour Party conference speech to the Cabinet, he stated: 'we have to secure Britain's future in a world ... driven by globalisation. ... We have to change and modernise ... to equip everyone for this changing world' (*The* (Brighton) *Argus*, 22 September 2005, p. 6). This changing world is one in which Britain must be at the forefront of cheap labour providers:

> My vision is of a Britain made for globalisation – the location of choice and the place for business to be ... And just as we have met our inflation target in every year since 1997 we will meet our inflation target in future years so that businesses can plan ahead, invest for the future with confidence, grow and prosper. And as I made clear ... seeking discipline in public sector pay,

I will resist inflationary pressures from wherever they come, safeguarding Britain's fiscal position today and for the future.
(Speech by the Chancellor of the Exchequer Gordon Brown MP,
at the CBI Annual Conference in London, 28 November 2005:
The Labour Party, 2005)

In June 2006, the day before the union leadership sell-out of a major higher education dispute, Brown announced a public sector wage freeze, promising that public sector reform will be 'stepped up, broadened, developed and intensified' (see Cole, 2006a, p. 17).

As we have seen, theo-conservatism, hegemonic in the US, is used to describe members of the Christian Right, referring in general to those people who believe that God's Law ought to play a larger role in public life. They also maintain that the more socially convervative aspects of that Law ought to be enforced. Although there are no clear and hard distinctions, 'theo-cons' can be distinguished from the Christian socialist tradition in Britain which focuses more on the welfare aspects of the Christian gospel: the Christian Left see Christianity and socialism as interconnected. While the policies of New Labour are most firmly aligned to the requirements of neo-liberalism, global capital and imperialism, the discourse of British ex-Prime Minister Tony Blair retains some historical remnants of Christian socialism (for an analysis of Christian socialism, and the trajectory from Tawney to New Labour, see Woolley, 2007).

Providing a direct link with Christian socialism, Blair's stated vision for the future is globalisation with 'power, wealth, and opportunity' in 'the hands of the many, not the few' (*Guardian*, 3 October 2001, p. 5), a globalisation combined with justice; globalisation as 'a force for good'. For Blair, this 'commitment to the poor and weak … not the contentment of the wealthy and strong' is to be achieved by the vacuous concepts of 'the power of community' (ibid., p. 4) and 'the moral power of a world acting as a community' (ibid., p. 5).

Blair's vision of benign globalisation needs to be seen in the light of the events of 9/11. Among other things, these events increased awareness in 'the developed world' that 'we' cannot just forget about more than half of humanity. In Blair's words: 'One illusion has been shattered on September 11: that we can have the good life of the west, irrespective of the state of the world' (*Guardian*, 13 November 2001, p. 10). So, is his vision of alleviating global inequalities within the context of world capitalism a viable one? I want to argue that globalisation with power, wealth and opportunity in the hands of many, not the few, is an oxymoron and that globalisation is, in fact, antithetical to social justice (see Chapter 5, pp. 56–57 for some statistics on the distribution of wealth and income).

Globalisation and neo-liberalism

First, I would argue that, rather than view globalisation as a new epoch (the current orthodoxy), the global movement of capital might more accurately be seen as a cumulative process and one that has been going on for a long time – in fact, since capitalism first began four or five centuries ago. Meiksins Wood (1998, p. 47), for example, argues that what we are seeing is not a major shift in capitalism, but capitalism reaching maturity (see also Cole 1998, 2005d). Globalisation is championed as the harbinger of free trade and is heralded by most as a new phenomenon. It is, in fact, as old as capitalism itself, but it is a phenomenon that alters its character through history (e.g. Cole, 1998). This is because one of the central features of capitalism is that, once rooted, parasitic-like, it grows and spreads. This double movement is thoroughly explored by Marx (1965 [1887]) in *Capital* and elsewhere (for a summary, see Sweezy, 1997).

Globalisation in the twenty-first century is pre-eminently neo-liberal. Martinez and García (2000) have identified five defining features of the global phenomenon of neo-liberalism:

1　*The rule of the market*

- the liberation of 'free' or private enterprise from any bonds imposed by the state no matter how much social damage this causes;
- greater openness to international trade and investment;
- the reduction of wages by de-unionising workers and eliminating workers' rights;
- an end to price controls;
- total freedom of movement for capital, goods and services.

2　*Cutting public expenditure*

- less spending on social services such as education and healthcare;
- reducing the safety-net for the poor;
- reducing expenditure on maintenance, e.g. of roads, bridges and water supply.

3　*Deregulation: reducing government regulation of everything that could diminish profits*

- less protection of the environment;
- lesser concerns with job safety.

4　*Privatisation: selling state-owned enterprises, goods and services to private investors, e.g.:*

- banks;
- key industries;
- railroads;
- toll highways;
- electricity;
- schools;
- hospitals;
- fresh water.

5 *Eliminating the concept of 'The Public Good' or 'Community'*

- replacing it with 'individual responsibility';
- pressuring the poorest people in a society to find solutions to their lack of healthcare, education and social security by themselves.

Global neo-liberalism was given a major boost in 1994, with the signing of the General Agreement on Trade in Services (GATS) at the World Trade Organisation (WTO). The aim of this agreement, which came into force in January 1995, is to remove any restrictions and internal government regulations in the area of service delivery that are considered to be 'barriers to trade'. The list of services of the GATS includes 12 types, subdivided in many others:

1 Business (accounting, computer science and related subjects, legal, marketing and correlated, medical and dental services, architecture, etc.);
2 Communication (telecommunication, mail, audiovisual, radio, motion picture etc.);
3 Construction and related engineering services;
4 Distribution (franchising, retail and wholesale, etc.);
5 Education (primary, secondary, higher, adult education and others);
6 Environmental (sewage, sanitation, disposal, etc.);
7 Financial (insurances, banking, leasing, asset management, etc.);
8 Health and related social services (hospital, other human health services, social, etc.);
9 Tourism and travel related (hotel, restaurant, travel agencies, etc.);
10 Recreational, Cultural and Sporting (news agency, libraries, archives, museums, theatre, sports, etc.;
11 Transports (maritime, aerial, railway, railroad, passenger, freight, maintenance and repair, towing, pipelines, warehouses, etc.);
12 'Other services not mentioned in any other place

(WTO, 2003, cited in de Siqueira, 2005)

Since February 2000, negotiations have been underway in the WTO to expand and 'fine-tune' the GATS. As GATSWatch (undated) has pointed out, these negotiations have aroused concern worldwide. A growing number of local governments, trade unions, non-governmental organisations (NGOs), parliaments and developing country governments are criticising the GATS negotiations and call for a halt on the negotiations. Their main points of critique are:

- Negative impacts on universal access to basic services such as healthcare, education, water and transport.
- Fundamental conflict between freeing up trade in services and the right of governments and communities to regulate companies in areas such as tourism, retail, telecommunications and broadcasting.

- Absence of a comprehensive assessment of the impacts of GATS-style liberalisation before further negotiations continue.
- A one-sided deal. GATS is primarily about expanding opportunities for large multinational companies.

(GATSWatch, undated)

As argued in Chapter 2, capitalism is, *by definition*, a system in which a minority (the capitalist class) exploits the majority (the working class) by extracting surplus value from their labour power. The globalisation processes, outlined above, now in hegemonic neo-liberal mode, with their emphases on 'the private' rather than 'the public', on greed rather than the welfare of humankind, serve to enhance this exploitation. Any idea of putting the control of globalised capital into the hands of the many is therefore not viable. Globalisation always has been and is a central feature in the maintenance and parasitic growth of capitalism.

Globalization and global environmental destruction

The unrelenting abuse of nature, viewed as a resource to plunder by global neo-liberal capitalism, has had disastrous consequences. Millions of poor people have been driven off their land, while whole areas of agricultural land have been damaged, and rainforests destroyed by mining, logging and oil companies. Our health is seriously at risk by the food we eat, genes are being engineered and modified, and 'global warming' is threatening the survival of life on the planet. I will deal with the effects of environmental destruction under the following headings: unhealthy food; genetic modification; the destruction of resources; and climate change.

Unhealthy food

The food that we eat in 'developed' countries is unhealthier than ever before. Many foods, for example, contain high levels of salt, sugar, saturated fats, preservatives, and are lacking in antioxidants and fibres. Food often contains E-numbers,[2] believed to be linked to disorders including allergies, neurological disorders, bowel disorders, cancer, heart disease and arthritis. In more recent years, further concerns have been raised that many of these additives may be of genetically modified (Wikipedia: http://en.wikipedia.org/wiki/E_number) (see below, for a discussion of genetic modification).

It is estimated that 70 per cent of the £20 million global annual food advertising budget is used to promote (unhealthy) soft drinks, sweets and snacks (Feldman and Lotz, 2004, p. 129).[3] Moreover, pesticides in food contain carcinogenics or hormone disrupting properties.

Much of what we eat has been modified. As Felicity Lawrence (2004, cited in Feldman and Lotz, 2004, p. 129), who worked anonymously in a chicken-processing factory, explains, water is routinely added to catering chicken, along with additives to hold it in:

> Chickens, like other animals, have become industrialised and globalised. We no longer know where they are produced or how they are processed. By the time we buy them in aseptic little packages, or processed into convenience meals, we have lost any sense of their origin.

Lawrence has some interested information, regarding an item that most of us would think of as a most healthy option. She reconstructed the contents of a 99 pence bag of washed and 'ready-to-eat' salad, and discovered it was in modified-atmosphere packaging (MAP), used to increase shelf-life and to keep the salad looking fresh for up to ten days, thus allowing supermarkets to get food from around the world where it is produced at the lowest wage-rates. As Lawrence (2004, cited in Feldman and Lotz, 2004, pp. 129–130) puts it:

> The salad is cut or separated out into individual leaves by gangs of workers, then washed in chlorine, dried and sorted before being packaged in pillows of plastic in which the normal levels of oxygen and carbon dioxide have been altered. Typically in MAP, the oxygen is reduced from 21% to 3% and the CO_2 levels correspondingly raised. This slows any visible deterioration or discolouring.

This process is thought to destroy many of the nutrients in the original salad. Moreover, the chlorine leaves residues of chlorinated compounds on the lettuce, some of which are known to cause cancer (Feldman and Lotz, 2004, p. 130).

Genetic modification

The last 25 years or so has seen a dramatic extension and deepening of global capitalism's penetration of nature for profit. For example, genetic modification, having first occurred in 1973, is an unprecedented incursion. Moreover, this knowledge is being privatised through patents on genes (Feldman and Lotz, 2004, p. 118). Paul Gilroy (2004, p. 84) has described these developments as the 'corporate control of the substance of life itself', linking 'the colonization of territory and human beings with the colonization of all life'. As Paul Feldman and Corinna Lotz (2004, p. 118) put it, 'the mapping of the human genome paves the way, potentially, for the wholesale alteration of the human species by corporations'. They cite Jeremy Rifkin (1998) who conjures up this nightmare vision:

> Imagine the wholesale transfer of genes between totally unrelated species and across all biological boundaries – plant, animal and human – creating thousands of novel life forms in a very brief moment of evolutionary time. Then, with clonal propagation, mass-producing countless replicas of these

new creations, releasing them into the biosphere to propagate, mutate, pro-
liferate, and migrate, colonising the land, water, and air.

(Rifkin, 1998, cited in Feldman and Lotz, 2004, p. 118)

This scenario, however, is more than a crazy dream since, as Rifkin points out,
'this is, in fact, the great scientific and commercial experiment underway'
(Rifkin, 1998, cited in Feldman and Lotz, 2004, p. 118). In 2004, the New
Labour Government announced that genetically engineered/modified (GE/GM)
maize could be grown in the UK, subject to national seed list and pesticide
approval. This crop will be fed to cows to make milk, but the milk will not be
labelled as GM (Feldman and Lotz, 2004, p. 130). It is the biotech corporations
who profit out of processes, which involve inserting genes randomly into
another sequence that may have taken hundreds of millions of years to evolve,
thus having unpredictable results (Feldman and Lotz, 2004, p. 130).

When US and Canadian farmers buy GE seeds, they usually tie themselves to
a contract which prevents them saving seed for use the following year, thus
forcing them to buy new patented seed each season.

Another form of genetic modification is nanotechnology, which is the manipulation of material, at the scale of the nanometre (one billionth of a metre – the
scale of atoms and molecules). Already hundreds of tonnes of nanoscale parti-
cles are appearing in consumer products, ranging from sunscreens to car parts
and paint (Feldman and Lotz, 2004, p. 135). There is a fear that nanoscale
robots, capable of manipulating molecules and reproducing, could pose a major
threat to global survival, analogous to the uncontrolled self-replicating of cancer
cells (Feldman and Lotz, 2004, p. 136).

Jeremy Rifkin (1998, cited in Feldman and Lotz, 2004, p. 137), has summed
up the dangers of genetic engineering as a whole:

> A handful of corporations, research institutions and governments could hold
> patents on virtually all 100,000 genes that make up the blueprint of the
> human race, as well as the cells, organs, and tissues that comprise the
> human body. They may also own similar patents on thousands of micro-
> organisms, plants and animals, allowing them unprecedented power to
> dictate the terms by which we and future generations will live our lives.

Destruction of resources

Intensive farming in the last 60 years and the turn to industrialised agriculture
under current globalisation have resulted in ecological catastrophe. As a result of
excessive tillage and fertiliser use, the removal of vegetation and over-grazing, it is
estimated that 10 to 20 per cent of the world's 1.5 billion hectares of cropland are
degraded to some degree (Feldman and Lotz, 2004, p. 127). Pesticide use has
grown 15-fold since 1950, and imposes a major health hazard, poisoning 3,000,000
people severely and killing 220,000 each year (Feldman and Lotz, 2004, p. 128).
Worldwide, the degradation of farmland has reduced cumulative food production

by approximately 13 per cent over the last 50 years. At the same time, about 20 per cent of irrigated land is damaged by a build-up of salt, which occurs when excess water evaporates (Feldman and Lotz, 2004, p. 128). Two-thirds of all fisheries are exploited at, or beyond, their sustainable limits (Feldman and Lotz, 2004, p. 128).

Of particular concern is the destruction of rainforests, home to more species of plants and animals than the rest of the world put together. In the 1970s, mining companies began pushing into the forests. Huge areas of tropical rainforest were destroyed to mine iron ore, bauxite for aluminium, gold and other minerals (Rainforest Live, 2006).

Mining activities need roads, the building of which further destroys the rainforests on a large scale. The roads are subsequently used not only by logging and mining companies, but also by settlers and poachers who exploit the forest even more. Mining companies often pay hunters to supply meat from the forest animals to feed the miners. Mining activities also cause severe pollution of rivers (Rainforest Live, 2006).

Some of the trees that grow in tropical rainforests such as teak, mahogany, meranti, ebony and rosewood are in great demand for timber by 'developed countries' such as the US, UK and Japan, and in order to meet this demand, at least 4.5 million hectares are logged each year. Hardwoods may take 100 years to mature so they cannot be easily replaced or farmed. Like mining companies, logging companies also bring mass destruction into the forests through road building, transporting the logs and the construction of sawmills (Rainforest Live, 2006).

The drilling and production of oil is also a great threat to large areas of rainforests: in the western edge of the Amazon rainforest, in the Yansuni National Park in Ecuador, in Nigeria, Colombia and Papua New Guinea. Once again, oil drilling involves cutting trees to make room for roads, but also for pipelines and oil machinery. In addition, the oil spills and pollutes rivers and streams, poisoning the wildlife as well as the water people drink. Not only is oil used as a fuel, but also to make plastic bags, bottles and cups and fabrics such as nylon and polyester (Rainforest Live, 2006).

Burning oil and other fossil fuels pollutes the atmosphere and contributes to global warming and climate change.

Climate change

One of the greatest threats to the survival of all the inhabitants, and indeed all living things on our planet, is the major change in the world's climate. The 'greenhouse effect' refers to an insulating layer created by heat-trapping gases in the atmosphere, which contain the sun's energy and allow life on earth to continue. 'Global warming' results from an increase in the heat-trapping gases in the atmosphere (Feldman and Lotz, 2004, p. 119). The idea that some of the gases in the atmosphere helped to warm the earth was first propounded by Joseph Fourier as early as 1824 and, by 1896, 'global warming' was broadly scientifically understood. It was predicted that a doubling of concentrations of the greenhouse gas (GHG) CO_2 would warm the earth by 4–5°C. It was also shown that such a doubling was possible through the burning of fossil fuels (coal, oil and natural gas) (Ward, 2005–2006, p. 13).

In the most comprehensive and the most accurate scientific projection yet of the potential effects of human-made global warming, Marko Scholze took 52 simulations of the world's climate over the next century, based on 16 different climate models, grouping the results according to varying amounts of global warming by 2010. The findings were that if global temperatures rise by an average of 3°C or more by the end of the century, more than half of the world's major forests will be lost (Jha, 2006).

Scholze said the effects of a 2°C category were inevitable, this being the temperature rise that will happen, on average, even if the world immediately stopped emitting greenhouse gases. This scenario predicts that Europe, Asia, Canada, Central America and Amazonia could lose up to 30 per cent of its forests (ibid.).

A rise of 2°C–3°C will mean less fresh water available in parts of West Africa, Central America, Southern Europe and the Eastern US, raising the probability of drought in these areas. In contrast, the tropical parts of Africa and South America will be at greater risk of flooding, as trees are lost. A global temperature rise of more than 3°C will mean even less fresh water. Loss of forest in Amazonia and Europe, Asia, Canada and Central America could reach 60 per cent (ibid.).

Scholze's scenarios echo research (Schellnhuber, 2005) which predicted that a 3°C rise in average temperatures would cause a worldwide drop in cereal crops of between 20 and 400 million tonnes, put 400 million more people at risk of hunger, and put up to three billion people at risk of flooding and without access to fresh water supplies (Jha, 2006).

At the time of writing (summer 2006), Peter Cox told the Royal Geographical Society annual conference that temperatures could rise by 8°C by 2100 because of a 'compost effect', which could see carbon dioxide levels increase 50 per cent faster than previously estimated (cited in Cassidy, 2006, p. 5). Global warming is damaging the soil's ability to absorb carbon emissions, and after 2050 the land will begin to release carbon into the atmosphere (Cox, cited in Cassidy, ibid.).

Following the discovery that the 1980s had experienced the six hottest years on record, since CE 1000 (AD), in 1989, the magazine, *Scientific American* announced a consensus among climate scientists and called for a 50 per cent cut in global fuel consumption and a stop to deforestation By 2000, the 1990s were the warmest decade on record (Ward, 2005–2006, p. 13). Currently, the six warmest years in descending order with the hottest first, have been 2005, 1998, 2002, 2003, 2004 and 2001 (Union of Concerned Scientists, 2006).

Glaciers in Greenland are slipping into the sea at a rate that doubled between 1996 and 2000, and the Antarctic ice cap, which holds 70 per cent of the world's water, is now losing water at the same rate as Greenland (Ward, 2006, p. 12). Mountain glaciers throughout the world are receding. To take just one example, the Gurschen glacier in Switzerland has sunk 20 metres in the last 15 years. Glaciers are important because they constitute 2 per cent of the world's water and 10 per cent of the world's surface. Sea levels, ecosystems and regional stream flows are all affected by the size of glaciers (Stephens, 2006, p. 8).

The Arctic ice pack has lost about 40 per cent of its thickness over the past four decades and the global sea level is rising about three times faster over the past 100 years compared to the previous 3,000 years, and some 50 million people a year have to deal with flooding (Feldman and Lotz, 2004, pp. 119–120). If the sea rises by one metre in Bangladesh, 13 million people will be displaced, while, in London, 1.25 million people are at risk from flooding from the Thames. At the same time, the Gobi desert expands by 10,000 square km per year (Kinnear and Barlow, 2005), and the destructive power of hurricanes has increased by 70 per cent in the last 50 years (Ward, 2005–2006, p. 13). Hurricane Katrina is but one horrific example (but one which nevertheless reminded the world that even in the 'affluent west' people do not all suffer equally from global warming).[4] Other likely outcomes of climate change include a major disruption of agriculture, resulting in more widespread water shortages and famine, in turn exacerbated by current processes of neo-liberal globalisation (see above). Still further consequences could be the spreading of tropical diseases to temperate zones (Ward, 2005–2006, p. 13). Already diseases such as malaria and dengue fever are starting to spread more widely (Kinnear and Barlow, 2005).

Carbon levels are currently 378 ppm (parts per million), compared to pre-industrial levels of 280 ppm and, at the speed of capital growth today, are predicted to rise to 550 ppm by 2030 and 840 ppm by 2100. This could result in a 6–11°C rise in temperatures which, given that when a rise of 6°C in global temperatures 251 million years ago wiped out 95 per cent of all species on earth, could have disastrous consequences for the planet and its inhabitants (Kinnear and Barlow, 2005). Cox's research (cited in Cassidy, 2006, p. 5) paints an even bleaker picture, predicting that, because of the aforementioned 'compost effect', carbon levels could rised to more than 1,000 ppm by 2100. Cox argues that the Amazonian rainforest would be lost unless urgent action is taken to keep carbon levels below 500 ppm (cited in Cassidy, 2006, p. 5).

The causal role of neo-liberal global capitalism in global warming is indisputable. An annual growth rate (GNP) of 3 per cent (the accepted rate for the developed world) means that production is doubled every 24 years, and there is a close correlation between GNP and the rate of increased fossil fuel use (Kinnear and Barlow, 2005). As Phil Ward (2005–2006, p. 14) puts it, 'the capitalist system … is incapable of downsizing except by means of destructive slump or war'. As argued earlier, capitalism is out of control 'set on a trajectory, the "trajectory of production" … powered not simply by value but by the "constant *expansion* of surplus value"' (Rikowski, 2001, cited in Chapter 2, p. 23).

Petroleum is the main fuel used by consumers, and cars are a major source of carbon dioxide emission, second to emissions from planes, but greater than buses, coaches, trains and the London Underground (Kinnear and Barlow, 2005). Driving one kilometre uses ten times the energy of walking or 40 times of cycling. Cars are the world's most advertised product, with $10 billion spent annually in the US alone, and rising (Woodcock, 2006, p. 12). In the US, in 2004, with a population of 293 million, there were 119 million drivers and 237 million motor vehicles. While the population has risen by just over 60 per cent since 1960, the number of motor vehicles has risen by over 300 per cent (US Department of Transportation, Federal Highway Administration, 2006). The US has greenhouse gas emissions as large as those of South America, Africa and the Middle East, Australia, Japan and Asia put together (Tickell, 2006, p. 27).

While the whole world clearly suffers as a result of global warming, it is the poor countries that suffer most, simply because they have the least resources to adapt. There is a consensus among scientists that cuts of at least 60 per cent in carbon dioxide emissions, and in some areas up to 90 per cent, are needed to halt climate change (Feldman and Lotz, 2004, p. 120). However, the Kyoto Protocol of 1997, which the US – the world's largest polluter – refused to ratify, aimed only to reduce emissions in industrialised countries by around 5.2 per cent below their 1990 levels by 2012. New estimates suggest cuts of only 1 to 2 per cent will actually be achieved (Feldman and Lotz, 2004, p. 120) Sustainable development (balancing economic, social and environmental issues) in a global neo-liberal capitalist economy is just not feasible.[5]

The connection between increased fossil fuel use and imperialist adventures in oil-rich countries is an obvious one. One of the primary reasons for US imperial expansion is, of course, to control access to, and the marketing of oil (the other being US capitalist hegemony). This, in turn, creates further environmental degradation and destruction, both in the US and worldwide. In the next chapter I will consider the role of the 'New Imperialism' in the twenty-first century, and will argue the case for a study of imperialisms to be a central feature of the curriculum. I will conclude this chapter with a consideration of key educational issues connected to global neo-liberal capitalism and environmental destruction.

Educational implications

Global neo-liberal capitalism

Students would benefit from engaging in an analysis of the mechanics of capitalist production and exchange. Marxism would be an obvious starting point. Such an analysis should have as central a discussion of the labour theory of value (LTV) (see Chapter 2, pp. 24–25) since this most clearly explains exactly *why* Marxists believe that capitalism is *objectively* a system of exploitation (the teaching of the LTV was, in fact, compulsory in secondary schools in the former Yugoslavia). Students could consider the concept of globalisation. Is it a new phenomenon, or is it as old as capitalism itself? Is it inevitable, as claimed by many. To what extent is the concept of globalisation ideological? Does it hide more than it reveals?

As outlined in this chapter, neo-liberal capitalism, in being primarily about expanding opportunities for large multinational companies, has undermined the power of nation states and exacerbated the negative effects of globalisation on such services as healthcare, education, water and transport. The effects on both the 'developed' and 'developing world' should be discussed openly and freely in the classroom.

Eco-socialism

McLaren and Houston (2005, p. 167) have argued that 'escalating environmental problems at all geographical scales from local to global have become a pressing reality that critical educators can no longer afford to ignore'. They go on to cite 'the complicity between global profiteering, resource colonization, and the wholesale ecological devastation that has become a matter of everyday life for most species on the planet' (ibid.). Noting the wealth of ecosocialist scholarship that has emerged in recent years (e.g. Williams, 1980; Benton, 1996; Foster, 2000, 2002; see also Feldman and Lotz, 2004), McLaren and Houston, following Kahn (2003), state the need for 'a critical dialogue between social and eco-justice' (ibid., p. 168). They call for a dialectics of ecological and environmental justice to reveal the malign interaction between capitalism, imperialism and ecology that has created widespread environmental degradation which has dramatically accelerated with the onset of neo-liberalism (ibid., p. 172; 'New Imperialism' is discussed in the next chapter). McLaren and Houston (ibid., p. 174) then propose an educational framework, of which the pivot is class exploitation but which also, following Gruenwald, 2003, interrogates the intersection between 'urbanization, racism, classism,[6] sexism, environmentalism, global economics, and other political themes'. The classroom is a good arena to discuss issues, ranging from what is happening in the immediate vicinity of the school, to issues at the national policy level, through to global issues, including the eco-social issues connected to the global survival of the planet. Students could begin by discussing the issues discussed in this chapter: the destruction of resources; unhealthy food; genetic modification; and climate change, including the threat posed by nuclear power. They could then interrogate the causes, and assess the likely chances of changes under neo-liberal capitalism and the 'New Imperialism' – for example, what can be done *now* to address these pressing issues, and how a world socialist system might do things differently.

8   The New Imperialism

Postmodern, transmodern and
Marxist perspectives

In this chapter, I begin by examining and critiquing a postmodern interpretation
of the 'New Imperialism', before examining what I perceive to reflect more
accurately the US reality, and epitomised by the *Project for the New American
Century*. I then address globalisation and the US Empire. I go on to analyse
US imperialism from transmodern and Marxist perspectives, respectively. This
includes a discussion of the transmodern concept of enfraudening (developed by
educational theorist David Geoffrey Smith in an important critique of current
US practice) and of the Marxist concept of racialisation. I conclude by arguing
that a critical consideration of imperialisms, old and new, should be central to
the curriculum.

Introduction

I argued at length in Chapter 5 about the dangers of postmodernism in educational
theory (in academia), specifically about the way in which it acts as an ideological
support for global and national capitalism. Now in the public as well as the academic domain (and therefore more dangerous), postmodernism is particularly pernicious in its protagonists' advocacy of 'the New Imperialism'.

The 'New Imperialism': a postmodern fantasy[1]

Robert Cooper (2002, p. 5) argues that postmodern imperialism takes two
forms. The first is the voluntary imperialism of the global economy, where
institutions like the IMF and the World Bank provide help to states 'wishing to
find their way back into the global economy and into the virtuous circle of
investment and prosperity' (ibid.). If states wish to benefit, he goes on, 'they
must open themselves up to the *interference* of international organisations and
foreign states' (ibid.; my emphasis). Cooper (ibid.) refers to this as a new kind
of imperialism, one which is needed and is acceptable to what he refers to as
'a world of human rights and cosmopolitan values': an imperialism 'which,
like all imperialism, aims to bring order and organisation' [he does not
mention exploitation and oppression] 'but which rests today on the voluntary
principle'.

While 'within the postmodern world, there are no security threats … that is to say, its members do not consider invading each other' (ibid., p. 3), that world, according to Cooper, has a right to invade others. The 'postmodern world' has a right to pre-emptive attack, deception and whatever else is necessary. As he puts it:

> Among ourselves we operate on the basis of laws and open cooperative security. But when dealing with more old-fashioned kinds of states outside the continent of Europe, we need to revert to the rougher methods of an earlier era – force, pre-emptive attack, deception, whatever is necessary to deal with those who still live in the nineteenth century world of every state for itself. Among ourselves, we keep the law but when we are operating in the jungle, we must also use the laws of the jungle.
>
> (ibid., pp. 3–4)

The second form of postmodern imperialism Cooper calls 'the imperialism of neighbours', where instability 'in your neighbourhood poses threats which no state can ignore'. It is not merely soldiers that come from the international community, he argues, 'it is police, judges, prison officers, *central bankers* and others' (my emphasis). 'Elections are organised and monitored by the Organisation for Security and Cooperation in Europe (OSCE). Local police are financed and trained by the UN' (ibid.). Cooper has in mind the European Union, which is, of course, engaged in a programme that is leading to massive enlargement. If this process is a kind of voluntary imperialism, Cooper suggests, 'the end state might be describes [*sic*] as a cooperative empire. "Commonwealth" might indeed not be a bad name' (ibid.). He concludes: 'that perhaps is the vision' but, in the context of 'the secret race to acquire nuclear weapons' and in 'the premodern world the interests of organised crime – including international terrorism [growing] greater and faster than the state … there may not be much time left [for the establishment of this empire]' (ibid., p. 6.).

So what is the background of this leading advocate of postmodern New Imperialism; of the legitimacy of a 'pre-emptive attack' on 'old-fashioned' non-European states, and of the need to establish a European Union Empire? Between 1999 and 2001, he was Tony Blair's Head of the Defence and Overseas Secretariat, in the British Cabinet Office. Now posted to Brussels in the capacity of Head of External Affairs for the EU, what the *Daily Telegraph* (25 October, 2003) describes as 'right-hand man to Javier Solana, Europe's foreign and security policy supremo', 'he retains close links with Downing Street, where his ideas are held in great respect' (*Daily Telegraph*, 25 August 2003).

While, as argued in Chapter 7, Blair is well-known for his belief in a benign globalisation and, while he is widely acknowledged to be Bush's 'poodle' (a reputation enhanced by an overheard conversation at the G8 summit in July, 2006, when Bush exclaimed, 'Yo Blair' and Blair said he'd knitted Bush a sweater), Blair is not generally known for his *intellectual* adherence to postmodern New Imperialism.

Julie Hyland (2002, p. 4) has argued that Cooper's thesis is fundamentally flawed. This is because central to it is an insistence that that there is no longer any real conflict of interests between the major powers. While Cooper places certain reservations with respect to the US and Japan, he is confident that they all have a vested interest in collectively policing the world. Hyland cites Lenin (1975, p. 111) who argued that all alliances between the major powers 'are *inevitably* nothing more than a "truce" in periods between wars'. As Lenin put it:

> Peaceful alliances prepare the grounds for wars, and in their turn grow out of wars; the one conditions the other, producing alternating forms of peaceful and non-peaceful struggle on *one and the same* basis of imperialist connections and relations within world economics and world politics.
>
> (Lenin, 1975, cited in Hyland, 2002, p. 4)

Cooper argues throughout, she goes on, as if the major powers can simply decide to set aside their differences in order to pursue a common political agenda. However, in reality, imperialism is not a policy, but 'a complex set of economic and social relations characterised by an objective conflict between the major powers over who controls the world's markets and resources' (ibid., p. 5). The struggle for oil, the source of power, she concludes, has not only been the major factor in Western imperial intervention, but is likely to be the key focus of potential conflict between the major powers (ibid.).

That a conflict of interests remains firmly on the agenda is not merely the province of the Left. Leading historian of Empire, Dominic Lieven, for example, who believes that 'the ideology of US empire is democratic and egalitarian' (2004, p. 25) cites 'bringing 1.25bn Chinese into the first world' as an indication that the ' "the great game" of empire is far from over' (ibid.).

The New Imperialism: the US reality

Transmodernist, David Geoffrey Smith (2003) provides detailed evidence that the US, in the twenty-first century, is engaged in a major imperial enterprise.

That this is the case is being recognised by a wide spectrum of political opinion, with wide support from neo-conservatives, and condemnation from liberals and Marxists (see, for example, Hyland, 2002; Young, 2002; Ferguson, 2004; Lind, 2004; Cole, 2004c; McLaren and Farahmandpur, 2006; Lieven, 2004; see Cole, 2004c for information on the political affiliation of these various writers).

In the real world, it is the US, of course, which is the key player in the New Imperialism, not the European Union – nor is that union likely to become, as Cooper desires, a European Empire or 'European Commonwealth'. *Guardian* columnist, the liberal Hugo Young, states unequivocally:

> the problem that Mr. Cooper ignores and that seems not to even trouble Mr. Blair any more is that the only [new world order] currently on offer is for the rest of the globe to be remade in America's image and in the interests

of the security of the US and its corporations. If there is any such thing as an acceptable postmodern imperialism, this most certainly is not it.

(Young, 2002, cited in Hyland, 2002, p. 8)

The reference to Blair underestimates (even in 2002) Blair's allegiance to US capitalism, in general, and to Bush in particular. In concluding that any new imperialist agenda needs to recognise that 'America is a threat to global order too' (Young, 2002, cited in Hyland, 2002, p. 8). Young also understates the very real threat posed by the US to the very existence of the world.

Epitomising the essence of the actually existing New Imperialism is the Project for the New American Century (see Peter McLaren's foreword to this book. It sets out its principles as follows:

- we need to increase defense spending significantly if we are to carry out our global responsibilities today and modernise our armed forces for the future;
- we need to strengthen our ties to democratic allies and to challenge regimes hostile to our interests and values;
- we need to promote the cause of political and economic freedom abroad;
- we need to accept responsibility for America's unique role in preserving and extending an international order friendly to our security, our prosperity, and our principles.

Such a Reaganite policy of military strength and moral clarity may not be fashionable today. But it is necessary if the United States is to build on the successes of this past century and to ensure our security and our greatness in the next (Project for the New American Century, undated).

'Increasing defense spending'; 'challenging regimes'; 'promoting political and economic freedom'; 'extending an international order' makes it abundantly clear that as long as the New Imperialism continues to exist, so too will (imperialist) wars.

As McLaren and Farahmandpur (2006) have argued:

> The United States was willing to put the whole world at risk of nuclear obliteration in order to carry out its Cold War anticommunist strategies; and now that communism has fallen onto global hard times that threatens its very existence, the United States places the world at a different – but no less execrable – risk by attempting to push through its neoliberal imperialist agenda that includes preemptive military strikes against any country that is deemed a threat to U.S. corporate or geostrategic interests.

Globalisation and the US Empire

Ellen Meiksins Wood (2003, p. 134) has captured succinctly globalisation's current imperialist manifestations:

> Actually existing globalization ... means the opening of subordinate economies and their vulnerability to imperial capital, while the imperial economy remains

sheltered as much as possible from the adverse effects. Globalization has nothing to do with free trade. On the contrary, it is about the careful control of trading conditions in the interest of imperial capital.

(cited in McLaren and Farahmandpur, 2006)

Globalisation is often used *ideologically* to justify the New Imperial Project. On 17 September 2002, a document entitled *National Security Strategy of the United States of America* (*NSSUSA*) was released which laid bare US global strategy in the most startling terms (Smith, 2003, p. 491). The report heralds a 'single sustainable model for national success: freedom, democracy and free enterprise'. Europe is to be kept subordinate to, and dependent on, US power, NATO is to be reshaped as a global interventionist force under US leadership, and US national security is claimed to be dependent on the absence of any other great power. The report also refers to 'information warfare', whereby deliberate lies are spread as a weapon of war. Apparently, a secret army has been established to provoke terrorist attacks, which would then justify 'counter attack' by US forces on countries that could be announced as 'harboring terrorists' (The Research Unit for Political Economy (RUPE), 2003, pp. 67–78, cited in Smith, 2003, pp. 491–492).

While the *NSSUSA* states that American diplomats are to be retrained as 'viceroys' capable of governing client states (RUPE, 2003, cited in Smith, 2003, p. 491), the New Imperialism, in reality, no longer seeks direct territorial control of the rest of the world, as did British imperialism for example, but instead relies on 'vassal regimes' (Bello, 2001, cited in Smith, 2003, p. 494) to do its bidding. This is because capital is now accumulated via the control of markets, rather than by sovereignty over territories. The New Imperialism does not require invading forces to stay for lengthy periods. It is, therefore, an imperialism *in absentia*. President Bush was thus partly right when he stated, in his 2003 State of the Union Address, that the US seeks to 'exercise power without conquest'. He was right in the sense that the US does not seek British imperialist-type *long-term colonial conquest*. What it seeks is what Benjamin Zephaniah (2004, p. 18) describes as 'cultural and financial imperialism'. This can involve sending in the troops in the short-term or, indeed, the longer term, or it can be done without armies.[2] As he puts it, with respect to the non-military option, 'they send in men in suits and they colonise the place financially' (ibid.).

Writing from a liberal perspective, Michael Lind (2004, p. 5) points out that this does not stop many neo-conservatives in the United States hankering after British imperialism (and in particular the young Winston Churchill) as their model. British neo-conservative popular historian and TV presenter Niall Ferguson, for whom the British Empire was relatively benevolent, has similar views. In a speech in 2004, he argued that the US Empire which 'has the potential to do great good' needs to learn from the lessons of the British Empire. First it needs to export capital and to invest in its colonies; second, people from the US need to settle permanently in its colonies; third, there must be a *commitment* to imperialism; fourth there must be collaboration with local elites. Success can only come, he concludes if the Americans are prepared to *stay* (Ferguson, 2004). More recently Ferguson (2005) argued that Bush is an 'idealist realist' who is 'clearly open to serious intellectual ideas'. Bush is a realist because he believes that power is 'far more important than law in the relations between states', and an idealist because he wants to spread 'economic and political freedom around the world'. Bush, he goes on, has picked up two main ideas from the academy, namely that free markets accelerate economic growth which makes democracy more likely to succeed, and democracies are 'much less likely to make war than authoritarian regimes'. Ferguson then offers the President a further idea. It helps to think of the US Empire (Ferguson's words not mine) 'as a kind of sequel to the British Empire'. The lesson to be learnt from that empire is the need to stay longer. 'Elections are not everything' and the danger posed to liberty in the US, and on the imperial front, he concludes, is less worrying than 'a decline in US power ... surely something about which idealists and realists can agree'.

Wall Street journalist, Max Boot, has gone so far as to state that 'Afghanistan and other troubled lands today cry out for the sort of enlightened foreign administration provided by self-confident Englishmen in jodhpurs and pith helmets' (cited in Smith, 2003, p. 490). A 'permanent' imperial occupation (of the British imperial kind) of Iraq and elsewhere is unlikely to happen. There are three reasons for this. First, it is not necessary (for reasons outlined above). Second it is not cost-effective. Paul Kennedy (1998) refers to this as 'the problem of imperial overstretch' which results in the dissipation of resources (economic, military and administrative) (cited in Smith, 2003, p. 498). Third, such actions would fail to achieve majority popular support, and would lead to what Waldon Bello (2002) describes as a 'crisis of legitimacy', the inability to convince others of one's moral right to rule (cited in Smith, 2003, p. 498).

Enfraudening and enantiomorphism: a transmodern perspective

Information warfare is a key imperialist strategy and modus operandi of capitalism; so is 'enfraudening the public sphere'. The major strength of transmodernism, I would argue, lies in its argument that European philosophers still are not facing the historical responsibilities of their legacies (Smith, 2004, p. 644). As I argued in Chapter 6, transmodernism makes an important contribution to an understanding of the legacy of the European invasion of the Americas, because it reveals how the imperialism in which contemporary US foreign policy is currently engaged has a specific and long-standing genealogy.

Smith (2003, p. 489) argues that the Bush Administration's 'war on terror' is being used to veil long-standing, but now highly intensified, global imperial aims. Following McMurtry (1998, p. 192), he suggests that, under these practices, knowledge becomes 'an absurd expression' (Smith, 2003, p. 489). Again, following McMurtry (2002, p. 55), Smith (2003, pp. 493–494) argues that the corporate structure of the global economy (dominated by the US, particularly through its petroleum corporations) 'has no life co-ordinates in its regulating paradigm' and is structured to misrepresent its indifference to human life as 'life-serving'. Thus we have terror in the name of anti-terrorism; war in the name of peace-seeking. Accordingly, US Secretary of State, Colin Powell (2003) is able to declare with a straight face and in a matter-of-fact tone that the 'Millennium Challenge Account' of the Bush Administration is to install 'freely elected democracies' all over the world, under 'one standard for the world' which is 'the free market system ... practiced correctly' (cited in Smith, 2003, p. 494). This provides the justification for the slaughter of hundreds of thousands of Iraqi children since 1990 through NATO bombing and the destruction of the public infrastructure (water, healthcare, etc.). This slaughter has, of course, taken on a new dimension since the March 2003 invasion and occupation of Iraq. Such justification is also given for the destabilisation of democratically elected governments throughout Latin America, Africa and Asia (Smith, 2003, p. 494).

Smith (2003, p. 494) describes this rhetorical process as enantiomorphic – whereby a claim is made to act in a certain way, when one actually acts in the opposite way. Enantiomorphism reached its zenith, I would argue, in the absurd claim nurtured by Bush and Blair that the invasion and occupation of Iraq was necessary because Saddam Hussein had weapons of mass destruction, which he was going to use on the West. There were also *reasonable* claims made that he tortured his people and was anti-democratic. The Americans and their allies were going there, we were told, to find the weapons of mass destruction, stop the people being tortured, and bring democracy. The reality is, of course, that not only did Saddam have no weapons of mass destruction (it is the Americans who have such weapons, and remain the only country that has dropped atomic bombs in warfare) but the Americans have continued the torture; and upheld the lack of democracy.

Transmodern 'narcissism' or racialising the Other: a Marxist analysis

While Smith's arguments on enfraudening and enantiomorphism are convincing, I have problems with the vague transmodern notions of 'narcissism' (see Chapter 6, note 4) in explaining the source of Western violence directed against the Other. As Paul Warmington (2006) has pointed out, the transmodern notion of 'narcissism' is problematic for Marxists. First, it represents essentialist notions of 'kinship'; a natural tendency to align oneself with one's 'own kind'. Second, because its psychosocial gloss does not take account of Marxist understandings of the material base of discourse, it inverts the historical relationship between imperialism and Otherness. Far from deriving from a narcissistic *alignment* with one's own kind and antipathy to the Other, I would argue, following Warmington (2006), that the Western violence that enforced capitalist imperialism (from the sixteenth century onwards) entailed a conscious and *strategic* (and traumatic) *alienation* from other nations (as well as from the West's own emergent liberal-democratic values). This historically specific alienation was achieved through contrived 'racial', cultural and spatial distinctions that served to mask the key contradictions of imperialist production. 'Race' and racialisation were key factors here.

The concept of 'race'

There is a consensus among certain geneticists and most social scientists that 'race' is a social construct rather than a biological given. That this is the case is explained succinctly by Steven Rose and Hilary Rose (2005) and I will summarise their arguments here. They point out that 'race' is a term with a long history in biological discourse. Given a rigorous definition by the evolutionist Theodosius Dobzhansky in the 1930s, 'race' applied to an inbred population with specific genetic characteristics within a species, resulting from some form of separation that limited interbreeding. 'In the wild', they go on, 'this might be geographical separation, as among finches on the Galapagos islands, or imposed by artificial breeding, as for example between labradors and spaniels among dogs' (ibid.). Early racial theorising also divided humans into either three (white, black, yellow) or five (Caucasian, African, Australasian, American and Asian) biological 'races', supposedly differing in intellect and personality. However, in the aftermath of Nazism, the UNESCO panel of biological and cultural anthropologists challenged the value of this biological concept of 'race', with its social hierarchies. When, in the 1960s and 1970s, genetic technology advanced to the point where it was possible to begin to quantify genetic differences between individuals and groups, it became increasingly clear that these so-called 'races' were far from genetically homogeneous. In 1972, the evolutionary geneticist Richard Lewontin pointed out that 85 per cent of human genetic diversity occurred *within* rather than *between* populations, and only 6–10 per cent of diversity is associated with the broadly defined 'races' (ibid.). As Rose and Rose explain:

> most of this difference is accounted for by the readily visible genetic variation of skin colour, hair form and so on. The everyday business of seeing and acknowledging such difference is not the same as the project of genetics.

For genetics and, more importantly, for the prospect of treating genetic diseases, the difference is important, since humans differ in their susceptibility to particular diseases, and genetics can have something to say about this. However, beyond medicine, the use of the invocation of 'race' is increasingly suspect. There has been a growing debate among geneticists about the utility of the term and, in autumn 2004, an entire issue of the influential journal *Nature Reviews Genetics* was devoted to it. The geneticists agreed with most biological anthropologists that for human biology the term 'race' was an unhelpful leftover. Rose and Rose conclude that 'whatever arbitrary boundaries one places on any population group for the purposes of genetic research, they do not match those of conventionally defined races'. For example, the DNA of native Britons contains traces of multiple waves of occupiers and migrants. 'Race', as a scientific concept, Rose and Rose conclude, 'is well past its sell-by date' (ibid.). Robert Miles (passim)[3] has forcefully argued that the very notion of 'race' should be rejected as an analytic category in the social sciences and, for these reasons, should be put in inverted commas whenever one needs to refer to it.

Racialisation

Miles (1987) has defined racialisation as an ideological[4] process that accompanies the appropriation of labour power (the capacity to labour), where people are categorised falsely into the scientifically defunct notion of distinct 'races'. As Miles puts it, the processes are not *explained* by the fact of capitalist development (a functionalist position). Racialisation, like racism, is socially constructed (see Chapter 9, pp. 117–119 for a discussion of, and a suggested definition of racism). In Miles's (1989, p. 75) words, racialisation refers to 'those instances where social relations between people have been structured by the signification of human biological characteristics [elsewhere in the same book, Miles (1989, p. 79) has added cultural characteristics] in such a way as to define and *construct* differentiated social collectivities' (my emphasis). 'The process of racialization', Miles states, 'cannot be adequately understood without a conception of, and explanation for the complex interplay of different modes of production and, in particular, of the social relations necessarily established in the course of material production' (1987, p. 7). It is this interconnection which makes the concept of racialisation inherently Marxist.[5]

Whereas, for postmodernists, discourse refers to the way in which different meanings are constructed by the readers of texts, for Marxists, any discourse is a product of the society in which it is formulated. In other words, 'our thoughts are the reflection of political, social and economic conflicts and racist discourses are no exception' (Camara, 2002, p. 88). While such reflections can, of course, be refracted and disarticulated, dominant discourses (e.g. those of the government, of big business, of large sections of the media, of the hierarchy of some trade unions) tend to directly reflect the interests of the ruling class, rather than 'the general public'. The way in which racialisation connects with popular consciousness, however, is via 'common sense'. 'Common sense' is generally used to denote a down-to-earth 'good sense' and is thought to represent the distilled truths of centuries of practical experience, so that to say that an idea or practice is 'only common sense' is to claim precedence over the arguments of Left intellectuals and, in effect, to foreclose discussion (Lawrence, 1982, p. 48). As Diana Coben (2002, p. 285) has noted, Gramsci's distinction between good sense and common sense 'has been revealed as multifaceted and complex'. For common sense:

> is not a single unique conception, identical in time and space. It is the 'folklore' of philosophy, and, like folklore, it takes countless different forms. Its most fundamental characteristic is that it is … fragmentary, incoherent and inconsequential.
>
> (Gramsci, 1978, p. 419)

The rhetoric of the purveyors of dominant discourses aims to shape 'common sense discourse' into formats which serve their interests. Drawing on, for example, W.E.B. Dubois and Elizabeth and Eugene Genovese, and underlining the fragmentary and incoherent role of 'common sense' in connecting racialisation to popular consciousness, Peter Fryer (1988) outlines the following argument. Modern racist ideology emerged with and from the Atlantic slave trade (which predated the 'mature' colonialism of the Indian sub-continent by 150 years) and was anomalous in that:

- at the point when Western European production was shifting towards free labour and was shifted by technological advances, it made itself increasingly reliant on a backward form of production, i.e. chattel slavery;
- at the point at which the emergent Enlightenment began to posit notions of individual freedom, the west embarked on conquest and enslavement, in order to secure servile labour systems (first in America, later in colonial Asia and Africa).

As Warmington (2006) argues, racialisation can be seen, therefore, as a project to rhetorically 'resolve' these contradictions, not merely to justify them in the sense of papering over their cracks but to construct a racialised 'justice' upon which to build brutal, servile production systems. In short, if liberty and the Enlightenment were morally and ideologically correct then they must necessarily be extended to all humanity (and this was the view of some dissident voices in the West). However, this extension was clearly impossible (both at home and abroad – but especially abroad in those continents that were, as Dubois wrote, being subjected to conquests that made them bear the largest burden of global pauperisation, conquests involving unprecedented levels of violence and displacement). Thus an ideology was required that placed the slave labour force outside the bounds of humanity and therefore outside the 'human rights' being tentatively proclaimed in Europe (clearly this ideology also infused racial folklore). Fryer (1988, p. 63) quotes Genovese and Genovese: '[The rising capitalist] class *required* a violent racism not merely as an ideological rationale but as a psychological imperative'.

I have recently (Cole, 2006c) addressed the origins of the New Imperialism, how 'the eclipse of the non-European' following the European invasion of 1492, consolidated by subsequent invasions and conquests, unleashed racialised capitalism, often gendered, on a grand scale. The expansion of capital entailed not only the beginnings of the transatlantic slave trade, but also the attempted enslavement, the massacre and the seizing of the land of indigenous peoples, both local and adjacent. Its legacy today includes a very high and disproportionate suicide rate for Native Americans in general, and continuing attacks on the reproductive rights of Native American women; the 'prison industrial complex' – a legacy of slavery – where 'people of color'[6] are disproportionately represented; human rights abuse at US borders; and continuing segregation in US cities. Racialised notions of 'like' and 'Other' ('black' and 'white', 'civilised' and 'savage') are *ends* (or mediators), the starting point being shifts in production (slavery and colonialism's forms of sixteenth to early twentieth century globalisation). 'Otherness' was a strategic, violent creation.

Under the New Imperialism, racialised 'Otherness' continues to be wielded as the tool that 'justifies' violence abroad, involving similar massacre and other human rights abuse that would be considered unjust at home. Rights at home cannot be extended abroad.[7] This duality is made explicit in the citation from Cooper, above, which juxtaposes 'ourselves' with 'those in the jungle' (see p. 99). Individuals such as Blair, whose intellectual adherence to postmodern New Imperialism is less explicit, are forced to somersault between contradictory 'good guy' positions on international order and justice: 'we're all the same' (therefore we must all live according to the dictates of 'globalisation'), and 'we're *not* all the same' (therefore, the sovereignty of some nation states can be dissolved). Once groups have become racialised via 'common sense', for example as 'savages' in the case of indigenous peoples, or sub-human and genetically inferior, as in the case of African slaves, genocide becomes less problematic (Cole, 2006c; see also McLaren, 1997). In a similar fashion, once Muslims are racialised as the Other (and the 'war on terror' knows no bounds) torture, humiliation and other human rights abuses, to which Guantanamo Bay and Abu Ghraib bear witness, becomes routine practice. Such practice is not confined to these locations. Former detainee, Moazzam Begg (Begg and Brittain, 2006) for one, recalls abuse in US and British military prisons in Pakistan, Afghanistan, Iraq and Egypt, as well as in Guantanamo Bay (see also Campbell and Goldenberg, 2004).

Such treatment is sustained by racialisation. Indeed, the historic a priori racialisation of Native Americans and African-Americans as sub-human, and Muslims as sub-human and terrorists serves to legitimate and facilitate their massacre, enslavement, torture, rape, humiliation and degradation. In the current era, global imperialist abuse involves psychological as well as physical abuse, with detainees denied halal meat, for example. In addition, sexual torture was, in May 2004, revealed as having occurred on a massive scale, and as having apparently been developed by intelligence services over many years. In particular the humiliation of the body stands in stark contrast to the Muslim importance of covering, and not exposing, flesh. Such abuse has also involved sexual humiliation. In 2003, US soldier Lyndie England, serving at the Abu Ghraib camp in Iraq, was charged with abusing detainees and prisoners by forcing them to lay in a naked pyramid with an aim to humiliate. The BBC (2004) reported that there 'were numerous incidents of sadistic and wanton abuse ... Much of the abuse was sexual, with prisoners often kept naked and forced to perform simulated and real sex acts'.

Such sexualised abuse is part and parcel of the racialisation of the Other in the pursuit of hegemony and oil. Global rule and the New Imperialism are, of course, first and foremost, about global profits. This connection to capital, national and international is outside the remits of both postmodernism and transmodernism, thereby rendering their use as a tool for analysis significantly lacking

Racialisation, under conditions of imperialism, is fired by what Dallmayr (2004, p. 11), has described above as 'the intoxicating effects of global rule' that anticipates 'corresponding levels of total depravity and corruption among the rulers'.

It will be clear from the above discussion that I am using the concept of racialisaton here in the sense of attributing *negative* characteristics to groups.

Describing people as 'white' is, of course, racialised discourse, and a discourse which overwhelmingly carries positive connotations. As Miles (1993) has argued, the process of racialisation is a dialectical process, so that racialising the Other is to simultaneously racialise the self. However, as Virdee (2006, p. 35) points out, Miles has no conceptual way of making a distinction between those projects of racialised formation that are motivated by racism and those that are motivated by antiracism. As Virdee (ibid.) puts it, 'both white supremacists demonstrating against the arrival of Hispanic migrants in the US and Hispanic-Americans countering such mobilisations are examples of racialized formation'. For a solution to Miles' shortcoming, Virdee (ibid., p. 38) turns to Omi and Winant (1989) who argue that a 'racial' project can only be 'defined as racist if and only if it creates or reproduces structures of domination based on essentialist categories of race'. Virdee concludes that this approach allows us to distinguish between racist and antiracist movements that are underpinned by the idea of 'race'. Thus, for example:

> the Civil Rights movement of the United States or the black movement in 1970s Britain which Miles defines as problematic because they try to combat racism using categories of thought invented by racists, can now employing Omi and Winant's approach be analytically defined as examples of anti-racist racial projects because they are not seeking to replace white supremacy with black supremacy but trying to challenge white supremacy by invoking the demand for citizenship and equal rights.

The racialisation of the 'Other' provides a more convincing explanation of the justification of conquest and enslavement by the West and of the 'New Imperialism' than the transmodern exaltation of basic naricissism as a causal factor. The concept of 'narcissism' is unconvincing because it *starts* from the opposition of 'like' and 'Other', and because it conflates ahistorical notions of 'Otherness' with historically specific forms of racialisation.

For Marxists, the historical and contemporaneous racialisation of the Other via 'common sense' must be connected historically and contemporaneously to changes and developments in the mode of production. In the current era of the New Imperialism, we live in a world, much of which is increasingly at the beck and call of the White House, where globalisation is portrayed as inevitable, and imperialistic designs are masked as 'the war against terror' and the promotion of democracy. If we are to transcend this hegemony, if we are to provide an alternative vision for our world, if we are to think in terms of a more genuine democracy, of democratic socialism, and an end to imperialism, racialisation and racism, then to what extent can we turn to education to redress the balance?

Imperialisms and the curriculum

Students need to be critically aware of systems of imperialism. Transmodernism and Marxism can be important in facilitating this. If we are to return to the teaching of imperialism, past and present, with integrity in schools and universities, the syllabus must, I would argue, incorporate the following, *in addition* to a critical analysis of the actual events themselves.

First, there must be a thorough and critical analysis of theories of imperialism, classical, Keynesian, postmodern *and* Marxist (e.g. Barratt Brown, 1976). This should include the connection between imperialism and modes of production. Second, as a case study, given its continuing historical legacy worldwide, there could be a discussion of the way in which British imperialism was taught in the past and why. Third, and allied to this, students need to be given the critical faculties and skills to deconstruct pro-British imperialist and/or racist movies and/or TV series, still readily available in the age of multiple channel, digital TV. Fourth, at a national level, students need a critical awareness of how British imperialism relates to and impacts on racism and racialisation, both historically and in the present (see Chapter 9), including the ability to make links with and understand current manifestations of nationalism, xenophobia, xenoracism and xenoracialisation, discussed in Chapters 8 and 9. Fifth, at a global level, students will need skills to evaluate the New Imperialism and 'the permanent war' being waged by the US with the acquiescence of Britain. Echoing Bunting (Chapter 9, note 9) Boulangé (2004) argues that it is essential at this time, with the Bush/Blair 'war on terror' and Islamophobia worldwide reaching new heights, for teachers to show solidarity with Muslims in schools today. For 'this will strengthen the unity of all workers, whatever their religion' (Boulangé, 2004, p. 24), and this will have a powerful impact on the struggle against racism in all spheres of society, and education in particular. In turn, this will strengthen the confidence of workers and students to fight on other issues. As I have argued, the particular strengths of the Marxist concept of racialisation would be the linking of forms of racism to modes of production.

According to the neo-conservative, Ferguson (2003):

> Empire is as 'cutting edge' as you could wish ... [It] has got everything: economic history, social history, cultural history, political history, military history and international history – not to mention contemporary politics (just turn on the latest news from Kabul). Yet it knits all these things together with ... a 'metanarrative'.

For Marxists, an understanding of the metanarrative of imperialism, past and present, does much more than this. Indeed, as both Marxists and transmodernists would concur, such an understanding takes us to the crux of the trajectory of capitalism from its inception right up to the twenty-first century; and this is why Marxists should endorse the teaching of imperialism, old and new. For a number of years, British imperialism was taught in British schools in ways that exalted the British Empire (e.g. Cole, 1992, 2004d; Cole and Blair, 2006). A critical and comprehensive study of British imperialism, on the other hand, would enable students to make connections between the treatment meted out to those in the former colonies and the experiences of Asian, black and other minority ethnic groups in Britain up to the twenty-first century (see, for example, Cole, 1992, 2004d; Cole and Blair, 2006; Cole and Virdee, 2006). Concepts of racism, racialisation, xenoracism and xenoracialisation would enable links to be made with the current demonisation of refugees, asylum seekers and twenty-first century migrant workers, for example from Eastern Europe (see Chapter 9). Of course, the role of education in general, and teaching about imperialism in schools in particular, has its limitations and young people are deeply affected by other influences and socialised by the media (hence the need for media awareness: see below), parents/carers and by peer culture. There is a need to reintroduce an *honest* evaluation of imperialism in British schools, the choice being between a continued enslavement by an ignorance of Britain's imperial past, or an empowered awareness of it. Such awareness would also begin to facilitate the process of understanding new imperialisms. An obvious link between the new US Empire and environmental issues is oil (see Chapter 7, pp. 92–96, for a discussion of the significance of oil in environmental destruction).

Education can either render current US imperialism as 'common sense', as inevitable, or even as benign, or education could put it under constant challenge. Education, by default, might aid its progress, or it could contribute to a critical awareness of US imperialism's manifestations and, from a Marxist perspective, the need for its demise, and replacement with a new world order.

In the next chapter, I turn to the last issue within educational theory to be considered in this book, namely, Critical Race Theory (CRT). Specifically, I will evaluate the potential of CRT in understanding racism in capitalist societies, as compared to the Marxist concept of racialisation. I will then address the crucial area of how racism can be undermined in schools. Having in this chapter addressed myself primarily to the US, Chapter 9 will be concerned with an understanding of racism in contemporary Britain.

9 Critical Race Theory and racialisation

A case study of contemporary racist Britain

This chapter begins with a Marxist critique of two central tenets of Critical Race Theory (CRT). I then go on to formulate my own preferred definition of the concept of racism, a wide definition, which I attempt to defend against those who argue for a narrower one. I then go on to look at contemporary racist Britain. Concentrating on British imperialism and its legacy, I utilise the the Marxist concept of racialisation, discussed in Chapter 8, to try to understand continuing anti-black racism and Islamophobia, along with newer xenoracism. Islamophobia, it is clear, has intensified dramatically in the aftermath of the London bombings of 7 July 2005 (7/7), while xenorcacism has increased considerably, with the enlargement of the European Union. Racialisation, it is argued has more purchase in explaining manifestations of racism in Britain today than CRT. In the final part of the chapter, I consider the implications for education.

Introduction

Critical Race Theory (CRT) is grounded in the 'the uncompromising insistence that "race" should occupy the central position in any legal, educational, or social policy analysis' (Darder and Torres, 2004, p. 98). Given this centrality, ' "racial" liberation [is] embraced as not only the primary but as the most significant objective of any emancipatory vision of education in the larger society' (ibid.) CRT was a reaction to Critical Legal Studies (CLS). CLS, in turn, represented a response by liberal lawyers and judges to the appointment of a number of Republican Federal judges during the presidency of Ronald Reagan. Those liberal legal scholars left in the law schools believed that the system of law reflected the privileged subjectivity of those in power and, believing that law cannot be unbiased and neutral, instituted CLS. CRT was a response to CLS, criticising the latter for its undue emphasis on class and economic structure, and insisting that 'race' is a more *critical* identity. CRT's pioneering legal scholars were Derrick Bell, Alan Freeman and Richard Delgado (DeCuir and Dixson, 2004, p. 26).

Critique of two tenets of Critical Race Theory (CRT)

CRT is a prominent paradigm in theorising about 'race' in the US. Here I focus on two ideas clearly associated with CRT: the first is that the concept of 'white supremacy' better expresses oppression in contemporary societies based on 'race' than does the concept of *racism*; and the second is the belief in the pre-eminence of 'race' rather than social class. I have this focus quite simply because, while CRT theorists overwhelmingly are concerned with US issues, and CRT is virtually unknown outside of the US, these aspects of it have recently been adopted *in toto* by arguably the most influential academic and writer on racism and education in Britain, David Gillborn.[1] I will critique each in turn.

White supremacy is not merely a feature of far-right political organisations but inherent in contemporary society

Gillborn (2005, p. 491) argues that 'white supremacy' is now mainstream and not the preserve solely of 'white supremacist hate groups' (see also Gilroy, 2004, who routinely uses the term 'white supremacy'). Furthermore, Gillborn claims that 'white supremacy' is useful in explaining oppression based on 'race' in western capitalist societies in general:

> critical work on race in the US has moved beyond 'commonsense' superficial readings of white supremacy as solely the preserve of obviously extreme racialized politics. Some scholars ... argue that mainstream political parties, and the functioning of agencies like the education system itself, are actively implicated in maintaining and extending the grip that white people have on the major sources of power in 'Western' capitalist societies.

'White supremacy' is not a new concept in the post-Civil Rights US. Indeed 'white supremacy' was advocated by leading US black intellectual and activist, bell hooks, in preference to racism many years ago. As she put it in 1989:

> As I write, I try to remember when the word racism ceased to be the term which best expressed for me the exploitation of black people and other people of color in this society and when I began to understand that the most useful term was white supremacy.
>
> (hooks, 1989, p. 112, cited in Gillborn, 2005, p. 485)

More recently, British writers Namita Chakrabarty and John Preston (2006, p. 1) have ascribed 'white supremacy', along with capitalism itself, the status of an 'objective inhuman [system] of exploitation and oppression'. In a similar vein, Gillborn (2006b, p. 320) has commended Ansley's (1997, p. 592) definition of 'white supremacy' as 'a political, economic and cultural *system* in which whites overwhelmingly control power and material resources' (my emphasis). While it is manifestly the case, as argued in this book, that *racism* is widespread in US and British society and elsewhere, there are two significant problems with the use of the term, 'white supremacy'. The first is that it lumps all white people together in positions of class power and privilege which, of course, is factually incorrect, both with respect to social class inequality in general, and, as will be shown in later in this chapter, with reference to the processes of xenoracialisation. I would argue, therefore, that while 'white supremacy' would most certainly have been an accurate description of US reality in the pre-Civil Rights era, the advocacy of the concept now in contemporary Britain and the US is misleading and incomplete. There are two reasons for this. The first is to do with the implication of 'a white power structure'. Gillborn (2005, pp. 497–498) states that we should reject the 'commonsense (white-sense?) view of education policy and the dominant understanding of the functioning of education in Western societies' in favour of 'the recognition that race inequity and racism are central features of the education system', and that they 'are not aberrant nor accidental phenomena that will be ironed out in time', but 'fundamental characteristics of the system'. While I would agree that common sense interpretations should be rejected (as we saw in Chapter 8, common sense is a central feature of the Marxist concept of racialisation), I would disagree that common sense in any way equates with *white sense*. While it is undoubtedly true that racism (including xenoracism – see below) has penetrated large sections of the white working class, and while it is clearly the case that members of the (predominantly though not exclusively) white *ruling class* are the beneficiaries of the common-sense view of education policy, it is certainly not white people as a whole who are in this hegemonic position, nor white people as a whole who benefit from current education policy, or any other legislation. Indeed the white working class, as part of the working class in general, consistently fares badly in the education system.

The second problem with Gillborn's position relates to his specific conclusion that '*education policy is an act of white supremacy*' (2005, p. 498). This has the unfortunate effect of equating institutional racism in education with the policies of far-Right racist movements and with fascism, and muddies the waters, thus preventing a rational analysis of racism. Marxists (and others) have consistently stressed the need to differentiate the specificities of fascism from everyday capitalist-imperialist practice. *Race Traitor* (2005) describes itself 'as an intellectual center for those seeking to abolish the white race'. It is an organisation that takes the dangers of 'white supremacy' to their limits and that calls for the abolition of whiteness. The organisation argues that 'the white race' is an historically constructed social formation, which consists of all those who partake of the privileges of the white skin in US society. Its position is that its 'most wretched members' share a status higher, in certain respects, than that of the most exalted persons excluded from it. In return, they give their support to a system that degrades them. For *Race Traitor*, the key to solving the social problems of our age is to abolish 'the white race', which, for them, means no more and no less than abolishing the privileges of the white skin. Until that task is accomplished, the organisation believes, even partial reform will prove elusive, because white influence permeates every issue, domestic and foreign, in US society. The existence of 'the white race' depends on the willingness of those assigned to it to place their racial interests above class, gender, or any other interests they hold. *Race Traitor* concludes that the defection of enough of its members to make it unreliable as a predictor of behaviour will lead to its collapse. One of its slogans is: 'Treason to whiteness is loyalty to humanity'.

Surprisingly, Gillborn (2005, p. 488) labels the political stance of Noel Ignatiev, and others at the journal, *Race Traitor* as Marxist.[2] This stance, which stresses 'abolition of the white race', and views such abolition as the 'key to solving the social problems of our age' bears absolutely no resemblance to Marxism whatsoever. Marxism does not advocate the abolition of *whiteness*; rather it seeks the abolition of capitalism and the liberation of the whole working class. Indeed, the central tenet of Marxism is the need for a class-, rather than a 'race'-based analysis of society.

I would argue, in addition, that the *style* in which *Race Traitor*'s ideological position is written is worryingly reminiscent of Nazi propaganda, and seriously open to misinterpretation.[3]

There is undue emphasis on social class, and oppression based on 'race' is the major form of oppression in contemporary societies

In an article which contains no social class analysis or analysis of capitalism, Gillborn (2006a, p. 27) encapsulates the CRT view on the centrality of 'race':

> CRT offers a challenge to educational studies more generally, and to the sociology of education in particular, to cease the ritualistic citation of 'race' as just another point of departure on a list of exclusions to be mentioned and then bracketed away. CRT insists that racism be placed at the centre of analyses and that scholarly work be engaged in the process of rejecting and deconstructing the current patterns of exclusion and oppression.

For Marxists, while recognising the crucial significance of identities other than social class, class exploitation and class struggle are constitutive of capitalism, and racism, as I shall argue, needs to be understood in terms of the role that racialisation plays in the retention and enhancement of capitalism by capital- ists. The problem with CRT is that it does not connect with modes of produc- tion. This means that CRT is incapable of analysing different forms of racism at different historical conjunctures of capitalism. A major strength of the Marxist concept of racialisation is that it does make these connections. This does not mean that CRT cannot provide insights into racism in capitalist societies.

One of CRT's founders, Richard Delgado (1995, as cited by Tate, 1996) argues that the stories of people of color come from a different frame of reference, one underpinned by racism, and that this therefore gives them a voice that is different from the dominant culture and deserves to be heard. Arguing in a similar vein, Dixson and Rousseau (2005, p. 10) define the concept of *voice* as 'the assertion and acknowledgement of the importance of the personal and community experiences of people of color as sources of knowledge'.

While, such insights are particularly illuminating for white people whose life experiences are restricted to monocultural settings, the crucial point for Marxists, however, is that people of color need always to be listened to *because* they have been racialised in class societies.[4] Racism can be best understood by both listening to and/or learning about the life histories and experiences of those at the receiving end of racism, and by objective Marxist analysis, which makes links with class and capitalism. There is thus considerable purchase in Zeus Leonardo's (2004) attempt to 'integrate Marxist objectivism and race theory's focus on subjectivity' (see also Maisuria, 2006). At the beginning of an article on racism in Britain, Alpesh Maisuria (2006, p. 1) explains his theoretical technique of linking state policy with his family's experiences of racism:

> I will … [highlight] events and legislation that have shaped and defined macro policy, and also the micro experiences of the Maisuria family. It is of huge important to establish a connection between macro politics and micro struggles in a liberal democracy to see how the state links with lived lives.[5]

Delgado and the return of social class

When CRT was originally envisioned, it was to be an intersection of 'racial theory' and activism against racism. However, a number of CRT theorists today are frustrated at the turn CRT has made from activism to academic discourse, and this has led to a reappraisal of the significance of social class.

Delgado (2003) noted above as one of CRT's founders, recently put forward a materialist critique of the discourse-focused trend of recent CRT writings which focus more on text and symbol and less on the economic determinants of Latino/a and black racial fortunes. Delgado's paper was the subject of a symposium, run by *The Michigan Journal of Race and Law*, entitled 'Going Back to Class: The Re-emergence of Class in Critical Race Theory'. University of Illinois at Chicago Philosophy Professor Charles Mills, a symposium panelist, said he favoured the combination of Marxism and CRT, which forms a kind of 'racial capitalism'. He said he agreed with Delgado on the belief, central to CRT, that class structure keeps racial hierarchy intact. The working class is divided by 'race', Mills said, to the advantage of the upper class, which is mainly composed of white elites (Hare, 2006).

University of California at Berkeley Law School Professor Angela Harris said CRT is essential in exposing how interconnected class, 'race' and sex can be: 'We need to pay attention to the intersections and understand how complicated these issues are', (cited in ibid.). As an example, she referenced the affirmative action disputes in higher education. The oft-cited argument that working-class whites are being rejected in favor of middle-class blacks and Latinos – who, the argument goes have a better chance of acceptance regardless of 'race' – is looking at class based solely on income (cited in ibid.). 'What CRT exposes is that class also needs to be looked at in terms of access to wealth and the racialization of class' (cited in ibid.). As for the future of CRT, Delgado envisions a new movement of CRT theorists to recombine discourse and political activism. 'I'm worried that the younger crop of CRT theorists are enamored by the easy arm-chair task of writing about race the word and not race in the world', Delgado concluded. 'A new movement is needed'.

For Marxists, these are promising developments and point towards a possible alignment between CRT and Marxism. However, any future alignment would need to have at its core a structural analysis of capitalism and capitalist social relations, combined with a critique thereof.

Racism

Shortly, following Cole, 2004e, I would like to offer my preferred definition of racism. This definition is a wide-ranging one and is contrary to the position of Robert Miles and his associates who are totally against inflation of the concept of racism (see Appendix 1). My argument for advocating, and indeed constantly developing, a wide-ranging definition of racism is as follows. Overt intentional racism, based on biology or genetics, whereby people are declared inferior on grounds of 'race', is now generally unacceptable in the public domain (it is freely available, of course, on Nazi and other overtly racist websites and far-Right outlets). Contemporary racism, nonetheless, might best be thought of as a matrix of biological and cultural racism. Following Cole (2004e, pp. 37–38), I would argue that, in that matrix, racism can be based on genetics (as in notions of white people having higher IQs than black people: see Herrnstein and Murray, 1994; and more recently Frank Ellis (Gair, 2006)) or on culture (as in contemporary manifestations of Islamophobia). Sometimes, however, it is not easily identifiable as either, or is a combination of both. A good example of the latter is when Margaret Thatcher, at the time of the Falklands/Malvinas war, referred to the people of that island as 'an island race' whose 'way of life is British' (Short and Carrington, 1996, p. 66). Here we have a conflation of notions of 'an island race' (like the British 'race' who, Mrs Thatcher believes, built an empire and ruled a quarter of the world through its sterling qualities (Thatcher, 1982, cited in Miles, 1993, p. 75)) and, in addition, a 'race', which is culturally, like 'us': 'their way of life is British'.[6]

There are also forms of racism which are quite unintentional, which demonstrates that you do not have to be *a* racist (i.e. have allegiance to far-Right ideologies) to be racist. Thus when somebody starts a sentence with the phrase 'I'm not racist but …', the undertone means that the next utterance will always be racist. The use by some people, *out of ignorance*, of the term 'Pakistani' to refer to everyone whose mode of dress or accent, for example, signifies that they might be of Asian origin is another example of unintentional racism (the use of the nomenclature 'Paki', on the other hand, I would suggest, is generally used in an intentionally racist way because of the generally known negative connotations attached to the word).

Racism can also be overt, as in racist name-calling in schools, or it can be covert, as in racist mutterings in school corridors.

For Miles (1989, p. 79), racism relates to social collectivities identified as 'races' being 'attributed with … negatively evaluated characteristics and/or represented as inducing negative consequences for any other'. Here I would also want to inflate Miles' definition to include, following Smina Akhtar, 'seemingly positive attributes'. However, ascribing such attributes to an 'ethnic group' will probably ultimately have racist implications, e.g. the sub-text of describing a particular group as having a strong culture might be that 'they are swamping *our* culture'. This form of racism is often directed at people of Asian origin who are assumed to have close-knit families and to be hard working, and therefore in a position to 'take over' *our* neighbourhoods.[7]

In addition, attributing something seemingly positive – '*they* are good at sport' – might have implications that 'they are not good' at other things. People of African-Caribbean origin, in racist discourse, are thought to have 'no culture', and to thus also pose a threat to 'us'. In education this is something that facilitates the underachievement of working class African-Caribbean boys who are thought to be (by some teachers) less academically able, and 'problems' (see below). Stereotypes and stratifications of ethnic groups are invariably problematic and, at least potentially, racist.

Racism can dominative (direct and oppressive) as in the apartheid era in South Africa, or it can be aversive, where people are excluded or cold-shouldered on grounds of racism (Kovel, 1988). In certain situations, racism may well become apparent given specific stimuli (for example, racism in the media and/or racist sentiments from a number of peers who might be collectively present at a given moment).

Elsewhere (Cole, 2004e, pp. 37–38), I have advocated a definition of racism which includes cultural as well as biological racism, intentional as well as unintentional racism; 'seemingly positive' attributes with probably ultimately racist implications as well as obvious negative racism; dominative racism (direct and oppressive) as opposed to aversive racism (exclusion and cold-shouldering) (cf. Kovel, 1988) and overt as well as covert racism. All of these forms of racism can be individual or personal, and they can be brought on, given certain stimuli. These various forms of racism can also take institutional forms and there can, of course, be permutations among them. I would argue, therefore, that, in order to encompass the multifaceted nature of contemporary racism, it is important to adopt a broad concept and definition of racism, rather than a narrow one, based, as it was in the days of the British Empire, for example, on notions of overt biological inferiority, even though there may also have been implications of cultural inferiority. I believe that the above conception and definition of racism both theoretically and practically better explains racism in contemporary Britain (and elsewhere) than CRT notions of 'white supremacy'. From a Marxist perspective, in order to understand and combat racism, however, we must relate it to historical, economic and political factors. I now turn to the Marxist concept of racialisation which I introduced in Chapter 7, and which makes the connection between racism and capitalist modes of production and thus is able to relate to these factors.

I would argue that, in making these connections, racialisation has more purchase in explaining and understanding racism in contemporary Britain than 'white supremacy'. Indeed, I would maintain that if social class and capitalism are not central to the analysis, explanations are ambiguous and partial.

British imperialism and its aftermath

In the old imperial era, in order to justify the continuance of 'the strong arm and brave spirit … of the British Empire' (Bray, 1911, cited in Hendrick, 1980, p. 166), and the ongoing and relentless pursuit of expanding capital accumulation, the African subjects of the colonies were racialised, in school textbooks, as 'fierce savages' and 'brutal and stinking' (Glendenning, 1973, p. 35), while freed West Indian slaves were described as 'lazy, vicious and incapable of any serious improvement or of work except under compulsion' (Chancellor, 1970, p. 240). At the same time, references were made to 'the barbaric peoples of Asia' (Cassel's *Class History of England*, cited in Chancellor, 1970, p. 122) and the most frequent impression conveyed about Indians and Afghans was that they were cruel and totally unfitted to rule themselves (ibid.).

In the post-Second World War period, not surprisingly given British colonial history, the British Cabinet racialised many of the African-Caribbean community as 'accustomed to living in squalid conditions and have no desire to improve' (the *Observer*, 1989), while their children were described, by one local education authority, as 'physically robust and boisterous, yet mentally lethargic'. At the same time the same LEA perceived there to be 'very real problems' with the 'domestic habits and personal hygiene of the Asiatics' as well as 'the problem of [their] eating habits' (Grosvenor, 1987, pp. 34–35). Children from minority ethnic groups (not a source of cheap labour, as were their parents) were racialised as problems to be dealt with in these post-war years.

Anti-black racism

The racialisation of black people in British society continues, and while this occurs often in 'seemingly positive' forms (e.g. prowess in sport and music), *obviously* negative racism continues unabated. As far as permanent exclusion from school is concerned, the latest figures (DfES, 2005), for example, show that 0.29 per cent of black Caribbean, black African and other black pupils are in this situation as compared with 0.14 per cent of white pupils (see Gillborn, 2006b for a most compelling account of how national assessment mechanisms actually *produce* inequality for black pupils). Anti-black racism is not confined to pupils. Recent research has shown that black teachers 'are isolated, maligned and robbed of proper pay and status' (Muir, 2006b, p. 15). The report states that 'racism has a major impact on the everyday experiences of black teachers. To encourage more black people to become teachers, racism in schools must be challenged' (cited in ibid.). One headteacher told researchers: 'times when I have been trying to recruit black staff and you have the entire governing body almost looking in your face and saying "not in our school". Even when they are the best candidate!' (cited in ibid.).

According to extensive research by Marian FitzGerald (2006), which under-lines the connection between 'race' and social class, yearly crime figures only reinforce the negative stereotype of young black men as 'a problem' to society.

FitzGerald argues (FitzGerald *et al.*, 2003; see also FitzGerald, 2006) that street crime is unrelated to ethnicity but has everything to do with poverty and social circumstances. Her research led her to conclude that the education system (primary school to GCSE secondary stage) was letting down black children especially in poor areas. As she puts it:

> In discussion, I'd see kids who were unmistakeably bright but when I got them to fill in a short survey at the end of class, it was obvious they were being sent out into the world with a standard of literacy which was lower than that of my 8 year old granddaughter even though they were nearly twice as old and just as bright. This meant their job prospects were poor; so their chances of legitimately earning the things they aspired to were very limited. Yet, as I knew only too well, those in the poorest areas were sur-rounded by crime and opportunities for crime. Also very few of them were white but that was simply because these were areas that most whites had long-since abandoned.
>
> (personal communication)

It would be easy to overlook this important social class dimension in conven-tional CRT analysis.

Racialisation and intensified Islamophobia in Britain post-7/7

The intensity of racialisation has increased since the suicide bombings of 7 July 2005 (7/7) when a coordinated attack was made on London's public transport system during the morning rush hour. 7/7 was an epochal moment, not only because of the loss of life and injury, but because it was the first time Britain had been attacked by a non-white homegrown presence. When Chancellor, Gordon Brown made the point as follows: 'we have to face uncomfortable facts that there were British citizens, British born, apparently integrated into our communities, who were prepared to maim and kill fellow British citizens' (Brown, 2006). It is worth noting here the use of ethnic majoritarin thinking in the phrase 'integrated into our communities'.

Those events have provided a pretext in this 'war' situation to be more ruth-less than ever before. For example, on the international stage, it is argued that the idea that 'friendly fire' and 'soft targets' that injure, maim or kill, often unarmed civilians, is justifiable in that context. Similarly, at home, human rights are being revoked with counter-terror raids on a massive scale on Asians on what appears to be consistently flawed 'intelligence'. Two most recent examples include the tragedy of Brazilian Jean Charles de Menezes who was shot dead by the police, and of the two young British Muslim men, Mohammed Abdulkayar and Abul Koyair, where the former was also shot in the Forest Gate area of East London. Abdulkayer has described the harrowing event, when he was shot as soon as the police officer had 'eye contact' with him (Muir, 2006a). The police proceeded to hit him in the face with their guns and, as he begged them to stop, one of them kicked him in the face, and kept telling him to 'shut the fuck up' (ibid.).[8] Whereas CRT might view these actions as a normal act of white supremacy, a Marxist interpretation would relate the events to ongoing processes of state racialisation.

I will now argue that racialisation and institutional racism post-7/7 need to be seen in the context of the convergence of the legacy of British imperialism, and current US imperialism, including the so-called 'war on terror' (see also Gilroy, 2004), as well as xenoracism and xenoracialisation (defined below).

Islamophobia is a key facilitator of racialisation by connecting aspects of the old (British) to the New (US) Imperialism in capitalism's ongoing quest for global profits. The traditional racist term 'Paki' co-exists with the newer racist term of abuse, 'Bin Laden', and Islamic head scarves – hijabs – are now a symbol for a 'cause for concern', with some educational institutions now for-bidding students to wear them. These connections between the old and new imperialisms are particularly obvious, for example, in discussions surrounding the case of British detainees of Pakistani origin at Guantanamo Bay (see below).

According to The Commission on British Muslims and Islamophobia (CBMI), Britain is 'institutionally Islamophobic', with hostility towards Islam permeating every part of British society (Doward and Hinsliff, 2004). The report produces a raft of evidence suggesting that, since 9/11, there has been a sharp rise in attacks on followers of Islam in Britain. Ahmed Versi, editor of the *Muslim News*, who gave evidence, said:

> We have reported cases of mosques being firebombed, paint being thrown at mosques, mosques being covered in graffiti, threats made, women being spat upon, eggs being thrown. It is the visible symbols of Islam that are being attacked.
>
> (cited in ibid.)

Shopkeepers in South and East London can vouch for some of these findings. In June 2006, a man specifically targeted shops because 'Islamic-looking' people owned them. He went through a ritual of opening the door and shouting 'here's a firebomb for you' and throwing in an explosive (Barkham, 2006). One month after the London bombing, the *London Metro* led with an unequivocal front-page headline 'Faith Hate Crimes Up 600% After Bombings' (Austin, 2005). The report accompanying this title noted:

> the number of attacks ... have soared ... There have been 269 faith hate crimes reported since the suicide blasts, compared to just 40 in the same three-and-a-half weeks last year [2004]. In the first three days after the attacks, there were 68 religious hate crimes in the capital. There were none in the same period 12 months ago [2004].
>
> (ibid., p. 1)

The backlash from 7/7 has also meant that Hindus have suffered as a consequence of racialisation. Although no figures are collated to differentiate racial groups, there is hard evidence to suggest that Hindus and Hindu buildings have suffered aggression. As a consequence, a 'hate crime' hotline has been created, and for protection and preservation, religious leaders have been forced to take security training (Bennetto, 2006).

In addition to being targeted by individual racists, people perceived to be Muslims have seen an increase in police attention. The Police and Criminal Evidence Act (1984) permitted stop and search measures on civilians only if there was 'reasonable suspicion'. State racialisation has increased dramatically under the Terrorism Act 2000 (section 44) which, against much opposition, introduced new powers that allows stop and search on a random basis without suspicion, intelligence, prior information or accountability. The Act legitimises racial profiling, and thus racialisation, by stating that 'there maybe circumstances ... where it is appropriate for officers to take account of a person's ethnic origin in selecting persons to be stopped in response to a specific terrorist threat' (Kundnani, 2006, p. 2). People who appear to be of Islamic faith (wearing a veil, sporting a beard, particularly if combined with carrying a backpack (see Austin, 2006, p. 21)) are immediately identified as potential terrorists and are five times more likely to be stopped and searched than a white person (Dodd, 2005).

In 2003, more than 35,000 Muslims were stopped and searched, with fewer than 50 charged for non-terrorism related and minor offences (Doward and Hinsliff, 2004). After the 7/7 attacks in London, the number of Asian and black people stopped and searched in London streets by police using anti-terrorism powers increased by more than 12 times (Kundnani, 2006, pp. 2–3). Unpublished figures from 7 July to 10 August 2005 showed that the transport police carried out 6,747 stops under anti-terrorism laws, with the majority in London, with Asian people accounting for 35 per cent of the total (Dodd, 2005). There can be no doubt that racial profiling is being adopted by the authorities and state-sanctioned racialisation is occurring, since Asian people make-up 12 per cent of London's population against 63 per cent of white people, meaning that there is huge disparity in the ratio of the population and those who were targeted by police for the application of the Terrorism Act 2000 (section 44). What is clear is that 'stop and searches' cannot be justified by the conviction rate for terrorism offences. Between 2000 and 2006 there have been five anti-terror acts. The result of these measures to combat the potential of attacks has led to the racialisation of huge numbers of people, despite New Labour MP Hazel Blears pledging that new the Terrorism Act 2000 'will not discriminate against Muslims' (Dodd, 2005). The Metropolitan Police alone reported that religious hate crimes in London had risen from around 40 in July 2004 to around 270 one year later (cited in Renton, 2006, p. 16).[9]

Much of the world in the twenty-first century is imbued with the vestiges of the old (British) and the New (US) Imperialism (cf. Gilroy, 2004). Thus there co-exist images of 'primitive barbarism' and violence, pertaining to both imperialisms. Just as in the days of the British Empire there is an ideological requirement for racialisation (e.g. Cole and Virdee, 2006). As Benjamin Zephaniah states, underlining the symbiotic relationship between old (British) and New (US) Imperialism:

> when I come through the airport nowadays, in Britain and the US especially, they always question me on the Muslim part of my name. They are always on the verge of taking me away because they think converts are the dangerous ones.
>
> (Zepheniah, 2004, p. 19)

This was by no means an isolated incident. Thousands of Asian people are given 'special' attention at security checkpoints. For example, the actors in the highly acclaimed film *The Road to Guantanamo*, were stopped at an airport after returning to England from Germany where the movie had been awarded the *Silver Bear Award*. They were intimidated with respect to making further 'political' movies, refused access to legal aid, had personal belongings including a mobile phone confiscated, and were verbally abused (BBC, 2006b).

Islamophobia, like other forms of racism, can be cultural or it can be biological, or it can be a mixture of both. Echoing quotes from old school textbooks where, for example, Asia was denigrated as 'a continent of dying nations rapidly falling back in civilisation', and where reference was made to 'the barbaric peoples of Asia' (see Cole and Blair, 2006, p. 74), the former Archbishop of Canterbury, Lord Carey, in 2004, defended a controversial speech in which he criticised Islam as a faith 'associated with violence throughout the world'. At the Gregorian University in Rome he said that Islam was resistant to modernity and Islamic societies had contributed little to world culture for hundreds of years (PA News and Booth, 2004). At the time of writing (summer 2006), the Pope is being rebuked for aligning himself, in a speech, with Bush's 'crusade' against Islam. The Pope cited a fourteenth-century Christian emperor who proclaimed: 'show me just what Mohammed brought that was new, and there you will find things only evil and inhuman, such as his command to spread by the sword the faith he preached' (Agencies, 2006). A more biological Islamophobic racism is revealed by Jamal al-Harith, a British captive freed from Guantanamo Bay. He informed the British tabloid, the *Daily Mirror* that his guards told him: 'You have no rights here'. al-Harith went on to say that: 'after a while, we stopped asking for human rights – we wanted animal rights. In Camp X-Ray my cage was right next to a kennel housing an Alsatian dog'. He had a wooden house with air conditioning and green grass to exercise on. I said to the guards, 'I want his rights' and they replied, 'That dog is member of the US army' (Prince and Jones, 2004).

Xenoracialisation and skin colour

It is not only black people and Muslims and those thought to be Muslim who have been racialised. Indeed, Miles (1987, p. 75) makes it clear that, like racism, racialisation is not limited to skin colour: 'the characteristics signified vary historically and, although they have usually been visible somatic features, other non-visible (alleged and real) biological features have also been signified'. I would like to make a couple of amendments to Miles's position. First, consistent with my preferred definition of racism (see above), I would want to add '*and cultural*' after, 'biological'. Second, the common dictionary definition of 'somatic' is '*pertaining to the body*' and, given the fact that people are sometimes racialised on grounds of clothing (e.g. the hijab), I would also want this to be recognised in any discussion of social collectivities and the construction of racialisation. Elsewhere (e.g. Cole, 2004f; see also Cole and Virdee, 2006), I introduced the concept of xenoracialisation (developing on from Sivanandan's discussion of xenoracism) to describe the process whereby refugees, economic migrants and asylum-seekers (often white) become racialised. Sivanandan (2001, p. 2; see also Fekete, 2001, pp. 23–24) has defined xeno-racism as follows:

> The other side of the coin of the 'fear or hatred of strangers' is the defence and preservation of 'our people', our way of life, our standard of living, our 'race'. If it is xenophobia, it is – in the way it denigrates and reifies people before segregating and/or expelling them – a xenophobia that bears all the marks of the old racism, except that it is not colour-coded. It is a racism that is not just directed at those with darker skins, from the former colonial countries, but at the newer categories of the displaced and dispossessed whites, who are beating at western Europe's doors, the Europe that displaced them in the first place. It is racism in substance but xeno in form – a racism that is meted out to impoverished strangers even if they are white. It is xeno-racism.

Xenoracism and xenoracialisation have increased considerably with the ongoing enlargement of the European Union, and the accompanying and continuing capitalist quest for cheaper and easier to exploit labour. Given the documented existence of xenoracism (see below; see also Fekete, 2002; *BBC News*, 2005a, 2005b; *Belfast Today*, 2006) and accompanying xenoracialisation it is important that in the current era, as well as through history, that racism directed at people with 'white skins' remains firmly on the agenda. Fates reminiscent of Abu Ghraib and Guantanamo Bay have also befallen for those in danger of their lives and seeking refuge. In 2006 it emerged that Home Office officials demanded sexual intercourse to process visa applications (Townsend and Doward, 2006). These kinds of degrading and humiliating experiences are all too common for those in desperation and in most need (ibid.).

On 29 June 2003, the British broadsheet newspaper, the *Observer* gave a cameo of xenoracism and of the ongoing process of xenoracialisation, a process, which, in Plymouth, a garrison town which sent 15,000 service personnel out of a total of 40,000 to Iraq, seems to be leading to (voluntary) incarceration. Attacks on asylum seekers have become routine in Plymouth, which started when an Iraqi was beaten up outside a supermarket in the city centre. In 2003 the newspaper interviewed a 20-year-old, who had arrived in Britain three years earlier. He said 'many times they swear at me in the street', 'it is upsetting when you smile and say "Hi" and someone says "Fuck you"' (ibid.). Refugee groups estimate as many as six times more xenoracist and racist incidents go unreported (ibid.).

Not all newspapers, of course, provide sympathetic coverage to such issues. Indeed, as Geddes (2003, p. 40) notes (certain red-top) newspapers play an intermediate role in downgrading the public perception of asylum seekers. He gives an example of the local newspaper in the coastal town of Dover, which ran a front page editorial in December, 1998, claiming that: 'iIllegal immigrants, asylum seekers, bootleggers and scum of the earth drug smugglers have targeted our beloved coastline. We are left with the back draft of a nation's human sewage and no cash to wash it down the drain' (ibid., p. 43). Even before the incidents of 7/7, the media influence on the issue of 'race' was evident. For example, *Daily Mail* Journalist Richard Littlejohn made 88 negative comments about asylum seekers in just 36 months (Burgis, 2006). (Leader of the BNP, Nick Griffin has described Littlejohn as his 'favourite journalist'.) Xeno-racialisation directed at Britain as a whole is clearly visible in a week's reading of Britain's most popular tabloid, the *Sun* (for which Littlejohn was a columnist). On 1 March, day one, we were told in the leader that 'endless appeals by failed asylum seekers have been a source of irritation for years' (p. 8). On day two, we heard that 'lottery chiefs have been blasted over grants given to help asylum rejects fight deportation' (*Sun*, 2 March 2004, p. 2). In the same edition of the paper, a reader wrote in to inform other readers that 'this Government will always be soft on asylum seekers, because they are scared of upsetting Left-wingers and union groups'. Everyone he knows, he went on, 'is sick of the asylum madness' (ibid., p. 37). Similar coverage went on all week, with the *Sun* rounding off this particular week's coverage of migration issues as follows. Saturday's *Sun* informed its readers that 'Tory MP Ann Winterton has blasted Britain's political correct culture'. This refers to a letter Winterton has written to all Tory MPs bemoaning the end of 'free speech' (*Sun*, 6 March 2004, p. 2). This was in response to negative reactions to a racist 'joke' she made about the death by drowning in Britain in February 2004 of 20 suspected 'illegal immigrants' (some of whom were known to the police as asylum seekers) working in conditions of extreme exploitation.

So how can we explain the current process of xenoracialisation? Capitalism always seeks cheap labour, and globalisation in the twenty-first century requires labour market flexibility. However, resurgent economic crises have intensified the contradictions faced by states. As Gareth Dale (Dale, 1999, p. 308) puts it with great clarity:

> On the one hand, intensified competition spurs employers' requirements for enhanced labour market flexibility – for which immigrant labour is ideal. On the other, in such periods questions of social control tend to become more pressing. Governments strive to uphold the ideology of 'social contract' even as its content is eroded through unemployment and austerity. The logic, commonly, is for less political capital to be derived from the compact's content, while greater emphasis is placed upon its exclusivity, on demarcation from those who enter from or lie outside – immigrants and foreigners.

In practical terms, in Britain in 2006, the enlarged European Union provides an abundance of cheap Eastern European labour, in particular from Poland. Capitalism also benefits from 'illegal' labour power, which is even cheaper. As Callinicos (2006) puts it, 'the interests of capital are best served by controls that are weak enough to allow immigrants in, but strong enough to keep illegal workers vulnerable and therefore easy to exploit'. As David Renton (2006, p. 12) argues, business welcomes migration but on its own terms, with migrant workers 'insecure, unpopular: a class of people who will remain as long as possible marginal and poor'. He goes on (ibid., pp. 12–13), 'economically, they will not feel confident to demand the same rights as the settled population', while the non-migrant majority is encouraged to see migrant workers as a threat. Thus, psychologically, it seems easier for non-migrants to ally with capital rather than the new arrivals. As Renton (2006, p. 13) concludes:

> The rich benefit from migration, their political representatives oppose it. The explanation for this paradox is to be found in a dual strategy for labour. Migrants must come, but they must also be disciplined. Without the differential treatment, wages would not fall, capital would not gain.

In this chapter I have examined instances of the multifarious nature of racism in British society and have argued that racism can only be fully understood via the concept of racialisation which links racism to processes of capitalist development. In focusing on issues of 'color' and being divorced from matters related to old and new imperialisms and to capitalist requirements with respect to the labour market, CRT is ill equipped to analyse racism either in the British context or elsewhere.

Racism and education

Marxism most clearly provides an explanation for xenoracism and xenoracialisation. Transmodernism and CRT certainly remind us that racism is central in sustaining the current world order, and transmodernism that there are 'suffering Others' and that we need to interact democratically with suffering Others, while in a similar vein, CRT stresses that we must listen to the voices of people oppressed on grounds of racism. However, neither do or can make the necessary connections to move towards challenging the system on which racism and racialisation feeds. Indeed CRT's advocacy of 'white supremacy' as an explanatory factor is counter-productive in the struggle against racism. CRT does not connect to modes of production, and is therefore unable to explain why Islamophobia, the 'war on terror' and other forms of racism are necessary to keep the populace on task for 'permanent war' and the accumulation of global profits. In Britain, 'Citizenship Education' is a potentially fruitful arena for antiracist inclusive practice. Citizenship classes became compulsory for pupils aged 11 to 16 in September 2002. Citizenship's architect, Bernard Crick's view was that the subject should educate young people to be politically literate using real issues. However, in general, it never really took off the ground in the way that Crick intended. An example of good practice, however, can be found at Pimlico School in Westminster. Marcus Bhargava has described how 'students learn how to mount campaigns and challenge decisions. They go out on the street, do vox pops, make trips to prison cells, and write to their local MP' (cited in Preston, 2006, p. 6). It is highly likely that racism figures in Bhargava's projects, since the implications of such activities for antiracist awareness and practice are obvious. Bhargava wants his pupils 'to have the willingness to transform their society' (ibid.). As he concludes, 'I think it has to be that grand aim. If they don't come out feeling that they have the ability to change society, then we haven't done our job' (ibid.).

Another way to challenge racism is for pupils to link up with local communities. Pupils need to be aware of how racism affects local community groups and of local struggles for better jobs, working conditions, health services, daycare facilities, housing and so on. A good example of a school working with the local communities is Pimlico School in Westminster and the work of Marcus Bhargava (cited above).

It is important to *interact* with local racialised communities, in the pursuit of reciprocal knowledge. It is absolutely crucial, in my view, for organisations representing racialised groups to link up with each other *and* with non-racialised white working class communities, and to develop strategies for reciprocal mutual support and well being and to undermine the growth of organisations like the BNP whose tactics are to divide rather than unite communities. Residents' associations and youth organisations might also be good inroads, in defending and enhancing the rights of *all* the members of the local community.

There is also a need to link up with national communities representing various interest groups, and, indeed to link up internationally. The UK Government's international strategy and the DfES Global Gateway (www.globalgateway.org) provides the opportunity to register schools and to link up with schools worldwide.

Linking up with communities facilitates an understanding of racism, Islamophobia and xenoracism, locally, nationally and internationally. Understanding processes of racialisation and xenoracialisation will inform the ways by which people become demonised because of their (perceived) indentities.

Classroom resources from the Institute of Race Relations

There are some excellent resources for challenging racism in schools provided by the Institute of Race Relations: www.irr.org.uk/education/resources/index.html; see also The Runnymede Trust: www.runnymedetrust.org; Friends, Families and Travellers: www.gypsy-traveller.org; Early Year Development and Childcare Partnership: www.childrenwebmag.com/content/view/290; and Insted Equality and Diversity in Education: www.insted.co.uk

10 Common objections to Marxism and a Marxist response

At this stage it may be productive to address some of the common objections to Marxism and attempt to respond to them.

How is the Marxist vision of socialism different from capitalism and why is it better?

As argued in Chapter 6 (pp. 80–81), Marxists do not have a blueprint for the future. However, there are certain features, which would distinguish world socialism from world capitalism. What follows are just a few examples.

Public services would be brought under state control and democratically run by the respective workforces. There would be universal free healthcare for all, incorporating the latest medical advances. There would be no private healthcare or private public transport. There would universal free comprehensive education for all and no private schooling. There would be free comprehensive leisure facilities for all, with no fee for health clubs, concerts etc. There would be free housing and employment for all. There would be full rights for women, for the LGBT (lesbian, gay, bisexual and transgender) communities, for all members of minority ethnic groups and for disabled people. There would be full freedom of religion. There would be no child pornography. There would be no war, no hunger and no poverty.

These are not made up, but form the platform for the Respect Coalition in Britain (here is a URL link to a free *Respect* pamphlet, *Another World is Possible*: www.respectcoalition.org/pdf/f473.pdf). This gives details of the policies of *Respect*, which campaigns on a broadly current-day Marxist platform. It is an umbrella organisation, which includes the Marxist Socialist Workers Party, among other constituencies. The Coalition has an MP, and 18 local councillors.

Marxism is contrary to human nature because we are all basically selfish and greedy and competitive

For Marxists, there is no such thing as 'human nature'. Marxists believe that our individual natures are not ahistorical givens, but products of the circumstances into which we are socialised, and of the society or societies in which we live or have lived (including crucially *the social class position* we occupy therein). While it is true that babies and infants, for example, may act selfishly in order to survive, as human beings grow up they are strongly influenced by the norms and values that are predominant in the society in which they live. Thus in societies which encourage selfishness, greed and competitiveness (Thatcherism is a perfect example) people will tend to act in self-centred ways, whereas in societies which discourage these values and promote communal values (Cuba is a good example) people will tend to act in ways that consider the collective as well as their own selves. As Marx and Engels (1976) [1845] put it, 'life is not determined by consciousness, but consciousness by life'. Unlike animals, we have the ability to choose our actions, and change the way we live, and the way we respond to others. Hence, in capitalist society, the working class *is* capable of transcending false consciousness and becoming a 'class for itself', pursuing interests which can ultimately lead to a just society. Socialism does not require as a precondition that we are all altruistic and selfless; rather the social and economic conditions of socialism will facilitate the development of such human capacities (Bowles and Gintis, 1976, p. 267).

Some people are naturally lazy and won't work

Unlike Saint-Simon, who, as we have seen (Chapter 2, p. 15) believed that we are 'lazy by nature', Marxists would argue that laziness, like other aspects of our 'nature' is most likely acquired through socialisation too, but even if it is not we can still choose to overcome our laziness. In a socialist world, there are sound reasons to work, in order to create cooperative wealth. Whereas in capitalist societies, a surplus is extracted from the values workers produce, and hived off by the capitalists to create profits (see Chapter 2, pp. 24–25), under socialism everything we create is for the benefit of humankind as a whole, including us as individuals. Thus the only incentive for most workers under capitalism: more wages (an incentive which is totally understandable, and indeed encouraged by Marxists, because it ameliorates workers' lives and lessens the amount of surplus for capitalists) is replaced by a much more worthwhile incentive, the common good.

Why shouldn't those who have worked hard get more benefits in life?

Again this viewpoint is a product of capitalist society, based on selfishness. If everything is shared, as in a socialist world, we all benefit by working hard. No one needs to go short of anything that they need for a good life. Of course, in capitalist societies, needs are created by advertisers for capitalists, and many of these (excessive amounts of clothes, or living accommodation beyond our personal requirements) we do not really *need*. Indeed, excess possessions in a capitalist world where most of the population has nothing or next to nothing (see Chapter 5, pp. 56–58) is obscene.

Marxism can't work because it always leads to totalitarianism

Marxists have learnt from Stalinism which was, in many ways, the antithesis of Marxists' notions of democratic socialism (see Chapter 6, pp. 78–79 for arguments, against transmodernist David Geoffrey Smith and his ascriptions to socialism as 'imposed', and in defence of socialism as a democratic process). Part of the reason for Stalinist totalitarianism is that socialism was attempted in one country, whereas Marx believed that, for it to work, it must be international. This meant that the Soviet Union, being isolated, had to concentrate on accumulation rather than consumption. Alone in a sea of capitalist states, the economy had to be geared to competing economically and militarily with the rest of the world, with workers' rights taking a back seat. There are no inherent reasons why these mistakes should be made again. To succeed, socialism needs to be international and democratic. Indeed, as Maunder (2006, p. 13) reminds us, whereas previous exploited classes, such as the peasantry, could rise up, seize lands and divide them up among themselves, workers cannot, for example, divide a factory, hospital or supermarket. Thus if workers do seize control of such institutions, they can only run them collectively. As Maunder (2006, p. 13) concludes: 'their struggles have a democratic logic that can lay the basis for a different way of running society'. Genuinely *democratic* socialism, where elected leaders are permanently subject to recall by those who have elected them, is the best way to safeguard against totalitarianism. It is bourgeois democracy, for example, in Britain and the US which in effect amounts to a form of totalitarianism. In these countries, citizens can vote every five years, having in reality a choice (in the sense of who will actually be able to form a government) of two main totally pro-capitalist parties, who then go on to exercise power in the interests of neo-liberal global capitalism and imperialism with little or no regard for the interests of those workers who elected them. There are, of course, some restraints on what they can get away with (minimum wage and European human rights legislation in Britain, for example.

Someone will always want to be 'boss' and there will always be natural 'leaders' and 'followers'

As argued above, Marxists believe in true democracy. If a given individual in socialist society attempts to exploit others, s/he will need to be controlled democratically and subject to permanent recall. Under capitalism, if people feel they are 'born to be followers' rather than leaders, this is most like to be due to their social class position in any given society and to their socialisation (see above). Under socialism, there will be more chance for all to take roles of responsibility if they want. Under capitalism, see certain people are educated for leadership positions in the society, while others are schooled to be exploited members of the working class (Bowles and Gintis, 1976; see also Chapter 3).

It is impossible to plan centrally in such a hugely diverse and complex world

In a socialist world, local, national and international needs will need to be coordinated fairly and efficiently. Given modern technology, this is easier now than ever before, and will become more and more so, as technology continues to develop. Under capitalism, technology is harnessed to the creation of greater and greater surplus value and profit. In a socialist world, technology would be under the control of the people for the benefit of the people as a whole; for universal human need rather than global corporate profit.

Someone has to do the drudge jobs, and how could that be sorted out in a socialist world

Technology already has the potential to eliminate most of the most boring and/or unpleasant jobs. Some of those that remain could be done on a voluntary rota basis, so that no one would have to do drudge jobs for longer than a very brief period (Fourier had a similar idea – see Chapter 2, pp. 17–18). Voluntary work under capitalism in the public sector abounds, and there is every reason to assume that such work would flourish much more under socialism.

Socialism means a lower standard of life for all

World socialism will only lower the standard of life for the ruling classes. There will not, for sure, be the massive disparities of wealth apparent in our present capitalist world (see Chapter 5, pp. 56–58). There will, of course, be no billionaires and no monarchy. If the wealth of the world is shared, then there will be a good standard of life for all, since all reasonable needs will be met and, to paraphrase Marx (see Chapter 2, p. 26), the principle will be from each according to his or her ability, to each according to his or her needs.

Socialism will be dull, dreary and uniform and we will all have less choice

This is a popular misconception related to the experiences of life under Stalinism. Life under socialism should be exciting, challenging and globally diverse, as different countries develop socialism to suit their own circumstances, but with a common goal. The intensively creative advertising (world) industry (now in private hands), under public control could be used for the common good, for example to increase awareness of the availability of free goods and services (health promotion, universal lifelong education, public transport and so on). We do not need the excessive branded products common in capitalist societies, and created by different capitalist firms to increase profits. A cursory glance at the website of one well-known supermarket in Britain revealed a total of over 60 different butters/margarines. It is not necessary for Western consumers to have this degree of 'choice' when most of 'the developing world' eats its bread without spreads. Moreover, in many cases the ingredients in the vast array of products will be very similar, while the huge amount of unnecessary plastic packaging clearly adversely affects the environment.

A social revolution will necessarily involve violence and death on a massive scale

It is, of course, capitalism that has created and continues to promote death and violence and terror on a global scale. Inequalities in wealth and quality of life cause death and disease in capitalist countries themselves, and the capitalist West's underdevelopment of most of the rest of the world and the massive disparity in wealth and health has the dire consequences that we saw in Chapter 5. In addition, imperialist conquest historically and contemporaneously unleashes death, terror and destruction on a colossal scale. Stalinism, and other atrocities, committed *in the name of*, but not in the spirit of socialism also shares this guilt, but as argued above there is no inherent reason why the historical perversities of Stalinism need to be repeated. As for the violence entailed in future social revolution is concerned, this is, of course, an unknown. However, as argued in Chapter 6, socialism is a majoritarian process not an imposed event which is not *dependent* on violence. It is, of course, inconceivable that a world social revolution would involve no violence, not least because of the resistance of the dominant capitalist class. However, there are no reasons for violence to be a strategic weapon. Anyone who has ever attended a mass socialist gathering, e.g. *Marxism 2006* in Britain (www.swp.org.uk/marxism/), can attest to the fact that violence is not, in any way, an organising tool of the socialist movement. Mass violence is the province of world capitalism. Moreover, Marxists oppose the terrorism unreservedly. Terrorism is reactionary, in that it diverts attention away from the class struggle. It militates against what Leon Trotsky has described as self-organisation and self-education. As he put it:

> The more 'effective' the terrorist acts, the greater their impact, the more they reduce the interest of the masses in self-organisation and self-education.... To learn to see all the crimes against humanity, all the indignities to which the human body and spirit are subjected, as the twisted outgrowths and expressions of the existing social system, in order to direct all our energies into a collective struggle against this system – that is the direction in which the burning desire for revenge can find its highest moral satisfaction.
>
> (Trotsky, 1909)

The working class won't create the revolution because they are reactionary

A number of times in this book I have stressed the fundamental tenet of Marxism that the working class are the agents of social revolution, and that the working class needs to become a 'class for itself' in addition to being a 'class in itself'. It is unfortunately the case that the world is a long way off such a scenario at the present conjucture. It is also the case that false consciousness hampers the development of class consciousness and the move towards the overthrow of capitalism. It is further the case that in a number of countries, Britain included, large numbers of workers are reactionary (backward-looking); many are conservative, sexist and racist, and a certain constituency of the working class is attracted to racist and fascist political parties. However there are examples of burgeoning class consciousness, witnessed for example by the growth of Left parties (see below) in Europe and by developments in South America, notably the Bolivarian Republic of Venezuela. It is to be hoped that as neo-liberal global imperial capitalism continues to reveal and expose its essential ruthlessness and contempt for those who make its profits that class consciousness will increase and that, in the words of Engels (see Chapter 2, p. 27), the working class will one day be in a position to undertake 'the momentous act it is called upon to accomplish', the overthrow of world capitalism and its replacement by world democratic socialism. Perhaps it should be pointed out here that Maxists do not idolise or deify the working class; it is rather, as I have argued, that the structural location in capitalist societies of the working class, so that, once it has become 'a class in itself' makes it the agent for change. Moreover the very act of social revolution and the creation of socialism mean the end of the very existence of the working class as a social class. As Marx and Engels (1975 [1845]) put it:

> When socialist writers ascribe this world-historic role to the proletariat, it is not at all...because they regard the proletarians as *gods*. Rather the contrary... [The proletariat] cannot emancipate itself without abolishing the conditions of its own life... It cannot abolish the conditions of its own life without abolishing all the inhuman conditions of ... society today which are summed up in its own situation...It is not a question of what this or that proletarian, or even the whole proletariat, at the moment, *regards* as its aim. It is a question of *what the proletariat is*, and what, in accordance with this *being*, it will historically be compelled to do. Its aim and historical action is visibly and irrevocably foreshadowed in its own life situation as well as the whole organisation of bourgeois society today.

Marxists just wait for the revolution rather than address the issues of the here and now

This is manifestly not the case. As I have argued earlier, Marxists fight constantly for change and reform, which benefits the working class in the short-run under capitalism (for example, Marxists are centrally involved with work in trade unions agitating for better wages) with a vision of socialist transformation in the longer term (increasing class consciousness in the unions is part of this process). As Marx and Engels (1977a [1847], p. 62) put it:

> The Communists fight for the attainment of the immediate aims, for the enforcement of the momentary interests of the working class; but in the movement of the present, they also represent and take care of the future of the movement.

The *Respect* coalition has this dual aim, combining reform (bullet point 2: 'the fight against') with a revolutionary vision (bullet point 2: 'the ultimate abolition' and bullet points 1, 3 and 4):

- The organisation of society in the most open, democratic, participative, and accountable way practicable based on common ownership and democratic control
- The fight against, and ultimate abolition of racism, sexism, and all other forms of discrimination on the grounds of religion, disability, age or sexual identity. Defend a woman's right to choose
- The abolition of all forms of economic exploitation and social oppression
- The promotion of peace and a system of global and national justice that provides protection from tyranny, prejudice and the abuse of power

> (Respect, undated, p. 3)

However, there is no illusion that getting into power in the local and national capitalist state will create socialism, but it does provide a space to spread the message. As Respect's first MP put it recently:

> We don't believe that the world can be changed in town halls and in parliament, but we believe that town halls and parliaments can be used to build a mass movement of people that *will* change things in this country for the better.

> (Galloway, 2006)

The choice is not between life in the neo-liberal global capitalist world or a return to Stalinism, but between the anarchic chaos of capitalism and genuine worldwide democratic socialism. There is a burgeoning recognition that this is the case from the mass global movements against globalisation and in the growing anti-neo-liberal politics throughout Latin America, from the Bolivarian Republic of Venezuela to Bolivia, from Argentina to Brazil. There is also growing support for Marxist parties in Europe, such as the German Linkspartei, Italian Rifondazione Comunista, Portuguese Bloco Esquerda, the Scottish Socialist Party, and, in England and Wales, Respect – the Unity Coalition.

Marxism is a nice idea, but it will never happen (for some of the reasons headlined above)

Bringing Marxism to the forefront is not an easy task. Capitalism is self-evidently a resilient and very adaptable world force. However, as we saw in Chapter 2, Marx argued that society has gone through a number of different stages in its history: primitive communism; slavery; feudalism; capitalism. It is highly likely that in each era, a different way of living was considered 'impossible' by most of those living in that era. However, each era gave birth, in a dialectical process, to another. Thus, though it may be extremely difficult to imagine a world based on socialist principles, such a world *is* possible if that is what the majority of the world's citizens come to desire and have the will to create. Marxists need to address the obstacles full on. As Callinicos (2000, p. 122) has argued, we must break through the 'bizarre ideological mechanism, [in which] *every* conceivable alternative to the market has been discredited by the collapse of Stalinism' whereby the fetishisation of life makes capitalism seem natural and therefore unalterable and where the market mechanism 'has been hypostatized into a natural force unresponsive to human wishes' (ibid., p. 125).[1] Capital presents itself 'determining the future as surely as the laws of nature make tides rise to lift boats' (McMurtry, 2000, p. 2), 'as if it has now replaced the natural environment. It announces itself through its business leaders and politicians as coterminous with freedom, and indispensable to democracy such that any attack on capitalism as exploitative or hypocritical becomes an attack on world freedom and democracy itself' (McLaren, 2000, p. 32).[2] However, the biggest impediment to social revolution is not capital's resistance, but its success in heralding the continuation of capitalism as being the only option. As Callinicos puts it, despite the inevitable intense resistance from capital, the 'greatest obstacle to change is not ... the revolt it would evoke from the privileged, but the belief that it is impossible' (2000, p. 128). As I have consistently argued, for socialism to be on the agenda, there is a need for the working class, as a whole to become, as well as a 'class-in-itself', a 'class-for-itself'. Given the hegemony of world capitalism, whose very *leitmotif* is to stifle and redirect class consciousness, and given the aforementioned reactionary nature of certain sections of the working class, restoring this consciousness is a tortuous, but not impossible task. Callinicos again:

> Challenging this climate requires courage, imagination and willpower inspired by the injustice that surrounds us. Beneath the surface of our supposedly contented societies, these qualities are present in abundance. Once mobilized, they can turn the world upside down.
>
> (2000, p. 129)

As we hurtle into the twenty-first century, we have some important decisions to make. Whatever the twenty-first century has to offer, the choices will need to be debated. The Hillcole Group expressed our educational choices as follows:

Each person and group should experience education as contributing to their own self-advancement, but at the same time our education should ensure that at least part of everyone's life activity is also designed to assist in securing the future of the planet we inherit – set in the context of a sustainable and equitable society. Democracy is not possible unless there is a free debate about all the alternatives for running our social and economic system. ... All societies [are] struggling with the same issues in the 21st century. We can prepare by being better armed with war machinery or more competitive international monopolies. ... Or we can wipe out poverty ... altogether. We can decide to approach the future by consciously putting our investment into a massive drive to encourage participation from everyone at every stage in life through training and education that will increase productive, social, cultural and environmental development in ways we have not yet begun to contemplate.

(Hillcole Group, 1997, pp. 94–95)

While the open-endedness of the phrase, 'in ways we have not yet begun to contemplate' will appeal to poststructuralists and postmodernists, for whom the future is an open book (see Chapter 5), this is most definitely not the political position of the Hillcole Group. Whereas, for poststructuralists and postmodernists, all we have is endlessly deconstruction without having *strategies* for change (see Chapter 5), for Marxists, the phrase is tied firmly to an open but *socialist* agenda.

For transmodernists like David Geoffrey Smith, the way forward is to 'desacralize capitalism' and to move towards a 'rethought liberal democracy', while for Enrique Dussel, the answer lies in an 'ex nihilo utopia'. These suggestions are no doubt well intentioned, but they are idealistic in the current historical conjuncture. Like the views of the utopian socialists, discussed in Chapter 2, neither Smith's nor Dussel's ideas engage with the nature of the contradictions within capitalism, the dialectic, and with the working class consciousness needed for revolutionary change. Unless education takes these issue on board, unless it has a notion that things can get better, it is a futile and reactionary endeavour.

Marxists are clear as to their role is in the debate over the future of our planet. As Sarup (1988, pp. 147–148) argues:

A characteristic of human beings is that they make a distinction between the 'real' and the 'ideal' ... Human beings have a sense of what is possible in the future and they have the hope that tomorrow will be better than today. Marxists not only have this hope, this orientation towards the future, but they try to understand the world, to develop a critical consciousness of it, and try to develop strategies for changing it. Of course, they realize that progress is uneven, not unilinear; because of the nature of contradiction there are inevitably negative aspects, sad reversals and painful losses. Marxists struggle for a better future for all, but they know that this does not mean that progress is guaranteed or that the processes of the dialectic will lead to the Perfect … It is important for people to support the Enlightenment project because education is closely connected with the notion of a change of consciousness; gaining a wider, deeper understanding of the world represents a change for the better. And this, in turn, implies some belief in a worthwhile future. Without this presupposition the education of people would be pointless.

An equitable, fair and just world can be foreseen neither through postmodernism/poststructuralism, nor through the more enlightened and progressive ideas of transmodernism and CRT. For Marxists, as global neo-liberal capitalism and imperial hegemony tightens its grip on all our lives, the choice, to paraphrase Rosa Luxembourg (1916), is quite simple: that choice is between barbarism – 'the unthinkable' – or democratic socialism.

Afterword

I have made no secret of my own theoretical orientation throughout this book. However, I have tried to present the arguments of others as honestly and as accurately as I can. I have looked at the origins of socialism and Marxist theory and at developments in Marxist theory and education and suggested a way forward in the impasse that represents Marxist sociology of education – by returning to Marx himself. I have examined the origins of postmodernism and poststructuralism in the thoughts of Nietzsche. I have also assessed poststructuralist and postmodernist claims that they are pursuing social change and social justice, and have argued that such claims do not fulfil their promise. I have examined the transmodern challenge, and found it to be an improvement on poststructuralism/postmodernism in focusing on the plight of the oppressed, but ultimately lacking in a viable way forward after capitalism.

I have also assessed the potential of Critical Race Theory and, while I have found it useful, in that it stresses that people of color speak from a unique experience framed by racism and, therefore, need to be listened to, I found it lacking in making connections to social class and therefore to neo-liberal capitalist modes of production and to imperialism. Marxism, I must conclude, presents the only viable, humane alternative to capitalism; that alternative is world democratic socialism.

People often ask me where an example of actually existing socialism can be seen. In 2006, I worked for a short spell at the Bolivarian University of Venezuela in Caracas, and have elsewhere outlined my experiences (Richards, 2006; Cole, 2007b). Suffice it to say here that in Venezuela there is a very real sense that a socialist revolution, driven by the working class, has begun. This is apparent, both in the pronouncements and activities of the government, and in the voices of the spokespersons for the working class. In terms of political participation, Venezuelans indicate that they are more politically active than the citizens of any other surveyed South American country (Wilpert, 2006). For this reason, it matters less about whether Chavez is a genuine revolutionary socialist (although I happen to believe that he is) and more that the revolution is being driven from below, which, as we have seen, is a necessary prerequisite for a successful socialist revolution. Time will tell to what extent this Bolivarian model of twenty-first century socialism will spread to other continents.

Appendix
Robert Miles and the concept of racism

Miles (1989) argues *against* inflating the concept of racism to include actions and processes as well as discourses. Indeed, he argues that 'racism' should be used to refer exclusively to an *ideological* phenomenon, and not to exclusionary practices. He gives three reasons for this. First, exclusionary practice can result from both intentional and unintentional actions (Miles, 1989, p. 78). I would argue, however, that the fact that racist discourse is unintentional does not detract from its capacity to embody racism. For its recipients, effect is more important than intention (see my definition of racism Chapter 9, p. 118). Second, such practices do not presuppose the nature of the determination, e.g. the disadvantaged position of black people is not necessarily the result of racism (ibid.). However, the fact that the 'disadvantaged postion of black people is not necessarily the result of racism' is addressed by Miles's own theoretical approach, a class-based analysis which also recognises other bases of unequal treatment. Therefore, I would argue, this recognition does not need the singling out that Miles affords it. Third, there is a dialectical relationship between exclusion and inclusion: to exclude is simultaneously to include and vice versa, e.g. the overrepresentation of African-Caribbean children in 'special schools' for the 'educationally subnormal' (ESN) in the 1960s involves both exclusion from 'normal schools' and inclusion in ESN schools (ibid.). I do not see the purpose of this attempt to privilege inclusion. The simultaneous inclusion of black people entailed by exclusion is, by and large, a negative inclusion, as in the case of Miles's own example of ESN schools. There are, of course, situations where exclusion on account of the application of positive labels leads to positive consequences for those thus labelled. The way monarchies and aristocracies are perceived is an obvious example. They are excluded from everyday life but included in very elite settings with multiple positive benefits. I fail to see how Miles's observation about the dialectical relationship between exclusion and inclusion informs an analysis of racism.

While I understand Miles's desire to retain a Marxist analysis, and not to reify racism (since describing actions and processes as 'racist' may forestall an analysis of various practices in different historical periods of capitalist development), it is my view, as I attempted to demonstrate in Chapter 8 with respect to the US, and in Chapter 9 with respect to Britain, that it is *precisely* the Marxist concept of racialisation (and xeno-racialisation) that enables, and indeed *requires*, a persistant and constant analysis of the multiple manifestations of racism in different phases of the capitalist mode of production in different historical periods. Indeed, I try to show in Chapter 8 that, contrary to Miles, not only should racism be inflated to incorporate actions, processes and practices, but that it should, in fact, be inflated considerably to include a *wide range* of actions, processes and practices. Miles's position on not inflating the concept of racism retains a fervent following in the Department of Sociology at the University of Glasgow where Miles first expounded his views on racism and racialisation. I attended a workshop there recently where some Marxist sociologists were quite insistent on defending Miles's position, and stressed the need to use *Marxist* terminology rather than the concept of racism (though no such terminology, Marxist or otherwise, was generally forthcoming).[1] One contributor went as far as to express the view that 'there is not a lot of racism out there'. Another, also following Miles, stated that racism should be narrowed down, and confined to the level of *ideas*, and that *actions* should not be described as racist. The same delegate found the concept of racialisation problematic, adding that people 'magically becoming racialised' is meaningless. Another delegate argued that, whereas once people were sure what racism was; now both in the UK and globally, it is difficult to understand what racism is. Miles and the Marxist defenders of his position are right to be wary of any tendency to call everything 'racist' and thereby to foreclose discussion. However, in my view, there are grounds for believing that if an action or process is perceived to be racist then it probably is. Indeed this is enshrined in the excellent (2000) Race Relations (Amendment) Act. What I think should distinguish a Marxist analysis of racism is the attempt to relate various instances of racism and (xeno-)racialisation to different stages in capitalist development, but also to relate them to political and other ideological factors. This is not to say that all individual or institutional instances of racism and (xeno-)racialisation are reducible to the economy (Miles acknowledges this as a functionalist position), but that racism and (xeno-)racialisation in capitalist countries needs to be understood in terms of stages in capitalist development. I take the position that there are striking similiarities in actions and processes of racism and (xeno-)racialisation directed against different people in differing economic, political and ideological circumstances. This is *not* to claim that racism is primary and that all else flows from it, which was the fear of one delegate at the workshop, but to stress the need for retaining the concept of racism, widening it and relating it to developments in capitalism.

Notes

1 Introduction: personal and political reflections on a life in education

1 The word 'communist' is a greatly misunderstood one. It was used by Marx to refer to the stage after socialism when the state would have withered away and when we would live communally (see Chapter 2, p. 26). In the period after the Russian Revolution up to the demise of the Soviet Union, the Soviet Union and other Eastern European countries were routinely referred to as 'communist' in the West. The Soviet Union, following Marx, actually referred to itself as 'socialist'. Socialists critical of the Soviet Union (e.g. Cliff, 1974) have referred to the Soviet Union and other Eastern European countries as 'state capitalist'.

2 The term 'Left' (or 'left-wing') originates from the French Revolution, when liberal deputies from the Third Estate (those who were not members of the aristocracy or the clergy, including peasants, working people and the bourgeoisie) generally sat to the left of the president's chair. The nobility generally sat to the right. It is still the tradition in the French Assemblée Nationale for the representatives to be seated left-to-right, according to their political alignment. As this original reference became obsolete, the meaning of the term has changed, and is now used to denote a broad variety of political philosophies and principles. In contemporary Western political discourse, the term is most often used to describe forms of socialism, social democracy or, in the sense in which the term is understood in the US, liberalism (http://en.wikipedia.org/wiki/Left-wing: accessed 12 July 2006).

3 This book was primarily a Marxist analysis of young people and the state. In hindsight, I regret the disablist title of the book. I use the term 'disablist' without any hesitation. Should the term 'political correctness' spring to any reader's mind, I would respond by saying that if there are any doubts about the negative use of 'blind' being offensive, then it is probable that the reader has not worked with a blind colleague or taught a blind student. The same applies with the term 'deaf'. The common expressions, 'are you blind' or 'are you deaf?' take on new (offensive) meanings when working with or teaching blind, sight-impaired, deaf or hearing-impaired students. 'Political correctness' is a pernicious concept invented by the radical Right, which, to my dismay, has become common currency. The term was coined to imply that there exist (Left) political demagogues who seek to impose their views on equality issues, in particular appropriate terminology, on the majority. In reality, nomenclature changes over time. Thus, in the twenty-first century, terms such as 'negress' or 'negro' or 'coloured', nomenclatures which at one time were considered quite acceptable are now considered offensive. Egalitarians are concerned with *respect* for others and, therefore, are careful to acknowledge changes in nomenclature, changes which are decided by oppressed groups themselves, bearing in mind that there can be differences among such oppressed groups. Thus, for example, it has become common practice to use 'working

class' rather than 'lower class'; 'lesbian, gay, bisexual and transgender' rather than 'sexually deviant'; 'disability' rather than 'handicap', 'gender equality' rather than 'a woman's place'. Using current and acceptable nomenclature is about the fostering of a caring and inclusive society, not about 'political correctness' (see Chapter 8, note 6 for a discussion on nomenclature and racialisation).

2 Socialism and Marxist theory

1 This chapter focuses on Europe because the utopian socialists, which Marx and Engels critiqued in their development of scientific socialism (see below), were, as we shall see, Europeans. This is not to imply that socialist thought was not occurring elsewhere in the world. One of the major strengths of Marxism is that it is non-Eurocentric (for a discussion, see Chapter 6, p. 76).

2 Sexist language was the norm before the advent of the twentieth century feminist movement. I will thus resist the temptation to comment each time it occurs. Today, sexist language tends to be absent from the printed word. When it occurs, one must presume that it is there out of ignorance, or because the writer is deliberately being sexist.

3 Engels (1884) was to develop these ideas in *The Origin of the Family, Private Property and the State*.

4 A dialectical view of history sees societies moving forward through struggle. Thus out of opposing forces (thesis and antithesis) a new form of society arises (synthesis). This in turn generates a new thesis and antithesis and ultimately a new synthesis and so on and so on.

5 Laissez-faire economics entails the running of the economy without regulation or interference from governments or other bodies. It has its modern day parallel in neo-liberalism. For a discussion of the characteristics of neo-liberalism, see Chapter 7, pp. 87–90; see also Hill, 2003, 2005a, 2006a, 2007; Hill *et al.*, 2008 for discussions related to neo-liberalism and education.

6 Terry Eagleton (2002, p. 3) makes a distinction between the term *proletariat* (originally those who served the state by producing children) and the term *working class*. While the former refers primarily to any kind of subservient labour, the latter denoted a position within the social relations of production. However, in current usage, the two terms have become synonymous.

7 'Forcible' does not necessarily imply or involve excessive violence (a charge often levelled at Marxists). Engels, for example, stated: 'if the social revolution and practical communism are the necessary result of our existing conditions – then we will have to concern ourselves above all with the measures by which we can avoid a violent and bloody overthrow of the social conditions' (Engels, 1975 [1845], p. 243). Engels believed that education could play a role in a peaceful transformation of society: 'the calm and composure necessary for the peaceful transformation of society can ... be expected only from an *educated* working class' (ibid.). Chapter 3 addresses the issue of Marxism and education. While Marxists recognise that violence has been perpetrated on a grand scale *in the name of Marxism* it is, in fact, neo-liberal capitalism that is currently unleashing unabashedly an orgy of violence, hitherto unprecedented, causing masses of avoidable deaths from world poverty and imperialist conquest (for a discussion of Marxism, social revolution and violence, see Chapter 10 of this book).

8 Marx argues that the origins of the capital held by capitalists lies in the forcible seizure of feudal and clan property, the theft of common lands and state lands, and the forced acquisition of Church property at nominal price. In other words, capitalism has its origins in theft and continues on the same basis (see Marx, 1965 [1887], pp. 717–733.

9 Recently there has been a challenge to the revolutionary role of the working class in the work of Michael Hardt and Antonio Negri (Hardt and Negri, 2000, 2004). According to them, the working class as a potentially revolutionary agent has now

been dissolved by a more amorphous body, 'the multitude'. 'The multitude' is not defined by the nature of its work or the precise relationship it has with capital. Instead the concept embraces all those who work, or who are impoverished by having been denied that opportunity. The power of 'the multitude' lies in its creativity and spontaneity. 'The multitude' is a networked citizenry whose creative labour produces the resources on which a future democracy will depend (for a critical analysis of the work of Hardt and Negri, see Hickey, 2006).

3 Marxist theory and education

1 For Marxists, on the other hand, as we have seen, the ultimate aim is the overthrow of capitalism by revolutionary means (for a discussion of revolution and violence, see Chapter 10, p. 133; see also the quote by Engels: Chapter 2, note 7).

2 The 'free school' movement in twentieth century Britain (more or less complete freedom for the child to learn what he or she wants to learn, or the freedom not to learn at all) is epitomised by the work of British educationalist, A.S. Neill (e.g. Neill, 1966).

3 While formal education did not occupy a major part of Marx and Engels' time; in a very real sense, the fostering of 'a full knowledge of the conditions and of the meaning of the momentous act [the proletariat] is called upon to accomplish', Engel's 'theoretical expression of scientific socialism' (Engels, 1977 [1892], p. 428) should, for Marxists, be an essential part of any education programme in capitalist societies (see Chapter 10 for a discussion of the constraints and potentials of education).

4 They also believed that combining education with labour would be of use in the construction of a socialist future.

5 This is not to say that schools should replace capitalist propaganda with socialist *propaganda*. Rather, it means that pupils be provided with a range of interpretations of why and how things happen, including Marxist interpretations, and should be constantly urged to ask whose history and literature is conventionally taught in schools and whose is left out; from whose point of view is the past and present examined (Cole, 2004a, pp. 159–160).

6 To what extent Althusser might have modified his views on education as being the dominant *ISA*, given the current hegemony of organised religion (distortions of Christianity and Islam) is open to debate. In addition, the proliferation of the mass media in its numerous guises might have encouraged Althusser to attribute a more central role to 'culture'. However, there is no denying the current power of education in distilling dominant ideologies (e.g. Cole, 2007a; Hatcher, 2006; Rikowski, 2005). In the UK, for example, 'education, education, education' is, as is well known, New Labour's mantra. While there is disagreement among Marxists about the precise relationship between education, privatisation and capitalist profits (e.g. Rikowski, 2005; Hatcher, 2006; see also Cole, 2007a), there is a general consensus that the education system is a very powerful force in the maintenance of capitalism.

7 The course is described as 'remarkable' because of the impact it had on British society at the time, including a debate in the House of Commons. This culminated in Gould (1977), which alleged Marxist penetration into British sociology.

8 This phrase is Glenn Rikowski's (see Rikowski, 2004a). By 'The Classical Age of Marxist Educational Theory', he means the period, 1970–1982, 'when Marxist educational theory was being taken seriously by those on the Left (and also by critics of the Left inside and outside the academy)'. As he explains, Bowles and Gintis and Willis were the main reference points for the classical age of Marxist educational theory, but there were also other strands that were part of the excitement of the times: Louis Althusser and Michael F.D. Young. Paulo Freire's (1970) *Pedagogy of the Oppressed*, which gave rise to the American Critical Pedagogy School, is important, and is currently making a comeback today in some universities in the US. In this chapter I am

concentrating, within the Classical Age of Marxist Educational Theory, on *SCA*. For a broader overview of the work of Bowles and Gintis as a whole around this time, and responses to it, see Cole, ed., 1988.

9 Neo-Marxism simply means 'new Marxism' and refers to attempts by Marxists to develop Marxist theory in the light of changing circumstances. Use of the term was popular in the Classical Age of Marxist Educational Theory, but is less used now. Perhaps this is due to the fact that many Marxists now lay more stress on the notion that Marxism is, as Jean-Paul Sartre (1960) noted a 'living philosophy', continually being adapted and adapting itself 'by means of thousands of new efforts'. To Sartre's observation, Crystal Bartolovich (2002, p. 20) has added, Marxism is a living *project*, 'neither simply a discourse nor a body of (academic) knowledge'. On this view, the prefix, 'neo' becomes redundant. As we shall see, *discourse*, which refers to the way in which different meanings are constructed by the readers of texts, is a very central concept for poststructuralists and postmodernists (see Chapters 4 and 5).

10 As noted above, Bowles and Gintis, in *SCA*, moved analysis *away* from traditional sociological concerns with functionalist explanations (how schools and other institutions 'function' to maintain cohesion in societies). It is somewhat ironic, therefore, that they have been (rightly) criticised for their own functionalism in *SCA*, albeit functionalism *within* Marxism.

11 There are some contradictions in the work of Althusser. For example, the criticisms of functionalism and determinism levelled at Bowles and Gintis above could also be applied to the *ISA* essay, which as Sarup noted above, implies that children are ejected en masse to fulfil their designated class roles in capitalist societies. In other writings, Althusser (e.g. Althusser, 1969, pp. 87–128), has been very much associated with 'relative autonomy theory'. For a discussion of Althusserian Marxism as a whole, including the *ISA* essay and 'relative autonomy', see, for example, Callinicos, 1976; Sarup, 1983.

12 Surprisingly, in *SCA*, Bowles and Gintis reject the content of schooling as instrumental in upholding capitalism. As they argue, the actual content of the curriculum has little role to play in this process (Bowles and Gintis, 1976)

13 A perennial problem for Marxists, who view the working class to be agents for revolutionary change, is the backward views and actions of (large) sections of the working class, Willis's lads (see above) being a prime example (see Chapter 10, p. 134 for a discussion).

4 Nietzsche, poststructuralism and postmodernism

1 According to Perry Anderson (1998, p. 3), contrary to conventional wisdom, modernism was born not in Europe or the United States, but in Hispanic America. We owe the concept of modernism (*modernismo* in Spanish), states Anderson (ibid.), to an aesthetic movement in the 1890s in Peru, associated with a Nicaraguan poet, Rubén Darío, signifying a 'declaration of cultural independence' from Spain. Thus, the origin of modernism bears no relation to its contemporary meaning.

2 Foucault paid his debt to Nietzsche for the genealogical conception of history in Foucault, 1977a.

3 Postmodernism (*postmodernismo* in Spanish), according to Anderson (1998, p. 3), like modernism, also surfaced in Hispanic America. In the 1930s, in the work of Frederico de Onís (ibid.), it was used to describe a conservative reaction within modernism, with particular respect to poetry (in contradistinction to 'ultra-modernism' which positively encouraged the radical impulses to modernism). Thus, like modernism, postmodernism bears no relation to its current meaning.

4 Accordingly, postmodern and poststructural *feminists* propose replacing unitary images of woman with a focus on women's multiple identities. Socialism and traditional feminism are seen as the product of a bygone age – the modern era (or modernity).

I am not specifically concerned here with feminism per se. Suffice it to say that I believe that the liberation of women cannot be divorced from the pursuit of a socialist future (for recent defences of Marxism, rather than postmodernism, as best representing the interests of women, see, for example, Kelly, 2002a, 2002b, 2006; Zavarzadeh, 2002).

5 Poststructuralism and postmodernism in educational theory: social change and social justice

1 The incursion of poststructualism/postmodernism into UK education circles, however, is a relatively recent phenomenon. For example, Ian Stronach and Maggie MacLure (1997, p. 32), note that the *British Education Index* had no postmodern entries between 1986 and 1991, one in 1992, two in 1993 and 15 in 1994. Thus, 1994 seems to be a significant milestone for British educational postmodernism. The publication in that year of Robin Usher and Richard Edwards' *Postmodernism and Education* heralded the 'arrival' of postmodernism within the British educational milieu. Three years later, Stronach and MacLure's *Educational Research Undone* and Stuart Parker's *Reflective Teaching in the Postmodern World* consolidated the position in Britain of postmodernism within educational research and pedagogy respectively (Rikowski and McLaren, 2002, p. 4). Poststructuralism/postmodernism in educational theory has a longer history in the US. The late 1980s and early 1990s saw an explosion of books and articles written from these perspectives (ibid.). This chapter draws on, develops and updates Cole, 2003a.
2 The 'Other' is a term derived from the philosopher, Emmanuel Levinas, and includes 'the poor, the stranger, the widow, or the orphan of the Jewish scriptures as well as contemporary anologates – those who are vanquished, forgotten, or excluded in any way from existing sociopolitical or cultural systems' (Barber, 1998, p. ix).
3 While I argue in this chapter against the notion that postmodernism and poststructuralism are themselves forces for social change, that is not to say that poststructuralists and postmodernists, as individuals, do not take actions in the pursuit of social change and social justice. However, if they take such action, their reasons for so doing so are different from those of Marxists. To take the example of strike action, Marxists would see most strikes as essentially struggles over surplus value. On picket lines and on strike workers become politicised, and we can see a move maybe towards workers being a 'class-for-itself' as well as a 'class-in-itself' (that the working class is a class-in-itself is, for Marxists, an objective fact). This is very different from Atkinson's reasons, as revealed in Atkinson and Cole, 2007. Her reasons for being on picket lines are to do with her multiple identities and issues of social justice. I think we both agree that we would support workers for reasons of social justice. Beyond that, I think our analyses differ.
4 For a defence of the recent work of McLaren, particularly in the light of Lather's critique, see Cole, 2005a.
5 The focus of this chapter, however, is not conceptual distinctions – thus, the fact that Atkinson identifies specifically with *postmodernism*; Baxter identifies with *feminist poststructuralism* and Lather describes herself both as a 'postmodern materialist feminist' (e.g. 1991, p. xix) and as a *feminist poststructuralist* (e.g. 2001) is not of concern. Here I am interested in their common claim that poststructuralism and postmodernism can be forces for social change and social justice.
6 The arguments in this section draw on Cole (2001). For Atkinson's reply to them, see Atkinson (2001). My ability (Cole, 2001) to comment on Atkinson's (2002) paper before it was published and her ability to respond to my critique relates to the fact that Atkinson kindly provided me with a copy of her (2002) paper while it was 'in press'.
7 Marx and Engels attempted to learn from the experiences of the Paris Commune of 1871 in their preface to the German Edition (1977b [1872]) of the *Manifesto of the*

Communist Party. In fact, the whole Marxist project is based on the belief that history is progressive. Thus, for example, we can learn from the earliest forms of primitive communism, but in the context of a dialectic of accumulative progressive change.

8 Alex Callinicos has written of the requirement to 'anticipate, at least in outline, an efficient and democratic non-market from of economic co-ordination' (2000, p. 133) – 'to give serious attention to models of democratic socialist planning … [to] a much more decentralized system of planning in which information and decisions flow horizontally among different groups of producers and consumers rather than vertically between centre and productive units' (ibid., p. 123). By contrast, the notion of the possibility of the existence of a benign form of global capitalism, as advocated, for example, by Tony Blair and others (see Chapter 7, pp. 86–87), represents 'an utterly ridiculous utopia' (Allman, 2001, p. 13).

9 Norman Geras (1983), for example, has a whole page of footnotes citing writings by those for and against the notion that Marx criticised capitalism as *unjust* (pp. 212–213). It is not only *North* American philosophers who have been interested in whether Marx was concerned with ethics. Argentinian philosopher, Enrique Dussel (e.g. Dussel, 2001), whose work on transmodernism is the subject of the next chapter, has undertaken a careful reading of all Marx's pre-*Capital* works, and has argued for an ethical reading of Marx.

10 Marx was, of course, suspicious of philosophers who had 'interpreted the world in many ways'. For him, the point was 'to change it' (1976b [1845], p. 123). Marx, however, had a more overtly *political* objection to basing socialist demands on principles of social justice; namely that this tends to limit these demands to social reform rather than social revolution. Focusing on the redistribution of income rather than the conditions of production fuel social democratic rather than socialist solutions (Callinicos, 2000, p. 29; see also p. 34).

11 This argument needs to be modified slightly, given the large growth in self-employment (builders, decorators, plumbers, etc.). Many such workers, however, tend to be on low to medium incomes and their economic and social position is reminiscent of skilled workers through most of the twentieth century. Various welfare programmes, in many cases now being minimised or phased out, also mean further modification of the argument.

12 This is reminiscent of British Conservative Party arguments, before the election of New Labour in 1997, that adopting the European minimum wage in Britain would ultimately be detrimental to workers' interests. The general Marxist position advanced does not preclude the fact that social democrats and socialists in capitalist parliaments are, at times, able to force issues that are in workers' interests, the European minimum wage being one such example. In addition, there have, of course, been rare historical exceptions among the ruling class – philanthropic capitalists, for example.

13 Atkinson (2001) agrees that 'the state' is a complex of institutions but, rather than applying this multiple model to capitalism, like Foucault, she uses it to look at 'systems of control beyond the economy and the labour market, focusing in particular on control, and "self-control", within educational systems' (p. 88). Her analysis, therefore, is divorced from capitalism and thus unable to theorise it.

14 This was brought home starkly to me on a trip to South Africa in 1995; I was asked to present a Marxist critique of postmodernism at a seminar attended by some leading (South African) postmodernists. Having spent considerable time in the townships and squatter camps, where Marxism clearly had some purchase on how to move forward, I asked what postmodernists could do for their inhabitants and was met with stony silence. As I put it at the time:

> Wake up worried about presenting an unprepared talk on postmodernism and Marxism. To my relief, I manage to defend my position quite well to a largely

hostile audience. My previous experiences in Cape Town and my stimulating discussions with the comrades in the township has given me new strengths. There is
something unusually refreshing about decrying the irrelevance of postmodernism
after talking at length to poor blacks.

(Cole, 1995, p. 16)

15 Atkinson's response to this point first made in Cole (2001) was 'well, possibly Socialism with a capital S (although I would suggest, "considered as one of many possibilities" rather than "ruled out"' (Atkinson, 2001, p. 90). Atkinson (Atkinson and
Cole, 2007) has since expanded on this point. As she puts it, 'it doesn't rule out the
possibility of a socialist interpretation of society ... which has useful ways forward,
along with a lot of other ways. So socialism as a perspective is not ruled out'.
16 Ideology, where false ideas mask reality, is a meaningless concept for postmodernists,
since, for them, language cannot represent reality.
17 Surrealism and other art forms have had and continue to have similar subversive functions including, for example, the characters of certain 'alternative' comedians. British
comedian Steve Coogan's character, Alan Partridge (BBC2), an archetypal icon of
modern white middle class male inadequacy, is a good case in point. Thus, given the
obnoxiousness of Partridge, the pro-capitalism, classism (see Chapter 7, note 6 for some
comments on classism), regionalism, sexism, racism, disablism, homophobia, which the
character portrays, serve to ridicule these *isms/phobia* (see Cole, 2005b, pp. 13–16). The
line between subversion and acclamation, however, is a thin one. Take Ricky Gervais'
Politics tour. This has the British comedian *as Gervais*, rather than as his incompetent
alter ego, David Brent (*The Office*, BBC2), celebrating negative attitudes towards women
and minority groups. Here we may find ourselves laughing at the *object* of the abuse
rather than, as with Coogan, laughing at the stupidity of the character. Even obviously
subversive art forms, however, do not, in themselves, provide directions for change.
18 In using the expression, 'by default', I mean that, because postmodernism and poststructuralism do not provide solutions for an alternative system to capitalism, they aid
in its retention. Baxter's (2006) attempts to use FPDA to get more women as 'cap-
tains of industry' may be seen as a more overtly pro-capitalist endeavour, assuming
that is that this would be generally be perceived by (male) capitalists as positive to
their interests. Despite her earlier assertion that 'a post-structuralist study ... is not
concerned with ... carrying a torch for a noble cause' (Baxter, 2002a, p. 17), she now
seems to have found one.

6 Transmodernism in educational theory: a step closer to liberation?

1 The same distinction can be applied between 'transmodernism' and 'transmodernity', as
between 'postmodernism' and 'postmodernity' (see Chapter 4, pp. 45–46), with transmodernism the movement associated with transmodernity, a perceived state of being.
2 For details of Dussel's many works, see the following website: http://translate.google.
com/translate?hl=en&sl=es&u=http://www.clacso.org/wwwclacso/espanol/html/libros
/dussel/dussel.html&sa=X&oi=translate&resnum=1&ct=result&prev=/search%3Fq%
3Denrique%2Bdussel%26hl%3Den%26lr%3D%26sa%3DG (accessed 5 August 2006).
3 It is nonetheless crucial for Marxists to engage in productive dialogue with transmodernists. Those who adhere to or accept all or some transmodern arguments are also
likely to be amenable to Marxist ones.
4 *Educational theory* is, in general, difficult to compartmentalise. It may appear a
particularly problematic descriptor in the context of the subject matter of this chapter,
which has little obvious *direct* reference to education. Broadly, I view educational
theory as that body of knowledge which appears primarily in theoretical educational

journals and books, and/or is presented at academic educational conferences. David Geoffrey Smith's groundbreaking paper (Smith, 2003) appeared in the very popular and influential journal, *Policy Futures in Education*. Subsequent responses to it (Cole, 2004c, 2005c) also appeared in *Policy Futures in Education*, as did Smith's reply (Smith, 2004). Smith (2003) has provided a trenchant critique of US imperialism, to which I return in Chapter 8.

5 It was Sigmund Freud (1991 [1914]) who postulated an early stage of primal narcissism. During this time an infant is preoccupied with itself and with its own pleasure, while being oblivious of the needs of others.

6 The analysis in this section of the chapter owes much to a discussion with Glenn Rikowski.

7 I would like to make a couple of personal points here with respect to my own involvement in analectical interaction. I must point out that I, for one, have a great respect for, and have learnt much from aboriginal peoples. Indeed, for me, one of the ways in which the living project of Marxism needs to grow is to accept spirituality, as opposed to *organised religion*, as an important component of the human condition. Having lived for a year in Canada, and also for a year in Australia, I have spent long periods in informal conversation with friends, who are members of indigenous communities. I have also engaged in more formal conversation with Australian Aboriginals (e.g. Cole, 1986a; Cole and Waters, 1987) and Native Canadians (e.g. Cole, 1988b). In Cole, 1988b (p. 9), I describe the work of 100 Native Canadian Women in establishing 'a worker-owned co-operative run in harmony with traditional beliefs' (this was an interview but, to my disgust, the magazine decided to publish it as an article, with the name of the Native Canadian woman I interviewed obliterated – a fact that will not surprise transmodernists). Marxists support all progressive reforms in capitalist societies, this 'worker-owned co-operative' being one example, with a view to a longer-term project of transformation to democratic socialism.

8 An important caveat to note here is that Dussel (2004) has argued, following Bartolomé de Las Casas, that violence against the oppressor can be justified. Thus, just as for Las Casas, armed struggle against the Spanish conquistadors was eternally justified so, for Dussel, such a struggle was and is justified in other historical periods. Dussel gives the example of George Washington in Boston in 1776, Che Guevara in Cuba in 1959 and, currently, the Hamas in Palestine and the Iraqi people against the invaders of their country.

9 To take just one example: in the Bolivarian Republic of Venezuela, under the leadership of President Hugo Chávez, the government is committed to 'economic, political, social and cultural transformation towards a "Socialism of the 21st Century"' (Muhr and Verger, 2006, p. 1; see also Cole, 2007b). With respect to HE, for example, where policy is firmly embedded in other socialist projects, such as land and income redistribution, free health and state-subsidised food (ibid., p. 12), the government has introduced *Municipalización*, a distinct, two-dimensional form of decentralisation, concerned with the democratisation of HE as it geographically de-concentrates the traditional university infrastructure and takes the university to where the people are, including factories and prisons (ibid., p. 8). Students are encouraged to 'learn through doing' and to 'support their neighbourhood in resolving real community problems'. In this way the university is at the service of the people, rather than being an elite institution divorced from society (ibid., p. 9).

10 The rest of this chapter draws on and develops Cole, 2005c, pp. 93–97.

11 Unlike Marxism, which is based on notions of 'conflict' and class struggle, Smith's solution, like Dussel's, is based on 'consensus', and, as such, is essentially liberal pluralist.

12 The *Sun*, a right-wing tabloid owned by the Murdoch Corporation, is Britain's most popular newspaper (average daily circulation over 3,000,000 copies). Tony Benn (Benn, 2006) has described the power of the Murdoch Empire as 'murdochracy'.

13 It should be noted that Labour was actually in power until 1979, but, as Hill (2001c, p. 14) points out, 'after Callaghan's Ruskin College speech, it changed its education policies'. In fact, in signalling the need to align schooling closely to the needs of industry, Callaghan's intervention went beyond the sphere of education and sowed the seeds of 'New Labour', with its essentially neo-liberal agenda (see Chapter 7).

14 Smith's use of brackets here indicates that he thinks the points he makes could also apply to Marxism per se.

15 At first sight, there would seem to be a contradiction here, in Dussel's notion of 'ancient cultures remaining intact' and 'creation *ex nihilo*'. Dussel seems to be arguing both for 'starting from nothing' *and* rebuilding from 'excluded aspects of cultures'. I think that what he means is that we need first to transform the capitalist state, and then to rebuild post-capitalist transmodernity after this, according to indigenous values. Dussel's position is that the must be 'transformed' rather than 'reformed' (personal correspondence).

16 This is not to say that we cannot *imagine* what a future socialist society might be like (see Chapter 5, notes 7 and 8).

17 The WTO is one of the most untransparent and undemocratic global institutions (Sardar and Davies, 2002, p. 72, cited in Beckmann and Cooper, 2004, p. 2), largely due to the tendency for decisions to be made in mini-ministerial gatherings of a select group of rich OECD (Organisation for Economic Cooperation and Development) member countries, which are dominated by the US and the European Union (Rady, 2002, cited in Beckmann and Cooper, 2004, p. 2; see also Cole, 2007a).

18 A theo-con is a conservative who believes that religion should play a major role in forming public policy. Both the term and the phenomenon are closely tied to the US Christian Right. This term first appeared in 1996 in an article by Jacob Heilbrunn in The New Republic, entitled, 'Neocon v. Theocon'. He wrote:

> The neoconservatives believe that America is special because it was founded on an idea – a commitment to the rights of man embodied in the Declaration of Independence – not in ethnic or religious affiliations. The *theocons*, too, argue that America is rooted in an idea, but they believe that idea is Christianity.
>
> (http://en.wikipedia.org/wiki/Theo-con)

19 Smith, 2004, p. 645, has denied that he is a 'romantic moralist', and accuses Marxism of 'arrrogance', which relates to 'the refusal of the European mind to entertain any form of logic outside of its own operating paradigm really seriously'. I have argued against this notion of Marxism being Eurocentric earlier in this chapter.

20 This is not to advocate or to condone violence. As we saw in Chapter 2, note 7, Engels was concerned to *avoid a violent and bloody* revolution (see also the discussion in Chapter 10, p. 133).

7 Globalisation, neo-liberalism and environmental destruction

1 The first part of this chapter draws on Cole, 2005d.

2 E-numbers are classified as follows: E100-E199 (colours); E200-E299 (preservatives); E300-E399 (antioxidants, acidity regulators); E400-E499 (thickeners, stabilisers, emulsifiers); E500-E599 (acidity regulators, anti-caking agents); E600-E699 (flavour enhancers); E900-E999 (miscellaneous); E1000-E1999 (additional chemicals) (E-number, 2006).

3 My indebtedness in the following section of the chapter to Feldman and Lotz's book *A World to Win* is self-evident. For updates to their and others' work on socialist ecology, see the website www.aworldtowin.net.

4 Hurricane Katrina brought a number of the horrors of racialised capitalism *in the US* to the forefront of the world's attention (for an analysis see, for example, Cole, 2006b).

5 A worrying, equally unsustainable, response to the threat posed by fossil fuels came from the Blair government, in its suggestion to build a new generation of nuclear power stations. While, nuclear power does not emit large amounts of carbon dioxide, there are a number of dangers in this proposal. George Monbiot (2006, p. 25) has prioritised three. First, to start building a new generation of nuclear power stations before it is known what to do with the waste produced by existing plants is grotesquely irresponsible (the government's advisors have determined only that it will be buried). Second, the world will never be rid of nuclear weapons, if it is not also rid of nuclear power. Every state that has sought to develop a nuclear weapons programme over the last 30 years has done it by manipulating its nuclear power programme. Third, renewed nuclear power programmes are not needed, since, were similar levels of the proposed investment in nuclear power relocated to investment in energy efficiency and carbon capture and storage, along with the use of the vast new offshore wind resources, which the Blair government identified, carbon dioxide emissions could be cut just as quickly and effectively. While truly sustainable development may not be possible in the global neo-liberal economic world system, this is not to say that we should not *press* for change in the here and now. On the contrary, Marxists fight constantly for change and reform which benefits the working class in the short-run under capitalism with a vision of socialist transformation in the longer term (see Chapter 10, pp. 134–135 for a discussion). For suggestions from Marxists as to what can be done to challenge environmental degradation and destruction now in the context of neo-liberal global capitalism and imperialism see, for example, Kinnear and Barlow, 2005; Ward, 2005–2006, 2006; International Socialist Group, 2006; Respect, undated). As a longer-term vision, Marxists look to a direct and conscious relationship with nature, to products planned for need, rather than commodity production for profit. Marxists need to learn from the environmental destruction associated with both capitalism and Stalinism. In short, Marxism entails the creation of a socialist world, with collective stewardship of natural resources and the creation of social products, rather than the madness associated with the ongoing relentless privatisation for profit of the natural resources of our world.

6 Classism refers to discrimination on the grounds of class. Marxists oppose classism, as they do all the other exploitative and discriminatory 'isms' (see Cole, 2005b, pp. 13–16). However, they do not believe that class equality is possible under capitalism, since capitalism's fundamental feature is the exploitation of one class by another (see Chapter 2).

8 The New Imperialism: postmodern, transmodern and Marxist perspectives

1 This chapter draws on and develops Cole, 2004d and Cole, 2004c (see also Cole 2005e). I am aware that many postmodernists and poststructuralists, including the educational postmodernists critiqued in Chapter 5, would totally reject the following arguments. Perhaps it is in the nature of postmodernism that widely differing views can be contained within one school of thought.

2 It seems that John Howard is pursuing the same policy in the South Pacific, sometimes with troops, sometimes without (Pilger, 2004, pp. 13–14; see also Skeers, 2006).

3 Miles is perhaps the foremost British Marxist analyst of 'race', racialisation and racism. Hence I will sustain his arguments to critical appraisal in this chapter and the next. See also the Appendix in this volume.

4 As Hill (2001c, p. 8) has pointed out, the influence of ideology can be overwhelming. He cites Terry Eagleton (1991, p. xiii) who has written: 'what persuades men and women to mistake each other form time to time for gods or vermin is ideology'. This observation is particularly applicable to the concept of racialisation.

5 In adopting Miles' definition of racialisation, I should make it clear that there are a

number of non-Marxist applications of the concept of racialisation. Indeed, the concept is a contested term, which is widely used and differently interpreted (for an analysis, see Murji and Solomos, 2005).

6 I use the nomenclature, 'people of color' (including the US spelling of 'color') when referring to the US, since that is the preferred nomenclature in that country. Nomenclature varies historical and geographically. In the contemporary British context, following Cole, 1993 and Cole and Stuart, 2005, I prefer the nomenclature, 'Asian, black and other minority ethnic' to the more common nomenclature, 'black and ethnic minority'. There are four reasons for this. First, the term 'black' once popular as an all-encompassing nomenclature had ceased to have that purchase from the late 1980s onwards: hence the need for the wider formulation. Second, with respect to this nomenclature, the omission of the word 'other' between 'and' and 'ethnic minority' implies that only 'ethnic minorities' (people of Cypriot and Irish origin, for example) are minority constituencies whereas black people are not. This is, of course, not accurate. Third, the use of the term, 'ethnic minority' has, in practice, meant that members of the dominant majority group are not referred to in terms of their ethnicity, with the implication that they do not have ethnicity (the sequencing of 'minority' before 'ethnic' does not carry this implication, since, the creation of a new formulation, together with the prioritising of the former over the latter, facilitates the conceptualisation of a *majority* ethnic group too). Fourth, 'black and ethnic minority' has the effect of excluding people of Asian and other origins who do not consider themselves 'black'. The fact that people of Asian origin form the majority of 'non-white' minority ethnic women and men is masked (Cole, 1993, pp. 672–673). Ideally, I believe in 'ethnic' self-definition. I recognise that there can be differences in preferred nomenclature among 'ethnic groups' in opposing certain usages of terms and in defending others (for my views on 'ethnicity', see Cole, 2003b). Satnam Virdee (e.g. forthcoming, 2008), has adopted the nomenclature 'racialized minority' as an all-encompassing term. This has the merit of being generally ahistorically applicable, and not confined to a given historical period. 'Asian, black and other minority ethnic' has the advantage of historic specificity, although this may well need adapting in the light of burgeoning xenoracism and xenoracialisation (see Chapter 9, pp. 124–126). In a very real sense, 'Asian, black and other minority ethnic' and 'people of color' are themselves racialised categories, albeit attempts at *positive* descriptors (my concern in this book is primarily with negative racialisation). Thus Virdee's preferred nomenclature does have an additional merit in avoiding nomenclature that is *itself* racialised. I am aware, of course, that nomenclatures change and I am not attempting to make a definitive statement. If readers can improve on it, this is of course to be welcomed. I would particularly welcome the comments on nomenclature from members of racialised groups.

7 In reality, as Avery Gordon (2006) has revealed, the torture and sadistic treatment of prisoners in imperial prisons reflect accepted civilian norms in the US prison-industrial complex in the US itself.

9 Critical Race Theory and racialisation: a case study of contemporary racist Britain

1 Gillborn (2006a, p. 20) has provided the following conceptual map of CRT:

Critical Race Theory: a conceptual map

Defining elements

• racism as endemic … 'normal' not aberrant nor rare: deeply ingrained legally and culturally;
• crosses epistemological boundaries;

- critique of civil rights laws as fundamentally limited;
- critique of liberalism: claims of neutrality, objectivity, colour-blindness, and meritocracy as camouflages;
- call to context: challenges ahistoricism and recognizes experiential knowledge of people of colour.

Conceptual tools

- story-telling and counter-stories;
- interest convergence;
- critical white studies.

The following critique of Gillborn should be read as comradely criticism and *esprit de corps*, in the pursuit of our common goal of understanding, undermining and ultimately ridding the world of the multiple inequities of racism. For a further development of my Marxist critique of CRT, see Cole, forthcoming, 2008.

2 I need to point out that Gillborn has since described labelling Ignatiev and *Race Traitor* as such as a temporary lapse of judgement (personal email correspondence), something which happens to all of us when we are meeting deadlines. However, I felt that, since Gillborn's description is in print, it needs to be commented on.

3 This was underscored recently in a discussion in a café with a Marxist friend who, when I mentioned the organisation *Race Traitor*, told me 'hush' in case we were misunderstood!

4 Cognisance of racialisation will ensure that the CRT concept of *voice* does not drift into postmodern *multivocality* (multiple voices) where everyone's opinion has equal worth. For a Marxist critique of multivocality, see Cole and Hill, 2002; for a Marxist critique of postmodernism, in general, see Chapters 4 and 5; see also, for example, Hill *et al.*, 2002a.

5 In Marxist theory, the capitalist state is more than mere government, and includes a range of institutions, including the hierarchy of the police, of the armed forces, the courts and so on (see Chapter 3 pp. 30–31 for a discussion of repressive (and ideological) state apparatuses; see also Cole, 2007b).

6 The rest of the chapter is informed by ongoing work and discussions with Alpesh Maisuria. His input is particularly apparent in the section on 'Islamophobia'.

7 Steve Fenton (2003, p. 164) has described making a distinction between the (ethnic) majority, an almost unspoken 'us', and members of minority ethnic communities as 'ethnic majoritarian thinking'. It is perhaps epitomised in the (1981) Rampton Report, *West Indian Children in Our Schools*. The distinction is underlined by the fact, for example, that British Muslims have to substantiate their allegiance to Britain. After the Forest Gate terror raid (discussed below), the media highlighted the fact that the Muslim brothers stated that they were 'born and bred' East Londoners and they 'loved Britain' (Getty, 2006, p. 5).

8 Abdulkayar worked as a supervisor in Tesco. Tony Blair's sanctioning of the police raid and shooting in Forest Gate, even after the men were released, would have been inconceivable if the person shot had been a white suburban Christian Tesco supervisor. Indeed, the raid would not have happened in the first place. Despite this, one of the delegates to the Glasgow workshop (see Appendix 1 for some observations on this workshop) expressed doubts that the police actions were racist.

9 In many ways, the racialisation of the Muslim communities of Britain, which involves pathologising and scapegoating is similar to the way in which 'black youth' were racialised in the 1970s and 1980s (e.g. Hall *et al.*, 1978; Cole, 1986b, pp. 128–133). Madeleine Bunting (2004, p. 15) has argued that it is crucial that socialists make allies with Muslims as a show of collective solidarity, particularly at a time when there is a debate about interpretations of Islam.

10 Common objections to Marxism and a Marxist response

1 Here, we have an ironic twist: the capitalist class and their representatives who used to deride Marxists for what they saw as the metaphysic of 'Marxist economic determinism', for what they (wrongly) perceived was a belief in the inevitability of social revolution, are the ones who now champion the *inevitability* of global neo-liberalism, the accompanying 'world-wide market revolution' and the consequent *inevitability* of 'economic restructuring' (McMurtry, 2000).
2 At the same time, globalisation, in reality in existence since the beginnings of capitalism, is hailed as a new and unchallengeable phenomenon, and its omnipresence used ideologically to further fuel arguments about capitalism's inevitability. As we saw, in Blair's words, challenging globalisation is tantamount to denying that autumn follows summer.

Appendix: Robert Miles and the concept of racism

1 An exception was the suggestion of one contributor that we should use 'Englishness' rather than racism. His argument was that 'Englishness' helps to explain the contemporaneous incorporation of previously racialised groups. My response would be that the connection between 'racism' and 'nationalism' implicit in 'Englishness' may be particularly close in the English context. Miles has, in fact, argued that while it cannot be argued that there is a necessary relation between 'race' and 'nation', such articulation is particularly strong in the case of England (Miles, 1989, pp. 89–90). As he puts it, 'English nationalism is particularly dependent on and constructed by an idea of "race", with the result that English nationalism encapsulates racism' and that 'the ideas of "race" and "nation", as in a kaleidoscope merge into one another in varying patterns, each simultaneously highlighting and obscuring the other' (Miles, 1989). Thus while the concept of 'Englishness' may explain a form of *racism* (exluding Others not considered to be 'English') at a specific juncture, for example, what *may* be occurring, in certain contexts, in England in 2006, 'racism' is a more useful *general* term to describe discourse, actions, processes and practices, both historically and contemporaneously.

References

Agencies (2006) 'Muslim Anger Builds over Pope's Speech', *Guardian*, 15 September. Online. Available at: www.guardian.co.uk/pope/story/0,,1873167,00.html (accessed 15 September 2006).

Ahmed, T. (2006) 'Why Islam is the New Marx', *The Australian*, 11 August, p. 14.

Allman, P. (1999) *Revolutionary Social Transformation: Democratic Hopes, Political Possibilities and Critical Education*, Westport: Bergin and Garvey.

Allman, P. (2001) 'Foreword', in M. Cole, D. Hill, G. Rikowski and P. McLaren, *Red Chalk: On Schooling, Capitalism and Politics*, Brighton: Institute for Educational Policy Studies.

Althusser, L. (1969) *For Marx*, New York: Random House.

Althusser, L. (1971) 'Ideology and Ideological State Apparatuses', in *Lenin and Philosophy and Other Essays*, London: New Left Books. Online. Available at: www.marx2mao.com/Other/LPOE70ii.html#s5 (accessed 27 July 2006).

Anderson, P. (1998) *The Origins of Postmodernity*, London: Verso.

Ansley, F.L. (1997) '"White Supremacy" (and what should we do about it)', in R. Delgado and J. Stefancic (eds) *Critical White Studies: Looking Behind the Mirror*, Philadelphia: Temple University Press.

Antonio, R.J. (1998) 'Mapping Postmodern Social Theory', in A. Sica (ed.) *What is Social Theory?: The Philosophical Debates*, Malden and Oxford: Blackwell.

Apple, M.W. (1979) *Ideology and Curriculum*, New York and London: Routledge.

Apple, M.W. (1982) *Education and Power*, Boston: Ark Paperbacks.

Atkinson, E. (2001) 'A Response to Mike Cole's "Educational Postmodernism, Social Justice and Social Change: An Incompatible Ménage-à-trois"', *The School Field*, 12 (1/2), pp. 87–94.

Atkinson, E. (2002) 'The Responsible Anarchist: Postmodernism and Social Change', *British Journal of Sociology of Education*, 23 (1) pp. 73–87.

Atkinson, E. (2003) 'Education, Postmodernism and the Organisation of Consent', in J. Satterthwaite, E. Atkinson and K. Gale (eds) *Discourse, Power, Resistance: Challenging the Rhetoric of Contemporary Education*, Stoke on Trent: Trentham Books.

Atkinson, E. and Cole, M. (2007) 'Indecision, Social Justice and Social Change: A Dialogue on Marxism, Postmodernism and Education', in A. Green, G. Rikowski and H. Raduntz (eds) *Renewing Dialogues in Marxism and Education: Volume 1 – Openings*, Basingstoke: Palgrave Macmillan.

Austin, S. (2005) 'Faith Hate Crimes Up 600% After Bombings', *Metro*, 3 August 2005.

Austin, S. (2006) '9/11 Cinema Goer is Mistaken for Terrorist', *Metro*, 9 June 2006.

Babb, P., Butcher, H., Church, J., Zealey, L. (2006) *Social Trends 36*, London: HMSO. Online. Available at: www.statistics.gov.uk/StatBase/Product.asp?vlnk=13675 (accessed 2 September 2006).

Baker, P. (1995) *Destruction and the Ethical Turn*, Gainesville: University Press of Florida.

Barber, M. (1998) *Ethical Hermeneutics: Rationalism in Enrique Dussel's Philosophy of Liberation*, New York: Fordham University Press.

Barkham, P. (2006) 'Suspect Arrested After Asian Shops Firebombed', *Guardian*, 3 May 2006.

Barret-Brown, M. (1976) *The Economics of Imperialism*, Harmondsworth: Penguin.

Bartolovich, C. (2002) 'Introduction', in C. Bartolovich and N. Lazarus (eds) *Marxism, Modernity and Postcolonial Studies*, Cambridge: Cambridge University Press.

Baudrillard, J. (1968) *Le Système des Objets*, Paris: Denoël-Gonthier.

Baudrillard, J. (1970) *La Société de Consummation*, Paris: Gallimard.

Baudrillard, J. (1972) *Le Miroir de la Production.* Paris: Casterman.

Baudrillard, J. (1981) *For a Critique of the Political Economy of the Sign*, New York: Telos Press.

Baxter, J. (2002a) 'A Juggling Act: A Feminist Post-Structuralist Analysis of Girls' and Boys' Talk in the Secondary Classroom', *Gender and Education*, 14 (1), pp. 5–19.

Baxter, J. (2002b) 'Jokers in the Pack: Why Boys are More Adept than Girls at Speaking in Public', *Language & Education*, 16 (2), pp. 81–96.

Baxter, J. (2002c) 'Competing Discourses in the Classroom: A Post-structuralist Analysis of Girls' and Boys' Speech in Public Contexts', *Discourse & Society*, 13 (6), pp. 827–842.

Baxter, J. (2002d) 'Is PDA Really an Alternative? A Reply to West', *Discourse & Society*, 13 (6), pp. 853–859.

Baxter, J. (2003) *Positioning Discourse in Gender: A Feminist Methodology*, Basingstoke: Palgrave, Macmillan.

Baxter, J. (2004) 'Analysing Spoken Language in the Classroom', in A. Goodwyn and A. Stables (eds) *Language and Literacy*, London: Sage.

Baxter, J. (2005) 'Putting Gender in its Place: Constructing Speaker Identities in Management Meetings', in M. Barrett and M.J. Davidson (eds) *Gender and Communications at Work*, Aldershot: Ashgate Publishing Ltd.

Baxter, J. (2006a) ' "Do We Have to Agree with Her?" How High School Girls Negotiate Leadership in Public Contexts', in J. Baxter (ed.) *Speaking Out: the Female Voice in Public Contexts*, Basingstoke: Palgrave Macmillan.

Baxter, J. (ed.) (2006b) *Speaking Out: The Female Voice in Public Contexts*, Palgrave: Macmillan.

Baxter, J. (2007a) 'Post-Structuralist Analysis of Classroom Discourse', in M. Martin-Jones and A.M. de Mejia *Encyclopedia of Language and Education*, Vol. 3, New York: Springer.

Baxter, J. (2007b) 'Feminist Post-Structuralist Discourse Analysis: A new Theoretical and Methodological Approach?', in J. Sunderland *et al. Theorectical and Methodological Approaches to Gender and Language Study*, Basingstoke: Palgrave.

BBC (2004) 'Chaos and Violence at Abu Ghraib'. Online. Available at: http://news.bbc.co.uk/1/hi/world/americas/3690097.stm (accessed 17 September 2006).

BBC (2006a) On this Day 20 July, 1957. Online. Available at: http://news.bbc.co.uk/onthisday/low/dates/stories/july/20/newsid_3728000/3728225.stm (accessed 15 July 2006).

BBC (2006b) 'Guantanmo Actors Held at Airport'. Online. Available at: http://news.bbc.co.uk/1/hi/entertainment/4736404.stm (accessed 22 June 2006).

BBC News (2005a) 'Three Suffer Unprovoked Beating' (news.bbc.co.uk/1/hi/england/dorset/4713593.stm: accessed 24 July 2006).

BBC News (2005b) 'Polish Student Assaulted by Gang' (news.bbc.co.uk/1/hi/england/tees/4710011.stm: accessed 24 July 2006).

Beckmann, A. and Cooper, C. (2004) 'Globalisation, the New Managerialism and Education: Rethinking the Purpose of Education in Britain', *Journal of Critical Education Policy Studies*, 2 (1). Online. Available at: www.jceps.com/print.php?articleID=31 (accessed 29 March 2005).

Begg, M. and Brittain, V. (2006) *Enemy Combatant: A British Muslim's Journey to Guantanamo and Back*, London: Free Press.

Belfast Today (2006) 'Polish Man Hurt in Vicious Attack' (www.belfasttoday.net/ViewArticle2.aspx?SectionID=3425&ArticleID=1532979: accessed 24 July 2006).

Benn, C. and Chitty, C. (1996) *Thirty Years On: Is Comprehensive Education Alive and Well or Struggling to Survive?* London: David Fulton.

Benn, T. (1996) *The Benn Diaries 1940–1990*, London: Arrow Books.

Benn, T. (2006) 'Speech to *Marxism 2006*', 9 July.

Bennetto, J. (2006) 'Hindus Caught in Backlash After July 7 Terror Attacks', *Independent*, news.independentco.uk/uk/crime/article336392.ece 4 January 2006.

Benton, T. (ed.) (1996) *The Greening of Marxism*, New York: Guilford Press.

Berki, R.N. (1975) *Socialism*, Letchworth: Aldine Press.

Beveridge, W. (1942) *Social Insurance and Allied Services (The Beveridge Report)*, London: HMSO.

Bhaerman, S. (2006) 'Unanswered Questions: Nonconspiracy Theorist David Ray Griffin Takes Aim at the Official 9–11 Story', 14–20 June. Online. Available at: bohemian.com/bohemian/06.14.06/david-ray-griffin-0624.html (accessed 18 September 2006).

Bottomore, T. and Rubel, M. (1978) *Selected Writings in Sociology and Philosophy*, Harmondsworth: Penguin Books.

Boulangé, A. (2004) 'The Hijab, Racism and the State', *International Socialism*, no. 102, Spring, pp. 3–26.

Bowles, S. and Gintis, H. (1976) *Schooling in Capitalist America: Educational Reform and the Contradictions of Economic Life*, London: Routledge and Kegan Paul.

Brown, G. (2006) 'The Future of Britishness', The Fabian Society, 14 January 2006.

Bunting, M. (2004) 'Look Past the Hijab', *Guardian*, 10 May, p. 15.

Burgis, T (2006) 'We are Staring Up at a Mountain Shrouded in Who-Knows-What', *Big Issue* May 2006 No 691.

Butler, J. (1990) *Gender Trouble: Gender and the Subversion of Identity*, London: Routledge.

Callinicos, A. (1976) *Althusser's Marxism*, Pluto: London.

Callinicos, A. (1989) 'Introduction', in A. Callinicos (ed.) (1989) *Marxist Theory*, Oxford: Oxford University Press.

Callinicos, A. (2000) *Equality*, Oxford: Polity.

Callinicos, A. (2003) *Social Theory: A Historical Introduction*, Cambridge: Polity.

Callinicos, A. (2006) 'Immigration and the US Ruling Class', *Socialist Worker*, 15 April.

Camara, B. (2002) 'Ideologies of Race and Racism', in P. Zarembka (ed.) *Confronting 9–11, Ideologies of Race, and Eminent Economists*, Oxford: Elsevier Science.

Campbell, D. and Goldenberg, S. (2004) 'Afghan Detainees Routinely Tortured and Humiliated by US Troops', *Guardian Unlimited*. Online. Available at: www.guardian.co.uk/afghanistan/story/0,1284,1245236,00.html (accessed 7 August 2006).

Carlin, B. and Hope, C. (2005) 'Modernise or Die, Blair and Brown Warn the Unions'.

Online. Available at: www.telegraph.co.uk/news/main.jhtml?xml=/news/2005/09/14/ntuc14.xml (accessed 2 September 2006).

Carnoy, M. and Levin, H. (1985) *Schooling and Work in the Democratic State*, Stanford: Stanford University Press.

Cassidy, S. (2006) '"Compost effect" may Cause Global Warming to Reach Crisis Point in 2050', the *Independent*, 1 September, p. 5.

Central Intelligence Agency (CIA) (2006) DCI Counterterrorist Centre, 9 June 2006. Online. Available at: www.cia.gov/terrorism/ctc.html (accessed 22 June 2006).

Chatrabarty, N. and Preston, J. (2006) 'Posturing Fear in a World of Performed Evil: Terrorists, Teachers and Evil Neo-Liberals', Paper presented at the Institute of Education, University of London, 30 June 2006.

Chancellor, V. (1970) *History for their Masters*, Bath: Adams and Dart.

Chomsky, N. (2001) 'The New War Against Terror. The Technology and Culture Forum at MITT'. Online. Available at: www.counterpunch.org/chomskyterror.html (accessed 8 August 2006).

Cliff, T. (1974) *State Capitalism in Russia.* Online. Available at: www.marxists.org/archive/cliff/works/1955/statecap/index.htm (accessed 8 August 2006).

Coben, D. (2002) 'Metaphors for an Educative Politics: "Common Sense," "Good Sense" and Educating Adults', in C. Borg, J. Buttigieg and P. Mayo (eds) *Gramsci and Education*, Lanham: Rowman & Littlefield.

Cohen, G.A. (1983) 'Review of A.W. Wood', *Karl Marx, Mind*, 92, p. 444.

Cohen, S. (1985) 'Anti-Semitism, Immigration Controls and the Welfare State', *Critical Social Policy*, 13, Summer.

Cole, G.D.H. (1971) *A History of Socialist Thought, Volume 1: the Forerunners, 1789–1850*, London and Basingstoke: The Macmillan Press.

Cole, M. (1983) 'Contradictions in the Educational Theory of Gintis and Bowles', *The Sociological Review*, 31 (3), pp. 471–488 (this is republished as Chapter 3 in M. Cole (ed.) *Bowles and Gintis Revisited: Correspondence and Contradiction in Educational Theory*, London: The Falmer Press).

Cole, M. (1986a) 'The Aboriginal Struggle: An Interview with Helen Boyle', *Race and Class*, XXXVII (4), pp. 21–33.

Cole, M. (1986b) 'Teaching and Learning about Racism: A Critique of Multicultural Education in Britain', in S. Modgil, G. Verma, K. Mallick and C. Modgil (eds) *Multicultural Education: the Interminable Debate*, Lewes: The Falmer Press.

Cole, M. (ed.) (1988) *Bowles and Gintis Revisited: Correspondence and Contradiction in Educational Theory*, London: The Falmer Press.

Cole, M. (1988a) 'Correspondence Theory in Education: Impact, Critique and Evaluation', in M. Cole (ed.) *Bowles and Gintis Revisited: Correspondence and Contradiction in Educational Theory*, London: The Falmer Press.

Cole, M. (1988b) 'As Long as the Sun Rises', *Interlink*, 5 February/March, p. 9.

Cole, M. (1992) *Racism, History and Educational Policy: From the Origins of the Welfare State to the Rise of the Radical Right.* Unpublished PhD thesis, University of Essex.

Cole, M. (1993) '"Black and Ethnic Minority" or "Asian, Black and Other Minority Ethnic": A Further Note on Nomenclature', *Sociology*, 27, pp. 671–673.

Cole, M. (1995) 'Don's Diary', *The Times Higher Education Supplement*, 7 July, p. 16.

Cole, M. (1998) 'Globalisation, Modernisation and Competitiveness: A Critique of the New Labour Project in Education', *International Studies in Sociology of Education*, 8 (3), pp. 315–332.

Cole, M. (2001) 'Educational Postmodernism, Social Justice and Social Change: An Incompatible Ménage-à-trois', *The School Field*, 12 (1/2), pp. 69–85.

Cole, M. (2003a) 'Might It Be in the Practice that It Fails to Succeed? A Marxist Critique of Claims for Postmodernism and Poststructuralism as Forces for Social Change and Social Justice', *British Journal of Sociology of Education*, 24 (4), pp. 487–500.

Cole, M. (2003b) 'Ethnicity, "Status Groups" and Racialization: A Contribution to the Debate on National Identity in Britain', *Ethnic and Racial Studies*, 26 (5), pp. 962–969.

Cole, M. (2004a) 'Rethinking the Future: the Commodification of Knowledge and the Grammar of Resistance', in M. Benn and C. Chitty (eds) *A Tribute to Caroline Benn: Education and Democracy*, London: Continuum.

Cole, M. (2004b) 'Fun, Amusing, Full of Insights, but Ultimately a Reflection of Anxious Times: a Critique of Postmodernism as a Force for Resistance, Social Change and Social Justice', in E. Atkinson, W. Martin and J. Satterthwaite (eds) *Educational Counter-Cultures: Confrontations, Images, Vision*, Stoke-on-Trent: Trentham Books.

Cole, M. (2004c) 'US Imperialism, Transmodernism and Education: a Marxist Critique', *Policy Futures in Education*, 2 (3 and 4), pp. 633–643. Online. Available at: www.wwwords.co.uk/pfie/content/pdfs/2/issue2_3.asp#15 (accessed 8 August 2006).

Cole, M. (2004d) ' "Rule Britannia" and the New American Empire: a Marxist Analysis of the Teaching of Imperialism, Actual and Potential, in the British School Curriculum', *Policy Futures in Education*, 2 (3 and 4), pp. 523–538. Online. Available at: www.wwwords.co.uk/pfie/content/pdfs/2/issue2_3.asp#7 (accessed 8 August 2006).

Cole, M. (2004e) ' "Brutal and Stinking" and "Difficult to Handle": the Historical and Contemporary Manifestations of Racialization, Institutional Racism, and Schooling in Britain', *Race, Ethnicity and Education*, 7 (1), pp. 35–56.

Cole, M. (2004f) F*** You – Human Sewage: Contemporary Global Capitalism and the Xeno-racialization of Asylum Seekers, *Contemporary Politics*, 10 (2), pp. 159–165.

Cole, M. (2005a) 'The "Inevitability of Globalized Capital" vs. the "Ordeal of the Undecidable": a Marxist Critique', in M. Pruyn (ed.) *Teaching Peter McLaren: Paths of Dissent*, New York: Peter Lang Publishing.

Cole, M. (2005b) 'Introductory Chapter: Education and Equality – Some Conceptual and Practical Issues', in M. Cole (ed.) *Professional Values and Practice: Meeting the Standards*, 3rd Edition, London: David Fulton.

Cole, M. (2005c) 'Transmodernism, Marxism and Social Change: Some Implications for Teacher Education', *Policy Futures in Education*, 3 (1), pp. 90–105. Online. Available at: www.wwwords.co.uk/pfie/content/pdfs/3/issue3_1.asp#9 (accessed 8 August 2006).

Cole, M. (2005d) 'New Labour, Globalization, and Social Justice: The Role of Education', in G. Fischman, P. McLaren and H. Sünker (eds) *Critical Theories, Radical Pedagogies and Global Conflicts*, Lanham: Rowman and Littlefield.

Cole, M. (2005e) 'Empires Old and New: a Marxist Analysis of the Teaching of Imperialism, Actual and Potential, in the British School Curriculum', in J. Satterthwaite and E. Atkinson (eds) *Discourses of Education in the New Imperialism*, Stoke-on-Trent: Trentham Books.

Cole, M. (ed.) (2006) *Education, Equality and Human Rights: Issues of Gender, 'Race', Sexuality, Disability and Social Class*, 2nd Edition, London: Routledge.

Cole, M. (2006a) 'UCU sell-out', *Post-16 Educator*, 13, July–August.

Cole, M. (2006b) ' "Looters and Thugs and Inert Women Doing Nothing": Racialized Communities in Capitalist America and the Role of Higher Education', *Journal for Critical Education Policy Studies*, 4 (1).

Cole, M. (2006c) 'The Eclipse of the Non-European: Historical and Current Manifestations of Racialization in the US', *Ethnic and Racial Studies*, 29 (1), pp. 173–185.

Cole, M. (2007a) 'Neo-liberalism and Education: a Marxist Critique of New Labour's Five
Year Strategy for Education', in A. Green, G. Rikowski and H. Raduntz (eds) *Renewing
Dialogues in Marxism and Education: Volume 1 – Openings*, Basingstoke: Palgrave
Macmillan.

Cole, M. (2007b) 'The State Apparatuses and the Working Class: Experiences from the
UK; Educational Lessons from Venezuela', keynote address to the BESA Annual
Conference, Bath Spa University.

Cole, M. (forthcoming, 2008) 'Critical Race Theory Comes to the UK: a Marxist
Response', *Ethnicities*.

Cole, M. and Blair, M. (2006) 'Racism and Education: from Empire to New Labour', in
M. Cole (ed.) *Education, Equality and Human Rights: Issues of Gender, 'Race', Sexuality, Disability and Social Class*, 2nd Edition, London: Routledge.

Cole, M. and Hill, D. (1995) 'Games of Despair and Rhetorics of Resistance: Postmodernism, Education and Reaction', *British Journal of Sociology of Education*, 16,
(2), pp. 165–218.

Cole, M. and Hill, D. (1999a) 'Into the Hands of Capital: The Deluge of Postmodernism
and the Delusions of Resistance Postmodernism', in D. Hill, P. McLaren, M. Cole and
G. Rikowski (eds) *Postmodernism in Educational Theory: Education and the Politics
of Human Resistance*, London: The Tufnell Press.

Cole, M. and Hill, D. (1999b) 'Ex-left Academics and the Curse of the Postmodern',
Education and Social Justice, 3 (1), pp. 28–30.

Cole, M. and Hill, D. (2002) 'Resistance Postmodernism: – Progressive Politics or Rhetorical Left Posturing', in D. Hill, P. McLaren, M. Cole and G. Rikowski (eds)
Marxism Against Postmodernism in Educational Theory, Lanham: Lexington Books.

Cole, M. and Skelton, B. (eds) (1980) *Blind Alley: Youth in a Crisis of Capital*, Orm-
skirk: Hesketh.

Cole, M. and Stuart, J.S. (2005) '"Do you Ride on Elephants" and "Never Tell them
you're German": the Experiences of British Asian and Black, and Overseas Student
Teachers in South-east England', *British Educational Research Journal*.

Cole, M. and Virdee, S. (2006) 'Racism and Resistance: from Empire to New Labour', in
M. Cole (ed.) *Education, Equality and Human Rights: Issues of Gender, 'Race', Sexuality, Disability and Social Class*, 2nd Edition, London: Routledge.

Cole, M. and Waters, H. (1987) 'Two Hundred Years – Who's Celebrating?', *New Mari-
times*, October, p. 16.

Cole, M., Hill, D. and Rikowski, G. (1997) 'Between Postmodernism and Nowhere: the
Predicament of the Postmodernist', *British Journal of Educational Studies*, 45 (2),
pp. 187–200.

Cole, M., Hill, D. Rikowski, G. and McLaren, P. (2001) *Red Chalk: On Schooling,
Capitalism and Politics, Mike Cole, Dave Hill and Glenn Rikowski in discussion with
Peter McLaren*, Brighton: Institute for Education Policy Studies.

Cooper, R. (2002) 'The Post Modern State'. Online. Available at: fpc.org.uk/
articles/169 (accessed 7 August 2006).

Crick, B. (1987) *Socialism*, Milton Keynes: Open University Press.

Daily Telegraph (2003) 25 October 2003. Online. Available at: www.derechos.
org/nizkor/excep/cooper.html (accessed 7 August 2006).

Dale, G. (1999) 'Capitalism and Migrant Labour', in G. Dale and M. Cole (eds) *The
European Union and Migrant*, Oxford: Labour.

Dallmayr, F. (2004) 'The Underside of Modernity: Adorno, Heidegger, and Dussel', *Constellations*, 11 (1), pp. 102–120.

Darder, A. (2002) *Reinventing Paulo Freire: a Pedagogy of Love*, Cambridge: Westview Press.

Darder, A. and Torres, R.D. (2004) *After Race: Racism after Multiculturalism*, New York and London: New York University Press.

DeCuir, J.T. and Dixson, A.D. (2004) '"So When It Comes Out, They Aren't That Surprised That It Is There": Using Critical Race Theory as a Tool of Analysis of Race and Racism in Education', *Educational Researcher*, 33 (5) June/July, pp. 26–31.

Delgado, R. (1995) *The Rodrigo Chronicles: Conversations about America and Race*, New York: New York University Press.

Delgado, R. (2003) 'Crossroads and Blind Alleys: A Critical Examination of Recent Writing About Race', *Texas Law Review*, 82 (1), pp. 121–152.

Department for Education and Skills (2005) *Higher Standards, Better Schools for all: More Choice for Parents and Pupils*, London: DfES.

Department for Work and Pensions (2004/2005) *Households Below Average Income*, London: Department for Work and Pensions.

Derrida, J. (1976) *Of Grammatology*, Baltimore: Johns Hopkins University Press.

Derrida, J. (1979) *Spurs: The Styles of Nietzsche*, Chicago: University of Chicago Press.

Derrida, J. (1990) 'Force of Law: The Mystical Foundation of Authority', translated by Mary Quaintance, *Cardozo Law Review*, 11, pp. 919–1070.

Derrida, J. (1992) 'Force of Law: The "Mystical Foundation of Authority"', in D. Cornell, M. Rosenfeld and D. Gray Carlson (eds) *Deconstruction and the Possibility of Justice*, London: Routledge.

de Siqueira, A.C. (2005) 'The Regulation of Education through the WTO/GATS', *Journal for Critical Education Policy Studies*, 3 (1), March. Online. Available at: www.jceps.com/?pageID=article&articleID=41 (accessed 2 September 2006).

Dixson, A.D. and Rousseau, C.K. (2005) 'And We Are Still Not Saved: Critical Race Theory in Education Ten Years Later', *Race, Ethnicity and Education*, 8 (1), pp. 7–27.

Dodd, V. (2005) 'Asian Men Targeted in Stop and Search. Huge Rise in Number Questioned Under Anti-Terror Laws', *Guardian*, 17 August. Online. Available at: www.guardian.co.uk/attackonlondon/story/0,16132,1550470,00.html (accessed 18 September 2006).

Domhoff, G.W. (2006) 'Wealth, Income, and Power'. Online. Available at: sociology.ucsc.edu/whorulesamerica/power/wealth.html (accessed 15 September 2006).

Doward, J. and Hinsliff, G. (2004) 'British Hostility to Muslims "Could Trigger Riots"'. Online. Available at: www.guardian.co.uk/race/story/0,11374,1227977,00.html (accessed 8 August 2006).

Dussel, E. (1995) *The Invention of the Americas: Eclipse of 'Other' and the Myth of Modernity*, New York: Continuum.

Dussel, E. (1996) *The Underside of Modernity: Apel, Ricoeur, Rorty, Taylor and the Philosophy of Liberation*, Atlantic Highlands: Humanities Press International.

Dussel, E. (2001) *Towards An Unknown Marx – A Commentary on the Manuscripts of 1861–63*, London: Routledge.

Eagleton, T. (1991) *Ideology*, London: Verso.

Eagleton, T. (2002) 'A Shelter in the Tempest of History', *Red Pepper*, February. Online. Available at: www.redpepper.org.uk/arts/x-feb02-eagleton.htm (accessed 6 November 2005).

162   *References*

Ebert, T.L. (1996) *Ludic Feminism and After: Postmodernism, Desire, and Labour in Late Capitalism*, Ann Arbor: University of Michigan Press.

Edgoose, J. (1997) 'An Ethics of Hesitant Learning: The Caring Justice of Levinas and Derrida', *Philosophy of Education*. Online. Available at: www.ed.uiuc.edu/EPS/PES-Yearbook/97_docs/edgoose.html (accessed 8 August 2006).

Engels, F. (1884) *The Origin of the Family, Private Property and the State*. Online. Available at: www.marxists.org/archive/marx/works/1884/origin-family/index.htm (accessed 2 September 2006).

Engels, F. (1890) 'The Materialist Conception of History: From a Letter To Joseph Bloch', London, 21 September. Online. Available at: www.socialistparty.org.uk/WhatIs MarxFrame.htm (accessed 8 August 2006).

Engels, F. (1962) [1877] *Anti-Duhring: Herr Eugen Duhring's Revolution in Science*, Moscow: Foreign Language Press.

Engels, F. (1975) [1845] 'Speeches in Elberfeld', *Marx and Engels, Collected Works, Volume 4*. Online. Available at: www.marxists.org/archive/marx/works/1845/02/15.htm (accessed 2 September 2006).

Engels, F. (1977) [1892] 'Socialism: Utopian and Scientific', in *Karl Marx & Frederick Engels: Selected Works in One Volume*, London: Lawrence and Wishart.

E-number (2006). Online. Available at: en.wikipedia.org/wiki/E_number (accessed 25 September 2006).

Fekete, L. (2001) 'The Emergence of Xeno-racism', Institute of Race Relations. Online. Available at: www.irr.org.uk/2001/september/ak000001.html (accessed 8 August 2006).

Fekete, L. (2002) 'Evictions Against Xeno-racist Neighbours', www.irr.org.uk/europebulletin/united_kingdom/extreme_right_politics/2002/ak000003.html.

Feldman, P. and Lotz, C. (2004) *A World to Win: a Rough Guide to a Future Without Global Capitalism*, London: Lupus Books.

Fenton, S. (2003) *Ethnicity*, Cambridge: Polity.

Ferguson, N. (2003) 'Prince and Empire are the Key to History', *Sunday Times*, 6 July 2003.

Ferguson, N. (2004) 'American Empire – who Benefits?', *Empire and the Dilemmas of Liberal Imperialism*, CD accompanying *Prospect*, March 2004.

Ferguson, N. (2005) 'Admit it, George Dubya's Medicine is Not all Bad', *Times Higher Education Supplement*, 18 March 2005. Online. Available at: www.thes.co.uk/search/story.aspx?story_id=2020398 (accessed 7 August 2006).

Fischman, G. and McLaren, P. (2005) 'Is there any Space for Hope: Teacher Education and Social Justice in the Age of Globalizaton and Terror', in G. Fischman, P. McLaren, H. Sunker and C. Lankshear (eds) *Critical Theories, Radical Pedagogies, and Global Conflicts*, Oxford: Rowman and Littlefield.

FitzGerald, M. (2006) 'Lies, damned lies and "ethnic" statistics: some challenges for British criminology'. Presentation to meeting of the British Society of Criminology, 6 December 2006.

FitzGerald, M., Stockdale, J. and Hale, C. (2003) *Young People and Street Crime*, London: Youth Justice Board.

Foster, J.B. (2000) *Marx's Ecology: Materialism and Nature*, New York: Monthly Review Press.

Foster, J.B. (2002) *Ecology Against Capitalism*, New York: Monthly Review Press.

Foster, J.B. (2006) 'Aspects of Class in the United States', *Monthly Review*, 58 (3), (July–August) pp. 1–5.

Foucault, M. (1972) *Archaeology of Knowledge and the Discourse on Language*, London: Tavistock.

Foucault, M. (1977a) 'Nietzsche, Genealogy, History', in D.F. Bouchard (ed.) *Language, Counter-Memory, Practice: Selected Essays and Interviews*, Oxford: Blackwell.

Foucault, M. (1977b) *Discipline and Punish: The Birth of the Prison*, New York: Vintage.

Foucault, M. (1979) *The History of Sexuality, Volume 1: an Introduction*, London: Allen Lane.

Foucault, M. (1980) *Power/Knowledge, Selected Interviews and Other Writings, 1972–1977*, edited by C. Gordon, Brighton: Harvester Press.

Foucault, M. (1983) 'Structuralism and Post-Structuralism', *Telos*, 55.

Foucault, M. (2001) [1964] *Madness and Civilization*, London: Routledge.

Fourier, C. (1820) *Theory of Social Organization*. Online. Available at: www.fordham.edu/halsall/mod/1820fourier.html (accessed 8 August 2006).

Fourier, C. (1830) *The New Industrial World*. Extract Online. Available at: arthur.u-strasbg.fr/~ronse/CF/fourier.html (accessed 14 September 2006).

Freire, P. (1970) *Pedagogy of the Oppressed*, New York: Continuum.

Freud, S. (1991) [1914] 'On Narcissism: An Introduction', *Contemporary Freud: Turning Points & Critical Issues*, New Haven: Yale University Press.

Fryer, P. (1988) *Black People in the British Empire*: An Introduction, London: Pluto Press.

Gair, R. (2006) 'Ellis Faces Disciplinary Charges'. Online. Available at: campus.leeds.ac.uk/newsincludes/newsitem3675.htm (accessed 8 August 2006).

Galloway, G. (2006) 'Address to Marxism 2006', *Forum: What Next for Respect*, CD 51, London: Bookmarks (available at: www.bookmarks.uk.com/cgi/store/bookmark.cgi).

Gane, M. (ed.) (1993) *Baudrillard Live: Selected Interviews*, London: Routledge.

Geddes, A. (2003) *The Politics of Migration and Immigration in Europe*, London: Sage.

Genovese, E. and Genovese, E.D. (1983) *Fruits of Merchant Capital: Slavery and Bourgeois Property in the Rise and Expansion if Capitalism*, Oxford: Oxford University Press.

Geras, N. (1983) *Marx and Human Nature: Refutation of a Legend*, London: Verso.

Getty, S. (2006) 'East Enders Say they Love London', *The Metro*.

Gibson, A. and Barrow, J. (1986) *The Unequal Struggle*, London: Centre For Caribbean Studies.

Gibson, R. and Rikowski, G. (2004) *Socialism and Education: An E-Dialogue*, conducted between 19 July–8 August, at Rich Gibson's *Education Page for a Democratic Society*. Online. Available at: www.pipeline.com/~rougeforum/RikowskiGibson DialogueFinal.htm (accessed 8 August 2006).

Gibson-Graham, J.K. (1996) 'Querying Globalization', *Rethinking Marxism*, 9 (Spring), pp. 1–27.

Gillborn, D. (2005) 'Education Policy as an Act of White Supremacy: Whiteness, Critical Race Theory and Education Reform', *Journal of Education Policy*, 20 (4) July, pp. 485–505.

Gillborn, D. (2006a) 'Critical Race Theory and Education: Racism and Antiracism in Educational Theory and Praxis', *Discourse: Studies in the Cultural Politics of Education*, 27 (1), pp. 11–32.

Gillborn, D. (2006b) 'Rethinking White Supremacy: Who Counts in "WhiteWorld"', *Ethnicities*, 6 (3), pp. 318–340.

Gilroy, P. (2004) *After Empire: Melancholia or Convivial Culture?* Oxfordshire: Routledge.

Gilroy, P. (2006) 'Multi-culture in Times of War', Professor Paul Gilroy, Anthony Giddens Professor in Social Theory Inaugural Lecture: 10 May. Online. Available at: www.lse.ac.uk/collections/sociology/events.htm (accessed 3 September 2006).

Giroux, H.A. (1981) *Ideology, Culture and the Process of Schooling*, Philadelphia: Temple University Press.

Giroux, H.A. (1983) *Theory and Resistance in Education: A Pedagogy for the Opposition*, South Hadley: Bergin & Garvey.

Glendenning, F.J. (1973) 'History Textbooks and Racial Attitudes: 1804–1969', *Journal of Educational Administration and History*, 5, pp. 35–44.

Gordon, A.F. (2006) 'Abu Ghraib: Imprisonment and the War on Terror', *Race and Class*, 48 (1), July–September, pp. 42–59.

Gordon, C. (ed.) (1980) *Power/Knowledge: Selected Interviews and Other Writings by Michel Foucault, 1972–1977*, New York: Pantheon Books.

Gould, J. (1977) *The Attack on Higher Education: Marxist and Radical Penetration*, London: Institute for the Study of Conflict.

Gramsci, A. (1978) *Selections from Prison Notebooks*, London: Lawrence and Wishart.

Green, A. (1994) 'Postmodernism and State Education', *Journal of Education Policy*, 9, pp. 67–83.

Grosvenor, I. (1987) 'A Different Reality: Education and the Racialisation of the Black Child', *History of Education*, 16 (4).

Gruenwald, D.A. (2003) 'The Best of Both Worlds: A Critical Pedagogy of Place', *Educational Researcher*, 32, pp. 3–12.

Hall, S., Critcher, C., Jefferson, T., Clarke, J. and Robert, B. (1978) *Policing the Crisis: Mugging, the State and Law and Order*, London: Palgrave Macmillan.

Hardt, M. and Negri, A. (2000) *Empire*, Cambridge: Harvard University Press.

Hardt, M. and Negri, A. (2004) *Multitude: War and Democracy in the Age of Empire*, London: Penguin.

Hare, B. (2006) 'Law Symposium to Feature Black Racial Theorists', *The Michigan Daily* 24 January 2006. Online. Available at: www.michigandaily.com/media/paper851/news/2005/02/04/News/Law-Symposium.To.Feature.Black.Racial.Theorists-1428501.shtml?norewrite&sourcedomain=www.michigandaily.com (accessed 24 January 2006).

Harman, C. (1996) 'Globalization: A Critique of a New Orthodoxy', *International Socialism*, no. 73, pp. 3–33.

Harman, C. (2000) 'Anti-capitalism: Theory and Practice', *International Socialism*, 88, pp. 3–59.

Hatcher, R. (2006) 'Privatisation and Sponsorship: the Re-agenting of the School System in England', *Journal of Education Policy*, 21 (5), pp. 599–619.

Hayes, C. (2006) '9/11: The Roots of Paranoia', *The Nation*, 283 (2) (25 December), pp. 11–14.

Heffernan, R. (1997) 'Exploring the Power of Political Ideas: the Rise of Neo-liberalism and the Re-orientation of Political Attitude in the UK 1976–1996, Paper Presented to the Political Studies Association Annual Conference, University of Ulster' (reported as New Labour, New Paradigm, *The Times Higher Education Supplement*, 11 April 1997).

Hendrick, H. (1980) 'A Race of Intelligent Unskilled Labourers: the Adolescent Worker and the Debate on Compulsory Part-Time Day Continuation Schools, 1900–1922', *History of Education*, 9 (2), pp. 159–173.

Herrnstein, R.J. and Murray, C. (1994) *The Bell Curve*, New York: The Free Press.

Hickey, T. (2002) 'Class and Class Analysis for the Twenty-first Century', in M. Cole (ed.) *Education, Equality and Human Rights*, London: Routledge/Falmer.

Hickey, T. (2006) '"Multitude" or "Class": Constituencies of Resistance, Sources of Hope', in M. Cole (ed.) *Education, Equality and Human Rights*, 2nd Edition, London: Routledge.

Hill, D. (2001a) 'The National Curriculum, the Hidden Curriculum and Equality', in D. Hill and M. Cole (eds) *Schooling and Equality: Fact, Concept and Policy*, London: Routledge.

Hill, D. (2001b) 'State Theory and the Neo-Liberal Reconstruction of Schooling and Teacher Education: A Structuralist Neo-Marxist Critique of Postmodernist, Quasi-Postmodernist, and Culturalist Neo-Marxist Theory', *The British Journal of Sociology of Education*, 22 (1), pp. 137–157.

Hill, D. (2001c) 'Equality, Ideology and Educational Policy', in D. Hill and M. Cole (eds) *Schooling and Equality: Fact, Concept and Policy*, London: Kogan Page.

Hill, D. (2003) 'Global Neo-Liberalism, the Deformation of Education and Resistance', *Journal for Critical Education Policy Studies*, 1 (1) www.jceps.com/index.php?pageID=article&articleID=7.

Hill, D. (2004a) *The Hillcole Group*. Online. Available at: www.ieps.org.uk.cwc.net/hillcole.html (accessed 3 September 2006).

Hill, D. (2004b) 'Enforcing Capitalist Education: Force-feeding Capital through/in the Repressive and Ideological Educational Apparatuses of the State', in E. Wayne Ross and D. Gabbard (eds) *Education and the Rise of the Security State*, New York: Praeger.

Hill, D. (2004c) 'Educational Perversion and Global Neo-liberalism: a Marxist Critique', *Cultural Logic: An Electronic Journal of Marxist Theory and Practice*. Online. Available at: eserver.org/clogic/2004/2004.html (accessed 8 August 2006).

Hill, D. (2004d) 'Books, Banks and Bullets: Controlling our Minds – the Global Project of Imperialistic and Militaristic Neo-liberalism and its Effect on Education Policy', *Policy Futures in Education*, 2, 3. Online. Available at: www.wwwords.co.uk/rss/abstract.asp?j=pfie&aid=2238&stat1=1 (accessed 8 August 2006).

Hill, D. (2005a) 'Globalisation and its Educational Discontents: Neo-liberalisation and its Impacts on Access, Equality, Democracy, Critical Thought, and Education Workers' Rights, Pay and Conditions', *International Studies in the Sociology of Education*, 15 (3), pp. 257–288.

Hill, D. (2005b) 'State Theory and the Neoliberal Reconstruction of Schooling and Teacher Education', in G. Fischman, P. McLaren, H. Sünker and C. Lankshear (eds) *Critical Theories, Radical Pedagogies and Global Conflicts*, Boulder: Rowman and Littlefield.

Hill, D. (2006a) 'Global Neo-liberalism, Inequality and Capital: Contemporary Education Policy in Britain and the USA', in E. Wayne Ross and R. Gibson (eds) *Neoliberalism and Education Reform*, Cresskill: Hampton Press.

Hill, D. (2006b) 'New Labour's Education Policy', in D. Kassem, E. Mufti and J. Robinson (eds) *Education Studies: Issues and Critical Perspectives*, Buckingham: Open University Press.

Hill, D. (2007) 'Critical Teacher Education, New Labour in Britain, and the Global Project of Neoliberal Capital', *Policy Futures in Education* 5(2), pp. 204–225. Online. Available at: www.wwwords.©.uk/pdf/viewmessage2.asp?j=pfie&vol=5&issue=2&year=2007&article=7_Hill_pFIE_5_2_web.

Hill, D. and Cole, M. (2001) 'Social Class', in D. Hill and M. Cole (eds) *Schooling and Equality: Fact, Concept and Policy*, London: Kogan Page.

Hill, D. and Kumar, R (ed.) (2008, forthcoming) *Global Neoliberalism and Education and its Consequences*, New York: Routledge.

Hill, D., Gabbard, D. and Macrine, S. (eds) (2008) *Neo-liberalism, Education and the Politics of Inequality*, London: Routledge.

Hill, D., Sanders, M. and Hankin, T. (2002a) Marxism, Class Analysis and Postmodernism', in D. Hill, P. McLaren, M. Cole and G. Rikowski (eds) *Marxism against Postmodernism in Educational Theory*, Lanham: Lexington Books.

Hill, D., McLaren, P., Cole, M. and Rikowski, G. (eds) (1999) *Postmodernism in Educational Theory: Education and the Politics of Human Resistance*, London: The Tufnell Press.

Hill, D., McLaren, P., Cole, M. and Rikowski, G. (eds) (2002b) *Marxism against Postmodernism in Educational Theory*, Lanham: Lexington Books.

Hillcole Group (1997) *Rethinking Education and Democracy: A Socialist Alternative for the Twenty-first Century*, London: Tufnell Press.

Hobsbawm, E.J. (1994) *The Age of Extremes*, London: Abacus.

Hodgson, G. (1999) *Economics and Utopia: Why the Learning Economy is not the End of History*, London: Routledge.

Holmes, C. (1979) *Anti-Semitism in British Society 1876–1939*, London: Edward Arnold.

hooks, b. (1989) *Talking Back: Thinking Feminist. Thinking Black*, Boston: South End Press.

Hughes, J. (2004) 'Liberation Philosopher Reflects on the Legacy of Colonialism and Offers a Vision of the Future'. Online. Available at: socrates.berkeley.edu:7001/Events/spring2002/04–05–02-dussel/index.html (accessed 8 August 2006).

Hyland, J. (2002) 'British Foreign Policy Adviser Calls for a New Imperialism', World Socialist Web Site 27 April. Online. Available at: www.wsws.org/articles/2002/apr2002/coop-a27.shtml (accessed 8 August 2006).

International Socialist Group (2006) 'Climate Change: the Biggest Challenge Facing Humanity', *Socialist Outlook*, 9, Spring. Online. Available at: www.isg-fi.org.uk/spip.php?article303.

Jessop, B. (1990) *State Theory: Putting Capitalist States in their Place*, Oxford: Polity Press.

Jha, A. (2006) 'Forecast puts Earth's Future under a Cloud', *Guardian*, 15 August. Online. Available at: www.guardian.co.uk/science/story/0,,1844789,00.html (accessed 15 August 2006).

Jones, A. (1993) 'Becoming a "Girl": Post-Structural Suggestions for Educational Research', *Gender and Education*, 5, pp. 157–166.

Jones, A. (1999) 'The Limits of Cross-Cultural Dialogue: Pedagogy, Desire and Absolution in the Classroom', *Education Theory*, 49(3), pp. 299–316.

Jung, C. (1989) *Memories, Dreams, Reflections*, New York: Random House.

Kahn, R. (2003) 'Paulo Freire and Eco-Justice: Updating Pedagogy of the Oppressed for the Age of Ecological Calamity'. Online. Available at: getvegan.com/ecofreire.htm (accessed 8 August 2006).

Karp, S. (1997) 'Equity Suits Clog the Courts', in *Funding for Justice. A Rethinking Schools Publication* (pp. 4–9), Milwaukee: Rethinking Schools.

Kealey, T. (2006) 'It's More than all Right for Some', *The Times Higher Education Supplement*, 28 July.

Keen, D. (2006) 'One Down – but There's Always One More to Go', *The Times Higher Education Supplement*, 16 June.

Kelly, J. (2002a) 'Gender and Equality: One Hand Tied Behind Us', in M. Cole (ed.) *Education, Equality and Human Rights: Issues of Gender, 'Race', Sexuality, Special Needs and Social Class*, London: Routledge/Falmer.

Kelly, J. (2002b) 'Postmodernism and Feminism: the Road to Nowhere', in D. Hill, P. McLaren, M. Cole and G. Rikowski (eds) *Marxism Against Postmodernism in Educational Theory*, Lanham: Lexington Books.

Kelly, J. (2006) 'Gender and Education: Change and Continuity', in M. Cole (ed.) *Education, Equality and Human Rights: Issues of Gender, 'Race', Sexuality, Disability and Social Class*, 2nd Edition, London: Routledge.

Kelly, J., Cole, M. and Hill, D. (1999) *Resistance Postmodernism and the Ordeal of the Undecidable.* Paper Presented at the British Educational Research Association Annual Conference, Brighton, September.

Kelsh, D. and Hill, D. (2006) 'The Culturalization of Class and the Occluding of Class Consciousness: The Knowledge Industry in/of Education', *Journal for Critical Education Policy Studies*, 4 (1). Online. Available at: www.jceps.com/index.php?pageID=article&articleID=59 (accessed 16 September 2006).

Kinnear, M. and Barlow, S. (2005) 'The Eco Crisis and What it Means', paper presented at *A Climate for Change – Tackling the Eco Crisis and Corporate Power* Conference, October. Online. Available at: www.aworldtowin.net/about/c4cConf.html. The website of the organisation, *A World to Win*, which organised the Conference is www.aworldtowin.net.

Kovel, J. (1988) *White Racism: a Psychohistory*, London: Free Association Books.

Kreis, S. (2004) 'Charles Fourier, 1772–1837 – Selections from his Writings'. Online. Available at: www.historyguide.org/intellect/fourier.html (accessed 3 September 2006).

Kreis, S. (2006) 'The Utopian Socialists: Charles Fourier (1)'. Online. Available at: www.historyguide.org/intellect/lecture21a.html (accessed 8 August 2006).

Kundnani, A. (2006) 'Racial Profiling and Anti-Terror Stop and Search', Institute of Race Relations. Online. Available at: www.irr.org.uk/2006/january/ha000025.html (accessed 8 August 2006).

The Labour Party (2005) 'A Britain Made for Globalisation', Speech by the Chancellor of the Exchequer Gordon Brown MP, at the CBI Annual Conference in London, 28 November. Online. Available at: www.labour.org.uk/index.php?id=news2005&ux_news[id]=gb05cbispeech&cHash=e0a570ea8c (accessed 7 August 2006).

Lather, P. (1984) 'Critical Theory, Curricular Transformation, and Feminist Mainstreaming', *Journal of Education*, 16 (1), pp. 49–62.

Lather, P. (1991) *Getting Smart: Feminist Research & Pedagogy With/in the Postmodern*, New York: Routledge.

Lather, P. (1998) 'Critical Pedagogy and its Complicities: a Praxis of Stuck Places', *Educational Theory*, 48 (4), pp. 487–497.

Lather, P. (2001) 'Ten Years Later, Yet Again: Critical Pedagogy and its Complicities', in K. Weiler (ed.) *Feminist Engagements: Reading, Resisting and Revisioning Male Theorists in Education and Cultural Studies*, London: Routledge.

Lawrence, E. (1982) 'Just Plain Common Sense: the "Roots" of Racism', in Centre for Contemporary Cultural Studies (ed.) *The Empire Strikes Back: Race and Racism in 70s Britain*, London: Hutchinson.

Lawrence, F. (2004) *Not on the Label*, London: Penguin.

Lenin, V.I. (1961) [1901–1902] *What Is To Be Done? Burning Questions of Our Movement, Lenin Collected Works,* Vol. 5, Moscow: Foreign Languages Publishing House. Online. Available at: www.marxists.org/archive/lenin/works/1901/witbd/ (accessed 5 August 2006).

Lenin, V.I. (1975) *Imperialism, the Highest Stage of Capitalism*, Moscow: Progress Publishers.

Leonardo, Z. (2004) 'The Unhappy Marriage between Marxism and Race Critique: Political Economy and the Production of Racialized Knowledge', *Policy Futures in Education*, 2 (3 and 4), pp. 483–493. Online. Available at: www.wwwords.co.uk/pfie/content/pdfs/2/issue2_3.asp#4 (accessed 8 August 2006).

Lieven, D. (2004) Imperial History, CD accompanying *Prospect*, March 2004.

Lind, M. (2004) Debate: After the War, CD accompanying *Prospect*, March 2004.

Lukes, S. (1982) 'Marxism, Morality and Justice', in G.H.R. Parkinson (ed.) *Marx and Marxisms*, Cambridge: Cambridge University Press.

Luxemburg, R. (1916) 'The War and the Workers – The Junius Pamphlet'. Online. Available at: h-net.org/~german/gtext/kaiserreich/lux.html (accessed 4 September 2006).

Lyotard, J.-F. (1971) *Discours, Figure*, Paris: Klincksieck.

Lyotard, J.-F. (1973) *Dérive à Partir de Marx et Freud*, Paris: Union Générale Editions.

Lyotard, J.-F. (1974) *Economie Libidinale*, Paris: Minuit.

Lyotard, J.-F. (2004) *The Postmodern Condition: A Report on Knowledge*, Manchester: Manchester University Press.

MacArthur, B. (2005) 'Will the Election Sun Shine on Blair or Howard?', TIMESONLINE, 28 January: Online. Available at: business.timesonline.co.uk/tol/business/industry-sectors/media/article507424.ece (accessed 6 August 2007).

MacKenzie, N. (1967) *Socialism*, London: Hutchinson.

McLaren, P. (1997) *Revolutionary Multiculturalism: Pedagogies of Dissent for the New Millennium*, Boulder: Westview Press.

McLaren, P. (1998) 'Revolutionary Pedagogy in Post-Revolutionary Times: Rethinking the Political Economy of Critical Education', *Educational Theory*, 48 (4), pp. 431–462.

McLaren, P. (2000) *Che Guevara, Paulo Freire and the Pedagogy of Revolution*, Oxford: Rowman and Littlefield.

McLaren, P. (2005) *Capitalists and Conquerors: Critical Pedagogy Against Empire*, Lanham: Rowman and Littlefield.

McLaren, P. and Farahmandpur, R. (1999a) 'Critical Pedagogy, Postmodernism and the Retreat from Class: Towards a Contraband Pedagogy', in D. Hill, P. McLaren, M. Cole and G. Rikowski (eds) *Postmodernism in Educational Theory: Education and the Politics of Human Resistance*, London: The Tufnell Press.

McLaren, P. and Farahmandpur, R. (1999b) 'Critical Multiculturalism and the Globalization of Capital: Some Implications for a Politics of Resistance', *Journal of Curriculum Theorizing*, 15 (4), pp. 27–46.

McLaren, P. and Farahmandpur, R. (2001) 'Educational Policy and the Socialist Imagination: Revolutionary Citizenship as a Pedagogy of Resistance', *Education Policy: An Interdisciplinary Journal of Policy and Practice*, 15(3), pp. 343–378.

McLaren, P. and Farahmandpur, R. (2002a) 'Breaking Signifying Chains: A Marxist Position on Postmodernism', in D. Hill, P. McLaren, M. Cole and G. Rikowski (eds) *Marxism Against Postmodernism in Educational Theory*, Lanham: Lexington Books.

McLaren, P. and Farahmandpur, R. (2002b). 'Recentering Class: Wither Postmoderism?: Towards a Contraband Pedagogy', in D. Hill, P. McLaren, M. Cole and G. Rikowski (eds) *Marxism Against Postmodernism in Educational Theory*, Lanham: Lexington Books.

McLaren, P. and Farahmandpur, R. (2006) 'Who Will Educate the Educators? Critical Pedagogy in the Age of the New Imperialism', in A. Dirlik (ed.) *Pedagogies of the Global: Transnationalism, Ethnicity and the Public Sphere*, Boulder and London: Paradigm Publishers.

McLaren, P. and Houston, D. (2005) 'Revolutionary Ecologies: Ecosocialism and Critical Pedagogy', in P. McLaren, *Capitalists and Conquerors: a Critical Pedagogy Against Empire*, Lanham: Rowman and Littlefield.

McMurtry, J. (1998) *Unequal Freedoms: The Global Market as an Ethical System*, Toronto: Garamond Press.

McMurtry, J. (2000) 'Education, Struggle and the Left Today', *International Journal of Educational Reform*, 10 (2), pp. 145–162.

McMurtry, J. (2002) *Value Wars: the Global Market Versus the Life Economy*, London: Pluto Press.

Maisuria, A. (2006) 'A Brief History of the British "Race" Politics and the Settlement of the Maisuria Family', *Forum: For Promoting 3–19 Comprehensive Education*, 48 (1), pp. 95–101.

Marable, M. (2006) 'Empire, Racism and Resistance'. Online. Available at: www.trumpetamerica.org/061222ta2116.html (accessed 8 January 2007).

Martin, P. (2005) 'Iraqi Election to Rubber-stamp Continued US Occupation', *World Socialist Web Site*. Online. Available at: www.wsws.org/articles/2005/dec2005/iraq-d16.shtml (accessed 16 December 2005).

Martin, P. (2006) 'US Senate Backs Indefinite Occupation of Iraq', *World Socialist Web Site*. Online. Available at: www.wsws.org/articles/2006/jun2006/sena-j23.shtml (accessed 7 August 2006).

Martinez, E. and García, A. (2000) 'What is "Neo-Liberalism" A Brief Definition', *Economy 101*. Online. Available at: www.globalexchange.org/campaigns/econ101/neoliberalDefined.html (accessed 3 September 2006).

Marx, K. (1965) [1887] *Capital, vol. 1*, Moscow: Progress Publishers.

Marx, K. (1966) [1894] *Capital, vol. 3*, Moscow: Progress Publishers.

Marx, K. (1969) [1863] *Theories of Surplus Value – Part One*, London: Lawrence & Wishart.

Marx, K. (1976a) [1885] 'The Eighteenth Brumaire of Louis Bonaparte', in K. Marx and F. Engels, *Selected Works in One Volume*, London: Lawrence and Wishart.

Marx, K. (1976b) [1845] *Theses on Feuerbach*, in C.J. Arthur (ed.) *Marx and Engels, The German Ideology*, London: Lawrence and Wishart.

Marx, K. (1993) [1889] *The Grundrisse: Foundations of the Critique of Political Economy*, London: Penguin.

Marx, K. (1996) [1875] *Critique of the Gotha Programme*, Beijing: Foreign Language Press.

Marx, K. and Engels, F. (1975) [1845] 'The Holy Family' in K. Marx and F. Engels *Marx and Engels Collected Works, Volume 4*, Moscow: Progress Publishers. Online. Available at: www.marxists.org/archive/marx/works/1845/holy-family/ch04.htm (accessed 7 August 2007).

Marx, K. and Engels, F. (1976) [1845] *The German Ideology Part I: Feuerbach. Opposition of the Materialist and Idealist Outlook A. Idealism and Materialism*. Online. Available at: www.marxists.org/archive/marx/works/1845/german-ideology/ch01a.htm (accessed 8 August 2006).

Marx, K. and Engels, F. (1977a) [1847] 'The Communist Manifesto', in K. Marx and F. Engels, *Selected Works in One Volume*, London: Lawrence and Wishart.

Marx, K. and Engels, F. (1977b) [1872] 'Preface to the German Edition of the Manifesto of the Communist Party', in K. Marx and F. Engels, *Selected Works in One Volume*, London: Lawrence and Wishart.

Maunder, J. (2006) 'Marxism and the Global South', *Socialist Worker*, 17 June.

Meiksins Wood, E. (1995) *Democracy Against Capitalism: Renewing Historical Materialism*, Cambridge: Cambridge University Press.

Meiksins Wood, E. (1998) 'Modernity, Postmodernity or Capitalism?', in R.W. McChesney, E.M. Wood and J.B. Foster (eds) *Capitalism and the Information Age*, New York: Monthly Review Press.

Meiksins Wood, E. (2003) *Empire of Capital*, London and New York: Verso.

Mencken, H.L. (undated) *The Philosophy of Friedrich Nietzsche: Nietzsche the Philosopher.* Online. Available at: www.geocities.com/danielmacryan/nietzsche17.html (accessed 8 August 2006).

Miles, R. (1987) *Capitalism and Unfree Labour: Anomaly or Necessity?*, London: Tavistock.

Miles, R. (1989) *Racism*, London: Routledge.

Miles, R. (1993) *Racism after 'Race Relations'*, London: Routledge.

Miller, R. (1989) 'Rawls and Marxism', in N. Daniels (ed.) *Reading Rawls: Critical Studies on Rawls' 'A Theory of Justice'*, Stanford: Stanford University Press.

Mojab, S. (2001) 'New Resources for Revolutionary Critical Education', *Convergence*, 34 (1), pp. 118–125.

Monbiot, G. (2001) 'Tinkering With Poverty', *Guardian*, 20 November, p. 17.

Monbiot, G. (2006) 'Sure, Nuclear Power is Safer Than In The Past – But We Still Don't Need It', *Guardian*, 11 July, p. 25.

Moore, R. (1988) 'The Correspondence Principle and the Marxist Sociology of Education', in M. Cole (ed.) *Bowles and Gintis Revisited: Correspondence and Contradiction in Educational Theory*, London: The Falmer Press.

Morgan, M. and Short, V. (2005) 'The Return of Dickensian London', World Socialist Website. Online. Available at: www.wsws.org/articles/2005/nov2005/lond-n22.shtml (accessed 8 August 2006).

Muhr, T. and Verger, A. (2006) 'Venezuela: Higher Education for All', *Journal for Critical Education Policy Studies*, 4 (1). Online. Available at: www.jceps.com/? pageID=article&articleID=63 (accessed 6 August 2006).

Muir, H. (2006a) ' "He looked at me and shot. As soon as he had eye contact, he shot me" ' *Guardian*, 14 June. Online. Available at: www.guardian.co.uk/terrorism/ story/0,,1796915,00.html (accessed 9 September 2006).

Muir, H. (2006b) 'Black Teachers Face Bullying and Racism, Survey Finds', *Guardian*, 8 September, p. 15.

Murji, K. and Solomos, J. (eds) (2005) *Racialization: Studies in Theory and Practice*, Oxford: Oxford University Press.

Murphy, P. (1995) 'A Mad, Mad, Mad, Mad World Economy', *Living Marxism*, 80 (June), pp. 17–19.

National Union of Education, Research and Culture, General Confederation of Labour, France (2002) untitled paper presented at the European Social Forum, Florence, 6–10 November.

Neill, A.S. (1966) *Freedom not License*, New York: Hart Publishing.

Nietzsche, F. (1964) [1873] 'On Truth and Falsity in their Ultramoral Sense', in O. Levy (ed.) *The Complete Works of Friedrich Nietzsche*, New York: Russell and Russell.

Nietzsche, F. (1968) [1906] *The Will to Power*, New York: Vintage.

Nietzsche, F. (1969) [1883–1885] *Thus Spoke Zarathustra*, Harmondsworth: Penguin.

Nietzsche (1982) [1887] *Basic Writings of Nietzsche*, translated by Walter Kaufmane, introduction by Peter Gay, New York: The Modern Library.

Observer (2003) 'Refugees Find No Welcome in City of Hate'. Online. Available at:

observer.guardian.co.uk/politics/story/0,6903,987273,00.html (accessed 24 September 2006).

Omi, M. and Winant, H. (1989) *Racial Formation in the United States: From the 1960s to the 1980s*, New York: Routledge.

Owen, R. (1820) *Report to the County of Lanark*. Online. Available at: web.jjay. cuny.edu/jobrien/reference/ob50.html (accessed 27 July 2006).

Paczuska, A. (1986) *Socialism for Beginners*, London: Unwin Paperbacks.

PA News and Booth, J. (2004) 'Carey Defends "Anti-Islam" Speech', TIMESONLINE. Online. Available at: www.timesonline.co.uk/article/0,,1–1052154,00.html (accessed 8 August 2006).

Parenti, M. (1998) *America Besieged*, San Francisco: City Lights Books.

Parker, S. (1997) *Reflective Teaching in the Postmodern World: a Manifesto for Education in Postmodernity*, Buckingham: Open University Press.

Parrish, R. (2006a) *Violence Inevitable: The Play of Force and Respect in Derrida, Nietzsche, Hobbes, and Berlin*, Lanham: Lexington Books.

Parrish, R. (2006b) Personal Correspondence.

Pearsall, J. (ed.) (2001) *Concise Oxford Dictionary*, Oxford: Oxford University Press.

Pennock, J.R. and Chapman, J.W. (eds) (1983) *Marxism*, New York: New York University Press (Nomos 26).

Pieterse, N. (1992) *Emancipations, Modern And Postmodern*, London: Sage.

Pilger, J. (2004) 'Of the token hangers-on who make up the Anglo-America "coalition of the willing", only Australia remains true to the über-sheriff in Washington', *New Statesman*, 5 April, pp. 13–14.

Postone, M. (1996) *Time, Labor and Social Domination: a Reinterpretation of Marx's Critical Theory*, Cambridge: Cambridge University Press.

Preston, M. (2006) 'Positive Action: Many Schools are Hopeless at Teaching Citizenship, according to Ofsted. What are They Doing Wrong?', 14 November 2006. Online. Available at http://education.guardian.co.uk/schools/story/O,,1946883,00.html (accessed 31 August 2007).

Price, R.F. (1977) *Marx and Education in Russia and China*, London: Croom Helm.

Prince, R. and Jones, G. (2004) 'My Hell In Camp X-ray' (www.therevival.co.uk/oldsite/ articles/myhell_campx.php).

Project for the New American Century (undated) Online. Available at: www. newamericancentury.org/ (accessed 16 September 2006).

Race Traitor 16, Winter (2005) Online. Available at: racetraitor.org/: (accessed 8 August 2006).

Rady, F. (2002) 'The "Green Room" Syndrome', *Al-Ahram Weekly*. Online. Available at: weekly.ahram.org.eg/2002/613/in4.htm) (accessed 8 August 2006).

Rainforest Live (2006) Online. Available at: www.rainforestlive.org.uk/index. cfm?articleid=214 (accessed 12 August 2006).

The Rampton Report (1981) *West Indian Children in Our Schools*, London: HMSO.

Rees-Mogg, W. (2005) Fagin, Shylock and Blair, TIMESONLINE, 31 January. Online. Available at: http://www.timesonline.co.uk/tol/comment/columnists/william_rees_ mogg/ article508569.ece (accessed 6 August 2007).

Renton, D. (2006) 'Does Capitalism Need Racism?', paper presented at the *Racism and Marxist Theory Workshop*, University of Glasgow, 7–8 September.

Respect The Unity Coalition (undated) *Another World is Possible: Policies of Respect – the Unity Coalition*, London: Respect the Unity Coalition. Online. Available at: www.respectcoalition.org/pdf/f473.pdf (accessed 8 August 2006).

Richards, H. (2006) 'So, What Drives Venezuela's Socialist Climber?', *Times Higher Education Supplement*, 2 December.

Rifkin, J. (1998) *The Biotech Century*, New York: Tarcher Putnam.

Rikowski, G. (1997a) 'Scorched Earth: Prelude to Rebuilding Marxist Educational Theory', *British Journal of Sociology of Education*, 18(4), pp. 551–574.

Rikowski, G. (1997b) 'Nietzsche's School? The Roots of Educational Postmodernism', a paper presented at the Education Research Seminar: *A Marxist Critique of Post-Modernism In Education*, School of Education, Inter-Area Group, University of Brighton, 19 November. Online. Available at: www.flowideas.co.uk/?page=articles&sub=Nietzsche[a]s%20School (accessed 8 August 2006).

Rikowski, G. (2000) 'That Other Great Class of Commodities: Repositioning Marxist Educational Theory', BERA Conference Paper, Cardiff University, 7–10 September. Online. Available at: www.leeds.ac.uk/educol/documents/00001624.htm (accessed 8 August 2006).

Rikowski, G. (2001) 'The Importance of Being a Radical Educator in Capitalism Today', Guest Lecture in Sociology of Education, The Gillian Rose Room, Department of Sociology, University of Warwick, Coventry, 24 May (available from Rikowskigr@aol.com).

Rikowski, G. (2002) 'Prelude: Marxist Educational Theory after Postmodernism', in D. Hill, P. McLaren, M. Cole and G. Rikowski (eds) *Marxism Against Postmodernism in Educational Theory*, Lanham: Lexington Books.

Rikowski, G. (2004a) *The New Marxist Educational Theory*, Lecture Notes for the EDU3004 module Education, Culture and Society, April, Education Studies, School of Education, University College Northampton (available from Rikowskigr@aol.com).

Rikowski, G. (2004b) 'Marx and the Education of the Future', *Policy Futures in Education*, 2 (3 and 4), pp. 559–571. Online. Available at: www.wwwords.co.uk/pdf/viewpdf.asp?j=pfie&vol=2&issue=3&year=2004&article=10_Rikowski_PFEO_2_3–4_web&id=195.93.21.133 (accessed 8 August 2006).

Rikowski, G. (2005) *Silence on the Wolves: What is Absent in New Labour's Five Year Strategy for Education*, Brighton: University of Brighton, Education Research Centre, Occasional Paper, May (available from ERC, University of Brighton, Mayfield House, Falmer, Brighton, BN1 9PH; email: Education.Research@brighton.ac.uk).

Rikowski, G. and McLaren, P. (2002) 'Postmodernism in Educational Theory', in D. Hill, P. McLaren, G. Rikowski and M. Cole (eds) *Marxism Against Postmodernism in Educational Theory*, Lanham: Lexington Books.

Rorty, R. (1982) *The Consequences of Pragmatism*, Brighton: Harvester.

Rose, S. and Rose, H. (2005) 'Why we Should Give up on Race: as Geneticists and Biologists Know, the Term No Longer Has Meaning', *Guardian*, 9 April 2005. Online. Available at: www.guardian.co.uk/comment/story/0,,1455685,00.html (accessed 8 August 2006).

Saint-Simon, H. (1817) 'Declaration of *Principles*' (*L'Industry*, vol. II). Online. Available at: www.eco.utexas.edu/~hmcleave/368simonprinciples.html (accessed 4 September 2006).

Saint-Simon, H. (1975) *Henri Saint-Simon 1760–1825: Selected Writings on Science, Industry and Social Organisation*, translated and edited by Keith Taylor, London: Croom Helm.

Sanders, M., Hill, D. and Hankin, T. (1999) 'Education Theory and the Return to Class Analysis', in D. Hill, P. McLaren, M. Cole and G. Rikowski (eds) *Postmodernism in*

Educational Theory: Education and the Politics of Human Resistance, London: The Tufnell Press.

Sardar, Z. and Davies, M.W. (2002) *Why do People Hate America?*, Cambridge: Icon Books.

Sartre, J.P. (1960) *The Search for Method (1st part). Introduction to Critique of Dialectical Reason.* Online. Available at: www.marxists.org/reference/archive/sartre/works/critic/sartre1.htm (accessed 8 August 2006).

Sarup, M. (1978) *Marxism and Education*, London: Routledge and Kegan Paul.

Sarup, M. (1983) *Marxism/Structuralism/Education*, Lewes: The Falmer Press.

Sarup, M. (1988) *An Introductory Guide to Post-Structuralism and Postmodernism*, London: Harvester Wheatsheaf.

Save the Children (UK) (2006) Online. Available at: www.savethechildren.org.uk/scuk/jsp/newhome.jsp?flash=true&gawcam=brd&gawadgrp=brd1 (accessed 4 September 2006).

Schellnhuber, H.J. (2006) (ed.) *Avoiding Dangerous Climate Change*, Cambridge: Cambridge University Press.

Schurmann, R. (1990) Heidegger on Being and Acting: From Principles to Anarchy (trans. C.M. Gros), Bloomington: Indiana University Press.

Seidman, S. (1998) *Contested Knowledge: Social Theory in the Postmodern Era*, Oxford: Blackwell.

Short, G. and Carrington, B. (1996) Anti-Racist Education, Multiculturalism and the New Racism, *Educational Review*, 48 (1), pp. 65–77.

Silver, H. (ed.) (1969) *Robert Owen on Education*, Cambridge: Cambridge University Press.

Sivanandan, A. (2001) 'Poverty is the New Black', *Race and Class*, 43 (2), pp. 2–5.

Skeers, J. (2006) 'Australian Government Outlines Pro-market Agenda for its Pacific Sphere of Influence', World Socialist Web Site, 28 June. Online. Available at: dev.wsws.org/articles/2006/jun2006/paci-j28.shtml.

Slaughter, C. (1975) *Marxism & the Class Struggle*, New Park Publications. Online. Available at: www.marxists.org/reference/subject/philosophy/works/en/slaughte.htm (accessed 8 August 2006).

Slott, M. (2002) 'Does Critical Postmodernism Help us "Name the System"?', *British Journal of Sociology of Education*, 23 (3), pp. 414–425.

Smith, D.G. (2003) 'On Enfraudening the Public Sphere, the Futility of Empire and the Future of Knowledge after "America"', *Policy Futures in Education*, 1 (2), pp. 488–503. Online. Available at: www.wwwords.co.uk/pdf/viewpdf.asp?j=pfie&vol=1&issue=3&year=2003&article=4_Smith_PFIE_1_3_web&id=80.3.64.11 (accessed 8 August 2006).

Smith, D.G. (2004) 'A Reply to Mike Cole', *Policy Futures in Education*, 2 (3 and 4), pp. 644–645. Online. Available at: www.wwwords.co.uk/pdf/viewpdf.asp?j=pfie&vol=2&issue=3&year=2004&article=16_Smith_PFIE_2_3–4_web&id=80.3.64.11 (accessed 8 August 2006).

Stephens, J. (2006) 'Act Now to Help Save our Planet', *The Argus*, p. 8.

Stronach, I. and Maclure, M. (1997) *Educational Research Undone: the Postmodern Embrace*, Buckingham: Open University Press.

Symonds, P. (2004) 'Long-time CIA "Asset" Installed as Interim Iraqi Prime Minister', World Socialist Web Site, 31 May. Online. Available at: www.wsws.org/articles/2004/may2004/iraq-m31.shtml (accessed 7 August 2006).

Sweezy, P. (1997) 'More (or Less) on Globalisation', *Monthly Review* 49 (4), pp. 1–4.

Tabb, W.K. (2006) 'The Power of the Rich', *Monthly Review*, 58 (3), July–August, pp. 6–17.

Tate, W.F. (1996) 'Critical Race Theory', *Review of Research in Education*, 22, pp. 201–247.

Taylor, G. (1993a) 'Socialism & Education: Saint-Simon', *General Educator: Journal of the Natfhe General Education Section*, Issue 24, September–October, pp. 15–18.

Taylor, G. (1993b) 'Socialism and Education: Fourier (Part 1)', *General Educator: Journal of the Natfhe General Education Section*, Issue 25, December, pp. 14–16.

Taylor, G. (1994a) 'Socialism and Education: 3. Fourier', *General Educator: Journal of the Natfhe General Education Section*, Issue 26, January–February, pp. 18–20.

Taylor, G. (1994b) 'Socialism and Education: 4. Owen and New Lanark', *General Educator: Journal of the Natfhe General Education Section*, Issue 27, March–April, pp. 18–21.

Taylor, G. (1994c) 'Socialism and Education: 5. Owen and Owenism', *General Educator: Journal of the Natfhe General Education Section*, Issue 28, May–June, pp. 20–21.

Taylor, G. (1995) 'Socialism and Education: 9. Marx on Education, Industry and the Fall of Capitalism', *General Educator: Journal of the Natfhe General Education Section*, Issue 35, July–August, pp. 19–22.

Tickell, C. (2006) 'To Save the Earth, Call Me. Al', *The Times Higher Education Supplement*, 22 September, p. 27.

Times Educational Supplement (2006) 'CONFERENCE REPORT: Schools not doing enough to tackle racism', 16 April 2006.

Townsend, M. and Doward, J. (2006) 'Cash for Asylum Scandle Hits Reid', *Guardian*. Online. Available at: politics.guardian.co.uk/homeaffairs/story/0,,1790105,00.html (accessed 4 September 2006).

Trifonas, P. (2000) 'Jacques Derrida as a Philosopher of Education'. Online. Available at: www.vusst.hr/ENCYCLOPAEDIA/derrida-education.htm (accessed 8 August 2006).

Trotsky, L. (1909) *Why Marxists Oppose Individual Terrorism*. Online. Available at: www.marxists.org/archive/trotsky/works/1909/tia09.htm (accessed 8 August 2006).

Tyler, P.E. (2002) 'Officers Say U.S. Aided Iraq in War Despite Use of Gas', *New York Times*, 18 August. Online. Available at: www.commondreams.org/headlines02/0818–02.htm (accessed 4 September 2006).

Union of Concerned Scientists (2006) 'Global Warming 101 2005 Vies for Hottest Year on Record'. Online. Available at: www.ucsusa.org/global_warming/science/recordtemp2005.html (accessed 10 August 2006).

US Census Bureau (2005) Online. Available at: www.census.gov/hhes/www/poverty/poverty04/pov04hi.html (accessed 8 August 2006).

US Department of Transportation, Federal Highway Administration (2006) 'Highway Statistics 2004'. Online. Available at: www.fhwa.dot.gov/policy/ohim/hs04/htm/dlchrt.htm (accessed 7 August 2006).

Usher, R. and Edwards, R. (1994) *Postmodernism and Education: Different Voices, Different Worlds*, London: Routledge.

Virdee, S. (2006) 'Race, Class and the Dialectics of Social Transformation', paper presented at the Racism and Marxist Theory Workshop, University of Glasgow, 7–8 September.

Virdee, S. (2008, forthcoming) *Racism and Capitalist Modernity*, Oxford: Polity.

Waite, G. (1996) *Nietzsche's Corps/e: Aesthetics, Politics, Prophecy, or, the Spectacular Technoculture of Everyday Life*, Durham and London: Duke University Press.

Ward, P. (2005–2006) 'A Large Scale Geophysical Experiment?', *Socialist Outlook*, 8, Winter, pp. 12–15.

Ward, P. (2006) 'Nuclear Juggernaut Moving into Top Gear', *Socialist Outlook*, 9, Spring, pp. 12–13.

Warmington, P. (2006) Personal Correspondence.

Weatherford, J. (1990) *Indian Givers: How the Indians of the Americas Transformed the World*, New York: Fawcett Books.

Williams, R. (1980) *Problems in Materialism and Culture*, London: Verso.

Willis, P. (1977) *Learning to Labour: How Working Class Kids Get Working Class Jobs*, Farnborough, Saxon House.

Wilpert, G. (2006) 'Poll: Venezuelans Have Highest Regard for Their Democracy', *ZNET* 20 December. Online. Available at: www.zmag.org:80/sustainers/content/2006–12/20wilpert.cfm (accessed 15 January 2006).

Winstanley, G. (1652) *Law of Freedom*, London: Penguin. Online. Available at: www.marxists.org/reference/archive/winstanley/1652/law-freedom/ch05.htm (accessed 12 September 2006).

Wittgenstein, L. (2001) *Philosophical Investigations*, Oxford: Blackwell.

Woodcock, J. (2006) 'Driving to Disaster', *Socialist Worker*, 29 July.

Woolley, R. (2007) *Tawney, Temple and Acquisitiveness: the Legacy of English Ethical Socialism*, Lampeter: Mellen Press.

Women and Equality Unit (2004) Equal Pay Act. Online. Available at: www.women andequalityunit.gov.uk/legislation/equal_pay_act.htm (accessed 3 September 2006).

World Development Movement (2001) *Isn't It Time We Tackled the Causes of Poverty?* London: World Development Movement.

World Development Movement (2006) *Your Legacy to the World Development Movement*, London: World Development Movement.

Young, H. (2002) 'Leader', *Guardian*, 29 March.

Young, M.F.D. (ed.) (1971) *Knowledge and Control: New Directions for the Sociology of Education*, London: Collier-Macmillan.

Young, R.M. (1998) Marxism And The History Of Science, *The Human Nature Review*. Online. Available at: human-nature.com/rmyoung/papers/pap104h.html (accessed 8 August 2006).

Zavarzadeh, M. (2002) 'On "Class" and Related Concepts in Classical Marxism, and Why is the Post-Al Left Saying Such Terrible Things About Them?'. Online. Available at: www.etext.org/Politics/AlternativeOrange/3/v3n3_onrc.html (accessed 8 August 2006).

Zephaniah, B. (2004) 'Rage of Empire', *Socialist Review*, No. 281, January, pp. 18–20.

Index

Abdulkayar, M. 121
Age of Extremes (Hobbsbawn) 38
Ahmed, T. xi–xii
al-Harith, J. 123
Althusser, L. 27, 30–1, 42
analogic reasoning 73–4
Antonio, R.J. 40
apartheid xiv–xiv, 83
Atkinson, E. 51, 62–6
Attlee, C. 1
Aymaran people 82

Baudrillard, J. 48–50, 55–6
Baxter, J. 62–6
Begg, M. 108
Bell, D. 112
Bello, W. 103
Benn, H. 83
Beveridge Report (1942) 1
Bhargava, M. 127
binary oppositions, breakdown of 49–50
Blair, T. 2, 5, 83, 86, 99, 100–1
Blaxter, J. 53
Blears, H. 122–3
Boot, M. 103
Boulangé, A. 110
bourgeois morality, Fourier's critique of 19–20
Bowles, S. xvii, 31–36
Brown, G. 83, 120
Buddhism 83
Bush, G.W. ix, xii, 99, 102–3, 103–4

Callaghan, J. 1, 4
Callinicos, A. 39, 60–1, 126, 136
Capital (Marx) 35, 88
capitalism
    conflict 23–4
    defeat of xv–xvi

education 30–6, 33–6
    expansionist tendency of 22, 95
    labour 16
    modernisation 86
    as only option 136–7
    racialisation 107
    racialism xiv
    social justice 61
    socialism 129
carbon dioxide emissions 95–6
Carey, Lord 123
Cattui, M. 82
Chakrabarti, N. 113
character formation, Christian view of 20–1
children, in phalanxes 18, 19
Christian socialism 87
Churchill, Sir W. 2
class struggle
    analogic reasoning 73–4
    economic conditions 22–3
    and 'race' 113, 115–16, 120
    Saint-Simon 16–17, 21
    socialist society xvii–xviii
Classical Age of Marxist Educational Theory (Rikowski) 33
climate change 93–6
Coben, D. 106
Cole, M. xvi–xix
    higher education, working in 4–6
    manual worker 3
    school teaching 3–4
    school years 2–3
commodities, and labour power 35
communal living 18–19
communism
    of Robert Owen 21
    socialism, origins of 14–15
Communist Manifesto, The (Marx) 23

communities 17–19
Confucius 83
Cooper, R. 98–100, 108
cooperative movement, founding of 21
correspondence principle
    autonomy *versus* social revolution
       34–5
    base/superstructure model 34
    functionalism 34
    labour power 35–6
    relative autonomy theory 34
    resistance 34, 35
Cox, P. 94
Crick, B. 14, 15, 16, 127
Critical Legal Studies (CLS) 112
Critical Race Theory (CRT) 5, 6
    British imperialism 119–20
    definition of 112
    Islamophobia 112, 120–4
    'race' and social class 113, 115–16,
      120
    'white supremacy' concept 112–15
    xenoracialisation 124–6
    xenoracism 112
    see also racism

Dale, G. 126
Dallmayr, F. 8
de Menezes, J.C. 121
deconstruction
    discourse 53–4
    social change 62–6
    supplementarity 54–5, 65
Delgado, R. 112, 115–17, 116–17
Derrida, J. 41, 44–5, 48, 53–4, 58–9, 60,
    63, 65
developing countries, and global
    capitalism 56–8, 83
dialectical praxis, of Marxism 67
Diggers movement 14
Dobzhansky, T. 105
Douglas-Home, Sir A. 4
drudge jobs 18
Dusserl, E. 6, 68–75

eco-socialism 97
economic determinism 79–80
Eden, Sir A. 2
Edgoose, J. 54
education
    capitalism 30–6
    correspondence principle 32–5
    funding of xiii
    and labour 29–30

New Sociology of Education (NSE)
    31–2
Repressive *versus* Ideological Sate
    Apparatuses 30–1
Schooling in Capitalist America (SCA)
    31–4
utopian socialism 28–9
elitism 28, 29
'emancipative reason', myth of 71
enantiomorphism 104
Engels, F. 17, 20, 21, 22, 23, 27, 29–30,
    41, 135
England, L. 108
Enlightenment
    modernity 37, 38
    totalising truth 46
environmental destruction
    climate change 93–6
    genetic modification 91–92
    resource destruction 92–3
    unhealthy food 90–101
Equal Pay Act (1970) 2
equality, and human nature 19
European Union 99, 100, 124, 126

Farahmandpur, R. 101
Feldman, P. 91–2
feminist poststructural discourse analysis
    (FPDA) 55, 56, 64–6
Ferguson, N. 102–3, 110
feudalism 22
Fitzgerald, M. 120
Flax, J. 60
food, unhealthy 90–1
fossil fuels 93, 95–6
Foucault, M. 40, 41–4, 59
Fourier, J. 17–20, 21, 29, 93
'free-schoolers' 28
Freeman, A. 112
French Revolution (1789-1799) 15
Fryer, P. 107

Gaitskill, H. 2
García, A. 88
GATS (General Agreement in Trade in
    Services) 89–90
genetic modification 91–2
genetics 105
genocide 71
Geras, N. 61
German Ideology, The (Marx and Engels)
    79
Gillborn, D. 113, 114–15
Gilroy, P. 6, 69, 91

Gintis, H. xvii, 31–6
global neo-liberal capitalism
    deregulation 88
    'developing world' 56–8
    education 96–7
    GATS 89–90
    housing 57
    imperialism 82–4
    modernisation 86
    neoliberal globalism xii–xiii
    poverty 56–8
    privatisation 88
    public expenditure cuts 88
    'public good' concept 89
    rule of market 88
globalisation
    capitalism 90
    concept of 86
    education 96–7
    environmental destruction 85, 90–6
    global warming 85, 93–5
    labour power 35–6
    New Labour 86–7
Gramsci, A. 73
Grand National Consolidated Trade Union
    21
Gruenwald, D.A. 97

harmonian education 29
Harris, A. 116–17
Heath, E. 3, 4
Heffernan, R. 77
Hickey, T. 23–4, 26
Hill, D. xviii, 30, 31, 77
Hillcole Group of Radical Left Educators
    5, 136–7
history
    dialectic view of 20, 21
    materialist conception of 22
Hobbsbawn, E. 38
housing, and global capitalism 57
Houston, D. 97
Howard, M. 77
Hyland, J. 100
Hypolite, J. 63

Ignatiev, N. 115
imperialism
    as acceptable xii
    British 102–3, 110–11, 119–20, 123
    capitalism xiv
    neo-liberal 82–4
    see also 'New Imperialism'
In Place of Strife (White Paper 1969) 3

individual interest, problems of 20
Industrial Revolution 20
information warfare 102, 103
Institute for Radical Left Educators 5
Institute of Race Relations, classroom
    resources for 128
International Monetary Fund (IMF) 82, 98
Iraq war ix, 104
Islamophobia
    biological 123–4
    counter-terrorism 120–1
    cultural 123
    institutional 121–2
    police stop-and-search powers 122–3

Jones, A. 59, 65
Jung, C. 81
justice 59–62

Kavanagh, T. 77
Kennedy, P. 103
Keynesian economy 77
knowledge
    Enlightenment 46
    metanarratives 47
    modern *versus* postmodern 46–7
    multiple discourses 47–8
Koyair, A. 121
Kyoto Protocol 96

Labour Party 2, 82
labour theory of value (LTV)
    capitalist system 25
    democratic socialism 26
    dialectical praxis 24
    education, as ideological state apparatus
        27
    Owen, Robert 21, 22
    scientific socialism 27
    state capitalism 26–7
    surplus value 24–5
    working class, and social revolution
        25–7
laissez-faire economics 21
Lather, P. 53, 62–6
Lawrence, F. 90–1
Learning to Labour (Willis) 33
Lenin, V.I. 72–3, 100
Leonardo, Z. 116
Letwin, O. 77
Levellers movement 14
liberation theology 68–84
Lieven, D. 100
Lind, M. 102

Littlejohn, R. 77, 125
Lotz, C. 91–2
Luxemburg, R. xiii–xiv, 138
Lyotard, J.-F. 45–8, 49

MacKenzie, N. 14
MacLure, M. 58
Macmillan, H. 2
Maisuria, A. 116
Major, J. 4
Marable, M. xiv, xv
Martinez, E. 88
Marx, K. 17, 21, 22, 23, 25, 29–30, 35,
  36, 41, 59, 72, 73, 88, 135
Marxism
  central planning 132
  democracy 129–30
  drudge jobs 132
  here and now 134–5
  human nature 129–30
  as impossible 136–8
  Islam xi–xii
  justice 60–2
  laziness 130
  social revolution, death and violence
    involved in 133
  socialism, and capitalism 129
  standard of living 132
  terrorism x
  totalitarianism 131
  uniformity 132–3
  'vulgar' 79–80
  work, benefits of 130
  working class, as agents for change 134
Maunder, J. 82, 131
McLaren, P. 55, 67, 97, 101
McMurty, J. 103–4
Meiskins Wood, E. 83, 101–2
metanarratives, rejection of 45–6, 66
Miles, R. 105, 106, 109, 117, 118, 124,
  140–1
Miller, R. 62
Mills, C. 116
mining 93
modernity
  aristocratic society 38–9
  elitism 39, 40
  French Revolution 38
  modernism 37–67
  naturalism, and anti-naturalism 38
  perspectivism 39–40
  'will to power' 39, 40
modified-atmosphere packaging (MAP)
  91

Moore, R. 32
More, Sir T. 14

nanotechnology 92
narcissism 104, 109
National Seaman's strike 3
*National Security Strategy of United States
  of America (NSSUSA)* 102
'New Christianity' 16
New Harmony community village 21
'New Imperialism'
  curriculum 109–11
  postmodernism 98–100
  transmodernism 103–9
  US Empire 101–3
  US reality 100–1
New Labour 4, 5, 92
  see also Blair, T.
New Lanark cotton mills (Owen) 20
New Racial Domain xiv–xv
New Sociology of Education (NSE)
  31–2
Nietzsche, F. 38–40

Omi, M. 109
'ordeal of the undecidable' 58–60
Organisation for Security and Cooperation
  in Europe (OSCE) 99
Other
  racialisation of 104, 107–9
  suffering, and transmodernism 75, 82
Owen, R. 13, 20–1, 22, 26, 29

Paine, T. 76–7
Parenti, M. xiv
Parrish, R. 54
Pearsall, J. 71
peasants' revolts 14
pesticides 92
phalanxes 17–19
postmodernism
  as agent for change 62–3
  Cole's work xvii
  knowledge, nature of 46–8
  localism 63–4
  metanarratives 45–6
  'New Imperialism' 98–100
  non-dualism 64
  postmodernity 45–6
  of 'reaction' *versus* 'resistance'
    55–6
  'responsible anarchism' 58–60
  sign, political economy of 48–50
Postone, M. 73

poststructuralism
　deconstruction 41, 44–5
　emancipatory potential of 65–6
　genealogical analysis 42–3
　power, diffusion of 40, 41–44
　versus structuralism 40–1
　transformative possibilities of 64–6
poverty, and global capitalism 56–8
Powell, C. 104
power 40
　difference 42, 60
　as diffuse 41–2, 43
　history 41
　knowledge 43
　perspectivism 42
　power/discourse formations 41–2
　schools/prisons 43–4
press, right-wing popular in Britain 77
Preston, J. 113
Price, R.F. 29
Project for the New American Century 98, 101

Quispe, F. 82

Race Traitor 114–15
racialisation
　'common sense' 106–7
　discourse 106
　imperialism 108–11
　narcissism 104, 107–9
　racialised capitalism 107
　transmodernism 106–9
　see also Islamophobia;
　　xenoracialisation
racism 77
　anti-black 119–20
　dominative *versus* aversive 118
　education 126–8
　exclusion/inclusion 140
　forms of 117–19
　Marxist analysis of 140–1
　New Racial Domain xiv–xv
　seemingly positive attributes 118
　unintentional 117–18, 140
rainforest destruction 93
Reagan, R. xii, 112
Reform Act (1832) 21
Renton, D. 126
Repressive State Apparatuses (RSAs)
　versus Ideological Sate Apparatuses
　　(ISAs) 30–1
Respect Coalition 129, 135
Rifkin, J. 91–2

Rikowski, G. xviii, 23, 34–5, 39, 79, 80–1
Rorty, R. 45
Rose, H. 105
Rose, S. 105
Rumsfeld, D. ix

Saddam Hussein 104
Saint-Simon, H. de 13, 15–17, 16, 21, 28, 130
Sampson, A. 57
Sarup, M. 31, 33, 42–3, 45, 137–8
Scholze, M. 94
Schooling and Society (OU) 31, 33
Schooling in Capitalist America (SCA) 31–4
Seidman, S. 44, 49
September 11 attacks ix, 87
sexual liberation 19
Slaughter, C. 73
slave trade 22, 107
Slott, M. 25–6, 36
Smith, D.G. 6, 68–84, 100, 103, 137
social justice 59–62
socialism
　agrarian communism 14–15
　biblical references 13
　Diggers movement 14
　education xvii–xix
　Levellers movement 14
　slave rebellions 13–14
　state 70
　support for xvi
Socialisme ou Barbarie 46
Solana, J. 99
Soviet Union
　Marxism, and legacy of x–xi, 131
　state capitalism 26–7
Stalinism 131
Stronach, I. 58
structuralism 40–1
　see also poststructuralism
surplus value 22, 24–5, 61
Sutherland, P. 82
Sweezy, P. 88

Taoism 83
terrorism, war on ix–x, 103–4, 110
Terrorism Act (2000) 122, 123
Thatcher, M. xii, 1, 4, 5
Thatcher government, 1979 1, 4
Thesis on Feuerbach (Marx) 73
trade unions 87
transmodernism
　Analectic Interaction 74–5

analogic reasoning 72–4
anti-Eurocentrism 71
bourgeois democracy, British style
    77–8
educator, role of 81–84
'enfraudening' 76
'ethical hermeneutics' 68–9
imposition, *versus* majoritarian
    revolution 78–9
liberal democracy, *versus* democratic
    socialism 76–8
liberation theology 68–9
Marxism, 'vulgar' 79–80
modernity, critique of 70–1
oppressor, liberation of 75
postmodernism, critique of 72
South, oppression of 71, 76
totalising synthesis, rejection of 69–70
utopianism, and blueprints for the future
    80–1
Trotsky, L. 133
Trump, D. xii

Upper Clyde Shipbuilders work-in 3
Utopia (More) 14
utopian socialism
    education 28–9
    Fourier, Charles 17–20, 21
    history, materialist conception of 22–4
    labour theory of value 24–7
    Marxist critique of 21–7
    Owen, Robert 20–1
    revolutionary changes, absence of 22
    Saint-Simon, Henri de 15–17, 21
    'scientific socialism' 22
'utopic multiculturality' 82–4

'vassal regimes' 102
    see also 'New Imperialism'
Venezuela, socialist revolution in 139
violence, Western 71
Virdee, S. 109

Waite, G. 39
'war on terror' ix–x, 103–4, 110
Warmington, P. 104, 107
Watkins, K. 82
Weatherford, J. 76
'white supremacy' concept
    'common sense' 114
    and education 127
    education policy 114
    Race Traitor organisation 114–15
    'white power structure' 114
    see also racialisation; racism
Willis, P. 33
Wilson, H. 3
Winant, H. 109
Winstanley, G. 14–15
Winterton, A. 125
Wittgenstein, L. 47
World Bank 98
World Trade Center attacks ix
World Trade Organization (WTO) 82, 89

xenoracialisation 124–6

Young, H. 100–1

Zavarzadeh, M. 54–5, 65
Zephaniah, B. 102, 123